1996

The **FASB**
The People, The Process, and the Politics

Paul B. W. Miller, Ph.D., C.P.A.
Professor of Accounting
University of Colorado at Colorado Springs

Rodney J. Redding, Ph.D., C.P.A.
Associate Professor of Accounting
Gettysburg College

Paul R. Bahnson, Ph.D., C.P.A.
Assistant Professor of Accounting
University of Montana

Third Edition

IRWIN
Burr Ridge, Illinois
Boston, Massachusetts
Sydney, Australia

To:

Diana, David, and Greg

Brenda, Mike, and Kim

Kathie, Sara, and Andy

© RICHARD D. IRWIN, INC., 1986, 1988, and 1994

Senior sponsoring editor: Jeff Shelstad
Developmental editor: Margaret Haywood
Marketing manager: John Biernat
Project editor: Ethel Shiell
Production manager: Laurie Kersch
Cover designer: Laura Gunther
Art manager: Kim Meriwether
Art studio: Accurate Art
Compositor: Bi-Comp, Inc.
Typeface: 10/12 Times Roman
Printer: R. R. Donnelley

Library of Congress Cataloging-in-Publication Data

Miller, Paul B. W.
    The FASB : the people, the process, and the politics / Paul B. W.
Miller, Rodney J. Redding, Paul R. Bahnson.—3rd ed.
        p.   cm.
    Includes bibliographic references and indexes.
    ISBN 0-256-08276-6
    1. Financial Accounting Standards Board. 2. Accounting—
Standards—United States. I. Redding, Rodney J. II. Bahnson,
Paul R. III. Title.
HF5616.U5M534 1994
657′.021873—dc20   93–5703

Printed in the United States of America

1 2 3 4 5 6 7 8 9 0 DOC 0 9 8 7 6 5 4 3

FOREWORD

The 20 years that have passed since the founding of the Financial Accounting Standards Board give it a life nearing that of its longest-lived predecessor. Few could have predicted the events of those two challenging decades but the Board's viability and influence have been demonstrated time and time again in both domestic and international arenas. In particular, the Board's Conceptual Framework and its open and participatory process have dramatically changed the nature, methods, and language of debate about accounting issues.

The Board is a unique private sector organization that has no statutory authority but that nonetheless bears a responsibility granted by Congress to the Securities and Exchange Commission. Success in this unusual role is possible because of the tension between the SEC and the private business sector. The SEC is empowered to set accounting standards but is also less than overly prepared or eager to exert that power. Many managers within the business sector, in turn, would rather operate under few, if any, standards and prefer that those standards be established outside the government. Thus, actions that permit or even cause the Board to fail create the risk that the SEC would be required to take over standard setting.

As a result, the Board occupies a very fragile position. Although it was created to be an instrument of change, it must do its work in a world that fiercely protects the status quo. Because each constituency tries to use the system to defend its own particular interests, the FASB requires nurturing by those who want it to succeed, especially those who believe that the public's interest is paramount. That nurturing can only be accomplished if the public interest dimensions of financial accounting and reporting are fully understood by all who participate in the process.

Miller, Redding, and Bahnson have written a flavorful book that is filled with insight available only to diligent, informed observers of standard setting. As a result, those who study this book will understand more about the need for standards, the process used to create them, the major participants in that process, and the immense difficulty of balancing the public interest against the individual interests of the numerous constituents. This deeper understanding is essential to responsible participation in the standard setting process and to the survival of a viable, independent Board that is capable and worthy of its responsibilities. This book will be invaluable to those readers who have either or both of these objectives in mind.

> **Raymond C. Lauver**
> *FASB Member 1984–1990*
> New Canaan, Connecticut
> November 1993

PREFACE

The overall goal of this third edition of *The FASB: The People, the Process, and the Politics* is the same that we pursued in the first two editions—we want to provide a complete, clear, and objective description and evaluation of the Financial Accounting Standards Board. Despite the significance of its work, the power vested in it, and its relatively small size, the FASB is neither aloof nor impersonal but is very much involved in personal and institutional interactions with its constituencies. After 20 years of setting the direction for progress in financial accounting and reporting, the Board remains focused on its main objectives and sensitive to the interests of those who are affected by its activities. Despite the many criticisms directed toward them from all corners, the people of the FASB continue to carry out their process amid the significant and varied political forces that they are subjected to.

ORGANIZATION AND NEW FEATURES OF THE THIRD EDITION

Perhaps the most important new feature for the third edition is the addition of Dr. Paul Bahnson as our coauthor. Paul is a former member of the FASB's staff through his service as a postgraduate intern during his doctoral studies. He is now a member of the faculty of the University of Montana, and has continued to keep an eye on the Board through his teaching and research. His specific contributions to the project are too numerous to mention, and much of what we have accomplished is due to his efforts.

The book begins with a Prologue that consists primarily of five articles from the business press about a financial reporting issue: mark-to-market accounting for investments. Through the articles, the reader can see the issue emerge, attract attention from regulators, create controversy, and then receive an authoritative resolution, despite the heavy opposition leveled against the FASB. This section of the book provides a bird's-eye view of what the Board is, what it does, and how political factors affect its activities.

As in the prior editions, Chapter 1 lays a foundation for the rest of the book. It provides a macrolevel explanation of the reasons for the importance of financial accounting for the operation of the capital markets and the overall economy. New to this edition is an explicit discussion of the noninvesting public's interest in financial reporting. The chapter also explains why accounting issues need to be resolved authoritatively, and then describes why the FASB was formed and the sources of its authority. The chapter also considers the question of whether the Board is political, and comes to the conclusion that it clearly is.

Chapter 2 examines the structure for setting standards that was created in response to the proposal by the Wheat Study Group of the American Institute of Certified Public Accountants in 1972. It shows how this structure has been kept viable through both internal and external influences. A new section presents information about potentially negative changes in the composition of the board of trustees. This chapter has proven to be especially interesting in the prior editions because of its introductions to the people of the FASB. As before, we have not simply described positions in an organization chart but have provided information about the personalities of the people who give the organization its expertise and vitality. We have included new information on all seven Board members, including the two newest members appointed in 1993. We have expanded our description of the Research and Technical Activities staff, which often operates behind the scenes without the attention that is normally directed at the Board. The appendix to the chapter describes the FASB's two predecessor bodies (the Committee on Accounting Procedure and the Accounting Principles Board) and explains why they were disbanded and replaced.

In Chapter 3, we describe the due process that the FASB uses as it searches for the right questions and possible answers. Because we are relatively unhindered by the space limitations that affect other books, we are able to go beyond other published descriptions of these activities. We believe that readers will gain from learning that the system's flexibility allows it to adapt to changes in the environment and the unique factors surrounding each project, and that it makes a great deal of political sense to have a due process that includes all constituents. The third edition has several changes from the second. First, it now includes a full description of the hierarchy of authoritative sources of generally accepted accounting principles created in Statement of Auditing Standards No. 69 in 1991. Second, it has been revised to use the mark-to-market project to illustrate each of the stages of the process. Third, it includes five complete comment letters for this project in an exhibit that lets the reader see the kind of information that constituents provide to the Board, as well as letting them have a taste of the attitudes that the letter writers often display. As before, we are convinced that the chapter offers something new to virtually everyone who reads it.

Chapter 4 closely examines and evaluates the FASB's conceptual framework, which continues to have the distinction of being the Board's most important and controversial project. The analysis includes inside views that were made possible by Paul Miller's position as a faculty fellow on the Board's staff during the controversial recognition and measurement phase of the project. His status as a member of the staff team gave him special insights into the issues as well as the personal and political pressures that significantly affected the project's final form. The chapter also summarizes the contents of each of the six Statements of Financial Accounting Concepts in a way that is decidedly different from those provided in other places. A major change for the third edition came from a very useful suggestion from one of our reviewers. Specifically, this discussion has been moved one chapter earlier to allow the framework's concepts to be used in analyzing the issues described in the next chapter.

Chapter 5 describes a series of major accounting issues that have occupied the attention of the FASB and its predecessors over the last 50 years. Some issues must be resolved again when they take on new forms in different transactions and industries; other issues have reappeared simply because of growing dissatisfaction with a previous answer. As before, we did not set out to describe all major issues, but we do present enough to show readers how nontechnical factors affect accounting standards. As a result, it shows clearly that the standards-setting process is and has always been as much political as logical. The third edition includes several changes, including a series of short additions that show how the Conceptual Framework did affect or could have affected the FASB's standards. The chapter now presents a new section on issues related to employee compensation, including the very controversial projects on pensions, medical benefits, and compensation paid with stock. The chapter also has been updated to describe the requirements of new standards on consolidated financial statements, the statement of cash flows, employee health benefits, income taxes, and financial instruments.

Chapter 6 (previously called an *epilogue*) focuses on the FASB's future and the factors that are likely to affect its ability to continue fulfilling its mission. More so than any other chapter, Chapter 6 provides explicit descriptions of the political factors that affect the FASB. The contents of the chapter include the issues of whether standards setting should take place in the public or private sector, whether standards overload exists, and whether the Board is dominated by financial statement preparers. An important new feature for the third edition is a discussion of international accounting standards and issues, including a description of some of the steps the Board has taken in this arena. Another especially important addition is a detailed listing of actions taken by the Business Roundtable and other preparers with the apparent goal of diminishing the FASB's ability to create new standards. This section includes details that have not been widely published before.

WHO SHOULD USE THIS BOOK?

Our original concept for the first edition was that this book would be targeted for use in colleges and universities, primarily as a supplemental textbook for courses in intermediate accounting, advanced accounting, and accounting theory, as well as other courses where students need to learn about the political nature of standards setting. To help instructors in these settings, the book presents questions and exercises for each chapter at the end of the book. We have also prepared an Instructor's Manual that includes solutions and suggestions for conducting classes around the book.

In addition, the past has shown that this book has been an important resource in other settings. For example, a copy of the book is a standard component of the reading material provided to new FASB employees. We have also found that many journalists who cover financial reporting issues have read this book in order to gain a deeper understanding of the Board. It has also been especially gratifying to find numerous footnotes to the book in research papers and other textbooks, which indicates that it has become the standard reference work on the FASB.

Beyond these uses, we remain convinced that this book is highly suitable for continuing education for practicing accountants, regardless of whether they are engaged in public or private accounting. And, it should be read by others, particularly corporate managers, who need to understand much more about the Board and the important part it plays in their professional environment. By learning what this book has to offer, they can more easily cope with the changes that the Board produces.

ACKNOWLEDGMENTS

In expressing appreciation for the efforts of others, we need to begin with the many people of the FASB who helped us. At the top of the list for her patience, friendship, promptness, encouragement, and cheerful cooperation is Debbie Harrington, the Board's public relations counsel. Of course, we express great thanks to the chairman of the Board, Denny Beresford, and the other six members who were serving in 1993 (Jim Leisenring, Bob Swieringa, Joe Anania, Bob Northcutt, Tony Cope, and Neel Foster), each of whom kindly consented to give us some of their time and insights into their personal lives. The same sort of appreciation is expressed to Tim Lucas, director of Research and Technical Activities, and other staff members, including Jane Adams, Carl Bass, Teri List, Ann Perry, and Bob Wilkins. A special thanks goes to former Board member Ray Lauver for providing us with the book's foreword.

Thanks also to those who reviewed materials for us, including: Alan D. Campbell of Arkansas State University, Bruce E. Committe of University of Vermont, Raef Lawson of SUNY–Albany, and Tommy Moores of University of Nevada, Las Vegas.

We also benefited greatly from the efforts of Bradley-Allison Smith, a graduate student at the University of Colorado at Colorado Springs, for helping us compile the reading lists that appear at the end of each chapter.

Paul Miller
Rod Redding
Paul Bahnson

CONTENTS

PROLOGUE

The Life Cycle of an Accounting Issue

The following articles from the business press are presented here in order to illustrate a number of important points about the process used in the United States for setting financial accounting standards. The articles pertain to the Financial Accounting Standards Board's "mark-to-market" project, which produced a standard that created new practices to be used in accounting for investments in marketable equity and debt securities. The reader should observe the following specific points:

- While some standards-setting issues involve how to account for new events and transactions, others, like the issues in the mark-to-market project, are concerned with possible improvements in the accounting for transactions and events that have been around for a long time. The central issue in the mark-to-market project involved the question of whether companies (especially financial institutions) should report their investments at fair value instead of at the lower-of-cost-or-market, which was the required practice at the time this issue arose.
- Different groups within the financial reporting community had different positions on how investments should be reported. The groups included management, investors, creditors, investment analysts, independent auditors, and government regulators.
- Several groups can create generally accepted accounting principles. In this case, the Accounting Standards Executive Committee (AcSEC), a rule-making body of the American Institute of Certified Public Accountants (AICPA), first examined the issue and recommended that financial institutions disclose but not record fair values of their investments.

1

- The Securities and Exchange Commission (SEC), the federal agency with statutory authority to establish accounting rules for public companies, was not satisfied with AcSEC's decision and essentially nullified the rule before it was ever put into effect. The SEC did not propose an alternative rule but rather called on another institution within the accounting profession for additional guidance.
- The Financial Accounting Standards Board (FASB) took over the task of resolving this issue.
- The FASB's due process for resolving the issue involved a number of steps, beginning with adding the project to its agenda, continuing with much deliberation, and ending with the issuance of a Statement of Financial Accounting Standards. The elapsed time between the FASB's vote to add the issue to its agenda and the issuance of the Statement was 24 months.
- Although the FASB's due process has a required sequence of events, some variation within that sequence is necessary. For example, FASB member Jim Leisenring's reversal of his position early in 1992 during the process required the Board to reexamine the issues and increased the time used to resolve this issue.
- In addition, this project illustrates the influence that constituent groups attempt to bring to bear on the FASB through their input. The various groups that expected to be affected by the outcome of the project attempted to shape the Standard. Particular attention should be given to the September 21, 1992, article from *Accounting Today* that summarizes the views of several interested groups, including the managers of financial institutions.
- Everyone involved in the debate seemed to think that the numbers reported in the financial statements make a difference. Of course, this fact does not prove that financial accounting numbers actually affect decisions, but it does show that the information in the financial statements is thought to be important. Because the numbers are thought to be important, it follows that issues concerning them are also important.
- The reporters for the business press called on people from many different occupations for their views on the issue. The articles quote specific comments from corporate representatives, SEC and Treasury officials, an investment analyst, and a representative of an accounting firm. Also notice that the references made to comments by the FASB's director of Research and Technical Activities, a project manager, and a Board member. Because of the significance of Board member Jim Leisenring's changed positions on the issues, his comments were quoted directly in the press. Generally, only the FASB's staff speaks to the business press in order to allow Board members to keep their views to themselves, and to thereby provide them with more flexibility in reaching a consensus.

September 17, 1990

Rules Changes for Accountants Worrying SEC

BY KEVIN G. SALWEN AND SANDRA BLOCK
Staff Reporters of *The Wall Street Journal*

WASHINGTON—The Securities and Exchange Commission expressed dismay at new standards the accounting industry has adopted for financial institutions, and the agency urged that the standards be tightened sharply.

At issue is the way financial institutions, mostly banks and thrifts, account for debt securities they hold for investment. Under current accounting rules, such securities are marked at their cost, while debt securities held for short periods and used as trading assets are marked to market price.

The SEC, in a letter to an accounting industry panel, said the current method has "repeatedly proven to be irrelevant to valuing investment portfolios." The agency said all debt instruments should be marked to market price.

The letter—from Edmund Coulson, the SEC's chief accountant, and Robert Bayless, chief accountant of the SEC corporation finance division—follows an effort last week by the Accounting Standards Executive Committee of the American Institute of Certified Public Accountants to change the current rules. The committee voted Thursday to force banks to disclose in notes to the financial statements information about the amortized cost and market value of their investment holdings.

The SEC wasn't satisfied with the vote, which represents a significant pullback from earlier committee proposals that would have required financial institutions to report in financial statements themselves any changes in the portfolio value of debt held as investments. The committee's original plan drew protests from accountants and bankers, who argued that marking all debt securities to market would cause wide swings in earnings reports.

The SEC dismisses that view. "Any volatility is a product of a financial institution's investment portfolio," the agency said in its letter.

The SEC letter argues that the panel shouldn't "seek to redefine the distinctions between 'trading' and 'investment' securities, but to recognize that these distinctions cannot justify permitting a reporting company to overvalue assets."

SEC Chairman Richard Breeden made similar comments earlier last week to the Senate Banking Committee. He said Friday that he is worried that some banks' financial statements should carry the caution "once upon a time" at the top of the page.

Mr. Breeden cited the thrift crisis as a clear illustration of the flaws of the current accounting system. In an interview, he explained that in 1980, when Congress was considering the proposals to deregulate the thrift industry, S&Ls were showing a positive net worth of $36.2 billion. But, on a mark-to-market basis, their net worth was actually "somewhere between minus $78 billion and minus $118 billion," according to later research.

The failure of thrifts to reflect their true value accurately, Mr. Breeden said, "was a significant factor in delaying the understanding by the public of the actual condition of the thrift industry."

June 27, 1991

Rule-Makers Confront Accounting Issues of How Institutions Value Debt Securities

BY LEE BERTON

Staff Reporter of *The Wall Street Journal*

NEW YORK—Accounting rule-makers, under pressure from regulators, have decided to tackle one of the biggest accounting loopholes: how banks, thrifts, and other businesses value debt securities on their books.

Some bankers immediately assailed the idea, saying it would force banks to shed many bonds.

Under current accounting rules, financial institutions can engage in "gains trading" or "cherry-picking" with long-term bonds they hold. In such trading, the bank or thrift sells at year end only those bonds that produce financial gains. However, the institution continues to hold bonds that have fallen sharply in price, while valuing them at initial or historical value.

The Financial Accounting Standards Board, chief rule-making body for accountants, yesterday put on its agenda a project to force holders of debt securities for investment or trading purposes to book them at current, rather than historical, value.

Valuing debt securities as investments, but trading them without marking them to current market prices, "is one of the most abused concepts in accounting," says Janet Pegg, an accounting analyst for Bear, Stearns & Co.

Meeting in its Norwalk, Connecticut, headquarters, the FASB voted 6 to 1 to consider a new accounting rule that would end such financial reporting abuses. The Securities and Exchange Commission has for the past two years been pressuring accounting

rule-makers to tackle this issue. Indeed, George Diacont, the SEC's acting chief accountant, took the unusual step of attending yesterday's FASB meeting.

"While the SEC didn't say anything at the meeting, we know they view this project with some urgency," says Timothy Lucas, the FASB's research director. Mr. Lucas says that an exposure draft on "trading versus investment" treatment of debt securities may be issued by the end of this year, with a final rule expected late in 1992.

Although they concede there have been accounting abuses, both major and local banks strongly oppose dropping historical value accounting for investment portfolio accounts. Thomas Jones, executive vice president of Citicorp, says that "changing the rules may be overkill and could force some institutions to severely limit holdings of debt securities." Mr. Jones instead suggests that to check abuses, accounting rule-makers should institute a test that would show when bonds should be held at current rather than historical cost.

Marti Sworobuk, the IBAA's director of bank operations, says valuing the bonds at current market prices "would strongly discourage community banks from investing in local bond issues," which aren't rated and are difficult to value.

Last year, an accounting rule-making unit of the American Institute of Certified Public Accountants tried to issue a rule stopping the "gains-trading" loophole, but failed as a result of mounting pressure from financial institutions.

September 21, 1992

Banks Fire New Blast in Fair Value Wars

BY RICK TELBERG

WASHINGTON—Leading financial institutions are hoping that a new study by KPMG Peat Marwick will help brake accounting standards-setters' drift toward imposing additional market-value disclosures. Roughly 90 percent of the institutions surveyed by Peat said that as users of financial statements they stand against totally adopting fair-value accounting. Industry officials said they expected the study to be used to slow efforts by federal regulators and private-sector standards-setters to impose market-value disclosures as a tool in the early detection of troubled institutions. "I would hope that people step back after the first statements come out this spring before deciding to go any further," said Steven M. Roberts, an economist and Peat's principal in charge of its Washington advisory service for financial institutions. Peat conducted the study for the Association of Reserve City Bankers, a little-known group of some of the highest-ranking executives in the country.

"The study will make a major contribution to the debate over the issue of market-value accounting," said Richard Rosenberg, president of ARCB, "by not only demonstrating that bankers are doubtful about the usefulness of such information, but that users have serious questions about the same information."

Peat surveyed 35 investment banking firms as financial statement users and 64 commercial banks as preparers, and then met with another 40 investment firms in focus groups. 95 percent of the institutions surveyed said they would prefer traditional, historical-cost accounting, with fair-value disclosures as supplements. As a second choice, 76 percent said they would like no

fair-value information at all and 58 percent said they would like both. Only 26 percent endorsed a wholesale shift to an accounting model based on current values. And only 5 percent said fair value statements would provide a better picture of a company's financial health.

"Since the study shows that preparers and users are skeptical about the reliability, comparability and timeliness of fair value accounting, the study should give pause to those most intent on instituting market-value accounting in the banking industry," said John F. Ruffle, vice chairman of J. P. Morgan & Co.

Users were particularly concerned that fair value information would not be comparable between institutions, since preparers are free to choose their own methods, Roberts noted.

But users also faulted the current system for failing to provide adequate disclosures in four key areas—problem loans, loan concentration and credit quality, off-balance-sheet instruments such as swaps, and options and futures. The report also found striking differences in the expectations between users and preparers. For instance, at least half of all users said they expected only a 5 percent margin of error in fair value estimates. But three quarters of the preparers said they couldn't get that close. Users and preparers agreed, however, that fair value data will focus asset-allocation strategies on shorter term investments, contributing to the volatility of the capital markets in general and the particular institutions. Also, users and preparers agreed that the natural time lags between making a fair value estimate and actually issuing the statements will erode the relevance of the information.

January 16, 1992

FASB Balks on Current-Market Rules for Banks as Member Switches His Vote

BY LEE BERTON

Staff Reporter of *The Wall Street Journal*

NEW YORK—Following intense lobbying from banks, the Financial Accounting Standards Board backed off from proposing an accounting rule that would force companies to value investment securities at current market value.

The delay appears to bring the FASB into conflict with the Securities and Exchange Commission, which has been strongly urging the accounting group to issue current market rules for investment securities held by banks. Walter Schuetze, the SEC's new chief accountant, last week bluntly said that accounting standard-setters have looked at the "mark-to-market" issue long enough and that quick action is warranted to force banks and thrifts to use more up-to-date figures on the books.

The delay occurred because FASB member James Leisenring changed his vote on issuing the proposal, apparently becoming convinced by some of the banks' objections to the new standard.

The FASB was scheduled to issue the investment-security proposal in the first quarter and hold public hearings before issuing a final rule late this year or early in 1993. The chief rule-making body for accountants apparently had enough votes, 4 to 2, to issue the proposal, FASB staff members said.

But Mr. Leisenring took the FASB's staff and other FASB members by surprise when he switched his vote to negative from positive. This made the vote 3 to 3, not enough to issue the proposal.

Robert Wilkins, FASB project manager for the proposal, said he was "flabbergasted and surprised" by Mr. Leisenring's vote change. "The staff had issued a draft of the proposal which we had hoped to get out soon for exposure and public hearings," Mr. Wilkins added. "I guess it means we have more work to do before the board members are comfortable with this proposed standard."

Mr. Leisenring said in a telephone interview, "I think that the banks have some reasonable arguments that we might want to consider." He noted that Robert Northcutt will join the FASB as the seventh member in March and also could oppose the proposal. After Mr. Northcutt joins the FASB, a 5–2 vote will be required to issue an accounting rule. Mr. Northcutt couldn't be reached to comment.

Mr. Leisenring said that the FASB should consider some suggestions of bankers, who have asked that if assets are valued at current market prices, that liabilities of banks also be marked to market.

Donna Fisher, manager of accounting policy at the American Bankers Association said that banks "applaud this delay by the FASB and its willingness to look at the liability side of the balance sheet. But make no mistake about it, we still strongly disagree with market-value accounting for investment securities." Her position is that market value accounting "is difficult to obtain, costly and would be confusing to investors."

Timothy Lucas, the FASB's research director, said that despite Mr. Leisenring's vote change, "nothing I heard in the meeting [of the FASB yesterday] suggests that the board is giving up on the project" of marking investment securities to market.

April 14, 1993

FASB Votes to Make Banks and Insurers Value Certain Bonds at Current Prices

BY LEE BERTON

Staff Reporter of *The Wall Street Journal*

NEW YORK—The Financial Accounting Standards Board, despite continued opposition from financial institutions, decided to force banks and insurers to value certain bonds they hold for investment at current market values.

The rule will require financial institutions to value many of their debt securities at what they're trading for currently, rather than at initial cost, as many securities are valued now. Many accountants believe the change will more accurately reflect the institutions' financial situation.

But banks and insurance companies are strongly opposed to the rule, saying it will make their financial results more volatile and confusing. This "is a great disappointment to bankers who still believe it's a bad idea whose time should not have come," said Donna Fisher, manager of accounting policy for the 10,000 member American Bankers Association.

A spokesman for the 630-member American Council of Life Insurance said the bond-valuation rule will "cause wild swings in the amount of surplus [equity] reported by insurers" and "will force insurers to shorten bond maturities to reduce volatility for interest-rate change."

"The rule will make it tough to buy long-term, fairly illiquid bonds from local communities and could dry up capital available for loans, because we earn less on shorter-term bonds," asserted James Lauffer, chairman and president of First National Bank of Herminie in Irwin, Pa. Mr. Lauffer also is president of the Independent Bankers Association.

But FASB officials believe that the rule will make financial statements more accurate, and will stop "gains trading." The practice, also known as "cherry-picking," occurs when banks or insurers trade only those bonds that yield a profit while holding on to bonds whose price is down and marking them at cost.

The rule will "help standardize accounting by all entities for investment in debt securities and eliminate the diversity that makes comparisons between such entities difficult," said Robert Wilkins, a FASB project manager.

Under the rule, a company's bond portfolio is divided into three different categories. Bonds held to maturity can still be held at original cost. Bonds available for sale, which may or may not be traded before maturity, are to be marked to current value, with any reduction from original cost taken from shareholders' equity. Finally, bonds held only for trading purposes must be marked to current market price, with any unrealized losses charged against earnings.

The rule was approved when James Leisenring, an FASB member, shifted his vote to approval from an earlier vote of opposition last March. Mr. Leisenring said that while the current rule isn't his first preference, he feels that tabling the proposal, could have led to "chaos," because of divergent accounting treatments currently used by banks and insurers for bond portfolios.

Mr. Leisenring and others would have preferred to also mark-to-market certain liabilities held by banks. Timothy Lucas, research director of the FASB, said that a majority of the FASB, like Mr. Leisenring, "was sympathetic to looking at the liability side for similar treatment" as bonds held for investments. "It's a possibility down the road, as part of another FASB project on hedging," said Mr. Lucas.

1

Financial Accounting and the FASB

The primary goal of this book is to provide its readers with knowledge about the Financial Accounting Standards Board—its *people*, its *process*, and the *politics* of standards setting. This knowledge will help them understand more about an important part of the accounting profession, and thereby help prepare them for more successful careers, whether they have chosen to be accountants or to be involved with the business community in some other capacity.

By studying this book, the reader will be able to describe:

- The reasons for having a formal standards-setting process.
- The groups involved in the process.
- The methods used to set standards.
- How the FASB process is affected by such political practices as persuasion, negotiation, compromise, and consensus development.
- The FASB's Conceptual Framework project.
- Some controversial issues that the FASB has attempted to resolve.
- The prospects for the future of the FASB.

Furthermore, the reader will have a grasp of the history of standards setting as well as the current activities of the FASB.

This first chapter provides the basic foundation for much that is developed more completely in the rest of the book. In doing so, it answers the following questions:

- What is financial accounting, and why is it considered to be important?
- What groups are most interested in financial accounting, and what is the nature of their interest?
- Why should differences among these groups be resolved?
- What is the basic structure of the FASB?
- From where does the FASB derive its authority?
- What procedures does the FASB follow in setting standards?
- Is the FASB a political institution?

WHAT IS FINANCIAL ACCOUNTING, AND WHY IS IT CONSIDERED TO BE IMPORTANT?

As a brief definition, financial accounting is the practice of providing financial information about an economic entity to people who are not actively engaged in its management. Thus, it does not include management accounting, which is concerned with providing information to those who *are* actively engaged in managing the entity. Nor does it include regulatory accounting, which is used by entities in regulated industries (such as utilities, communications media, and financial institutions) to provide financial and other types of information to governmental bodies charged with protecting the public interest. Finally, it does not include the reporting of information to taxing authorities, such as the Internal Revenue Service.

Financial accounting is considered important because of the role it plays in the operation of the U.S. economy. The links in the relationship between financial accounting and the efficient operation of the economy are represented in Exhibit 1–1.

The Relationship between the Economy and Financial Accounting

In simple terms, the economy can be viewed as a means for generating wealth, which in turn provides for the necessities and amenities of life. The economy is also a means by which society accomplishes other goals, such as social stability, full employment, and improvement in the standard of living. Consequently, the efficient functioning of the economy is important for the standard of living of people in the United States and the rest of the world.

In order for the economy to operate, it must have *productive resources,* or goods that are used to produce more goods and services. These resources include such things as machinery, buildings, and inventory. For every dollar of output produced in the economy, more dollars are invested in productive resources. In order to support a gross domestic product of approximately $6 trillion, many more trillions of dollars must be invested.

EXHIBIT 1–1 Why Is Financial Accounting Important?

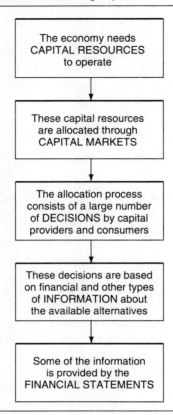

Where, then, do these capital resources come from? Many of them are generated by companies[1] through their own profitable activities. In contrast to this *internal* source, many other capital resources are raised *externally*; that is, companies obtain funds through investments by their owners, and through loans from nonowners (called *lenders* or *creditors*). The mutual satisfaction of the profit needs of the owners and creditors and the capital needs of the companies are achieved through the *capital markets*. In a broad sense, these markets include all transactions between capital providers and consumers. Thus, these markets encompass organized marketplaces, such as stock exchanges and options markets, as well as private situations, such as direct transactions between individual companies and their bankers or other creditors.

---

[1] Companies can include corporations, partnerships, and proprietorships. For convenience, the discussions in this book generally refer to public corporations and their stockholders.

The purpose of the capital markets is to allocate the available resources among those who want them. The mechanism of the allocation is the price of the resources, which takes the form of expected returns to investors and creditors. That is, investors and creditors will invest or loan their wealth only when they believe that they will receive an adequate profit (in the form of dividends, interest, and appreciation) in light of the risks they face. Likewise, corporations will acquire capital resources only when the cost of capital is appropriate for the circumstances.

Essentially, the capital markets allow many people and institutions to come together to do business. Alternative funding sources are considered by corporations, alternative investments are considered by stockholders and creditors, decisions are reached, and contracts are entered into. For example, corporations obtain resources by issuing stock, and thereby create new ownership rights. They also issue bonds in return for borrowed resources, and thereby create new creditors' rights. Additional borrowing takes place through leases and loans. Furthermore, the capital markets encompass transactions strictly between investors and creditors with no participation by a corporation. (For example, stocks and bonds are traded between individuals.) These transactions are important because they involve many buyers and sellers and allow the market forces to work more effectively.

Thus, many, many decisions are reached in the capital markets, and the process of making them involves assessments of future events. In particular, risks and returns are assessed and prices are established through competition. Although market participants consider many other factors, their decisions are generally financial in nature, in the sense that they involve money.

The lifeblood of all rational decision making is *information*, which has the basic effect of reducing uncertainty about predictions of future events and conditions. In order to act rationally, providers of capital need information about the alternative uses of their resources. Similarly, rational corporate managers need to know about the costs associated with the available alternative sources of funds.

Although many different types of information come into play in making these decisions, *financial information* is especially important because it is expressed in terms of money, which serves as a common denominator for allowing different investment and credit opportunities to be compared.

One major source of some (but certainly not all or even most) of this financial information is the *financial statements* prepared and distributed by corporations, usually as part of a more encompassing financial report.[2] *Financial accounting* is the process by which these statements are prepared.

---

[2] A complete set of financial statements includes: (1) the statement of financial position (balance sheet), (2) the income statement, (3) the statement of cash flows, and (4) the statement of stockholders' equity. The notes to the financial statements are also integral to the report.

Types of financial information. There are many different types of financial information. Some of it is concerned with the future (such as forecasts), while some of it is historical in nature (such as financial statements). Some of it is general to the economy or broad sectors of it (such as reports on interest rates or market sizes), while some of it is specific to a particular entity (such as financial statements). Furthermore, some of the information is prepared by or on behalf of certain investors and creditors for their own benefit (such as recommendations from financial analysts or bond rating agencies like Moody's), while some of it is provided directly by corporations for distribution to all investors, creditors, and others (such as financial statements).

Summary. Financial accounting is considered to be important to the economy as a whole because it provides information that can be used in the capital markets to help investors and creditors make decisions that affect the allocation of capital resources among the participants in economic activity. If these decisions are made in the light of useful financial information, it is more likely that the economy will be more efficient. And, if the economy is more efficient, it is more likely that society's goals will be fulfilled.

Two Other Views on the Importance of Financial Accounting

From a behavioral perspective, financial accounting is important to many people because their personal standards of living depend on their knowledge of its practices. These people include independent auditors who review financial statements for their propriety, private accountants who prepare financial statements describing their employer corporations, and financial analysts who use financial statements to develop recommendations for their clients. Financial accounting also can be important to managers of corporations because their job security, compensation, status, power, and other aspects of their self-esteem may very well be affected by the picture of their performance provided in the financial statements.[3] An awareness of these behavioral factors is very helpful for comprehending the processes used for setting standards.

As a result of research into the capital markets, others have suggested that financial accounting may not be very important because they believe that the studies have shown that the markets are efficient in terms of their ability to process other kinds of information without waiting for financial statements to be published. In effect, they suggest that sophisticated mar-

---

[3] The importance of these effects has been suggested by numerous other authors. For more information, the following should be consulted: Dale Gerboth, "Research, Intuition, and Politics in Accounting Inquiry," *The Accounting Review,* July 1973, pp. 475–82; Charles Horngren, "The Marketing of Accounting Standards," *Journal of Accountancy,* October 1973, pp. 61–66; and Rose Watts and Jerold Zimmerman, *Positive Accounting Theory* (Englewood Cliffs, N.J.: Prentice Hall, 1986).

ket participants have access to private information that allows them to reach financial decisions without relying on the published statements. Other research has suggested that a company's management cannot mislead the capital markets by selecting accounting principles that make the company appear to be in better condition than it really is. For example, the research shows that a company's stock does not trade at a higher price simply because reported profits are higher when first-in, first-out (FIFO) is used to measure cost of goods sold instead of last-in, first-out (LIFO). Again, the implication is that financial accounting information is not important.

However, these arguments are incomplete in several respects. First, the research has been based on events and conditions occurring in the organized securities exchanges (primarily the New York Stock Exchange), which involve highly competitive markets with large numbers of securities, buyers, and sellers. Other sectors of the capital markets are not as well organized or competitive, with the consequence that useful new information is probably conveyed to other groups of investors and creditors through financial statements. Second, other research suggests that public financial statements are important to the efficiency of the capital markets because they provide information that allows market participants to validate their previous predictions and expectations about the company, its industry, and the economy. If the financial statements provide new information that was not anticipated, it is reasonable to expect security prices to change when they are published. In effect, the capital markets would have to make perfect predictions in order for the financial statements to be useless. Third, it has been argued that public financial reporting increases competition in the capital markets by making more information available to more market participants. This wider distribution of more information diminishes the advantages of private information that allows some market participants to gain advantages over others. In addition to providing more fairness for less sophisticated participants, the increased availability of useful information reduces the costs incurred in generating and interpreting private information. For example, a new requirement to report an employer's liability for future pension payments would give all investors access to this information about the obligation with the consequence that more sophisticated investors with private information would no longer have as great an advantage. Furthermore, the employer's cost of developing the published measure of the liability would be lower than the combined costs incurred by all investors in trying to estimate its amount on their own. In addition, the published number may be more useful than the more speculative estimates produced by investors without the detailed knowledge available to the employer.

As a result of all these factors, it is appropriate to conclude that useful financial reporting is important for the more efficient functioning of the capital markets in particular and the economy in general.

WHAT GROUPS ARE MOST INTERESTED IN FINANCIAL ACCOUNTING, AND WHAT IS THE NATURE OF THEIR INTEREST?

The Prologue and the preceding pages have identified several groups of people who are interested in financial accounting. This section examines them more closely and shows how they often have competing interests in the reporting process.

As indicated in the preceding discussions, the most important group affected by the usefulness of financial information is the *public at large*, even though the greater majority of this group is probably unaware of financial accounting practices and issues. Their interest lies in the advantages they enjoy when the capital markets work efficiently and thereby allow the entire economy to be more productive. From another perspective, the public has an interest in financial reporting to the extent that the information in the financial statements allows regulators and others to take corrective action more quickly because the problems are revealed earlier. One example of this effect can be found in the savings and loan crisis of the 1980s. Some observers have suggested that this industry's regulators were encouraged to ignore growing problems, because the financial statements provided to them were based on accounting principles that did not reflect changes in the fair values of the loans held by the institutions and the fair values of the assets held as security against those loans. If the huge declines of the values had been incorporated into the financial reports, the regulators might have been spurred to take action sooner, thereby avoiding some of the costs that occurred later in the crisis. Another example can be found in the FASB's action in the 1990s to increase the information reported in financial statements about the cost of medical benefits to be paid to retired employees. This information showed managers, employees, and others that the companies were so greatly obligated that they would be unlikely to pay the benefits when they came due. Once the requirement took effect, companies responded by reducing their benefits in order to reduce the obligations. Even though employees lost some benefits, the public's interest and the employees' long-term interests were protected because the new information identified a major problem sufficiently early to avoid the kind of catastrophe faced in the savings and loan industry.

As demonstrated by their participation in the deliberations on various issues, certain *government regulators* are interested in financial accounting because they are charged with the responsibility of protecting the capital markets from inefficiencies in allocating capital resources, including those created by publishing false or otherwise misleading information. The Securities and Exchange Commission (SEC) has this specific responsibility. Other regulators (such as the Interstate Commerce Commission and the Federal Energy Regulatory Commission) occasionally participate in the financial accounting standards-setting process when proposed standards will affect companies under their jurisdiction. Their participation in standards setting is quite appropriate because of the role they are supposed to fill. Their goal in participating is often to encourage the disclosure of more information to financial statement users.

Providers of capital resources are naturally quite interested because they may be able to affect their risks and expected returns by using financial accounting information. This group of *financial statement users* includes actual and potential investors and lenders. It also includes financial analysts (both independent practitioners and those employed by brokerage firms) who advise investors on the suitability of various alternative investments. They may participate in the standards-setting process in order to increase the likelihood that they (or their clients) will receive at least a fair price for their resources. Consequently, their goal in the process is often to increase the amount of information disclosed. On the other hand, certain sophisticated users of financial statements have access to private sources of information that they are able to use to increase their wealth; it is only reasonable to expect them to want to *limit* the amount of information provided in the statements.

Managers of corporations are interested in financial accounting because their companies' access to resources (and the prices of those resources) can be affected by financial accounting information. As mentioned previously, if the managers' own compensation (or other aspects of their well-being) might be affected by financial accounting information, they are especially interested in the message conveyed in the financial statements. Consequently, they participate in the standards-setting process in order to have more control over a significant part of their surroundings. In general, they are more in control when there are fewer requirements for the type and quantity of information to be presented in the financial statements.

Independent auditors are interested in financial accounting and standards setting because of their special role in auditing information reported to investors and creditors by companies. Specifically, their task is to add credibility to the information reported by management in the financial statements by performing an audit of the financial statements and attaching an opinion to them. Because their professional reputations and livelihoods depend on the perceived quality of their audits, auditors face the risk of a potentially high penalty for failure. Consequently, their participation in the standards-setting process is often directed toward producing more auditable information. This tendency for auditors to protect their self-interest is often balanced by a sense of concern for the public interest, which is usually more closely aligned with statement users' needs or the efficiency of the capital markets' allocations of resources.

Instructors of accounting constitute another group involved in financial accounting. They are interested in the standards-setting process because they commit their careers to understanding accounting and to helping others understand it. Of all the groups participating in the standards-setting process, they may be the most independent and objective because of their social role as educators and because they are not financially involved like the others. However, the political nature of the standards-setting process tends to limit the effectiveness of this group because its members have less power than the other participants.

In summary, a variety of groups are affected by and interested in financial accounting. They have different points of view and interests, even to the extent of having goals for the standards-setting process that are in direct or nearly direct opposition. Furthermore, they each have power and influence and attempt to affect the process in ways that protect or advance their interests. The next section deals with the question of why it is considered desirable to resolve their differences on financial accounting issues.

WHY SHOULD DIFFERENCES AMONG THESE GROUPS BE RESOLVED?

A fundamental premise underlying current financial accounting standards setting is that *uniformity* in the practices used by all reporting companies is generally preferable to diversity. The origins of this premise lie in the view that valid, and thus useful, comparisons among alternative investments can be made only if the financial information is *comparable*. As explanation, comparability exists when like events and conditions are described similarly and when unlike events and conditions are described differently. If significant real economic similarities or differences exist but are not revealed in the accounting reports, it is possible that users of those reports will not make efficient allocation decisions.[4]

From a behavioral perspective, uniformity is generally considered desirable because it helps protect financial statement users against managers' natural bias to prepare their statements so that their performance looks better than it may really be. If managers are constrained in their choices, it is argued, they are less able to provide biased information and better decisions are more likely to be made.

On the other hand, uniformity also helps protect corporate management against less scrupulous managers of other corporations who might attempt to gain an advantage in the capital markets by providing deliber-

---

[4] It should be noted that uniformity is not sufficient to produce comparability. For example, no U.S. company is allowed to recognize an asset for the results of its research and development activities. Even though all companies follow this uniform practice, their financial statements do not provide comparable information because some companies have obtained substantial value from their research efforts, while others have obtained less. Further, it is likely that all companies have obtained something of value but they all report a zero value on their statements of financial position. For a more complete discussion of these points, see Statement of Financial Accounting Concepts No. 2 (paragraphs 111–119), which was issued by the FASB in 1978.

ately misleading information. Furthermore, by following an authoritative external rule, management may be protected against after-the-fact allegations from unsuccessful investors that the company's financial statements made its securities appear to be better investments than they really were.

Uniformity protects auditors because the rules provide an external basis for their judgments. Specifically, a conclusion that the financial statements were prepared in compliance with published standards is more easily reached (and far more defensible) than a conclusion that the statements disclose the "truth" about the company. In attesting to compliance, the auditor's decisions are relatively objective and supportable with hard evidence. In reaching a judgment about truth, the outcome would tend to be more conjecture than fact, and the auditor would be exposed to a high risk of failure and demands for retribution by those who relied on the audit opinion.

Because of these considerations, there is general agreement that most participants (and the economy as a whole) are better off with the regulation of the flow of information from corporations to investors and creditors as accomplished by the establishment of a uniform set of accounting standards. The term *generally accepted accounting principles* is used to describe agreed-upon rules and guidelines.[5] As will be made clear later in this book, not everyone agrees that standards are needed or that they are cost effective.

Because different views exist on the question of what rule should be created to deal with a given situation (as seen in the Prologue), it follows that there must be some process for resolving the differences. That mechanism is presently located in the *Financial Accounting Standards Board* (FASB). In general terms, the FASB's role is to resolve issues concerning the usefulness of various types of financial information in particular circumstances. In performing this task, the FASB must gather and sift evidence about that usefulness while taking into consideration the interests of the various parties affected by its standards. The output of its process becomes part of GAAP.

The next three sections of this chapter deal briefly with the FASB's structure, the source of its authority, and its procedures. Subsequent chapters provide more detailed information.

---

[5] As described earlier in footnote 1 on page 10, most of the discussion in this book focuses on corporations that have issued securities to the public. However, many other companies (including corporations, partnerships, and proprietorships) are required to issue financial statements in accordance with GAAP by state laws, by contracts with other parties (usually lenders and suppliers), or in order to qualify to be considered for a loan or other financial arrangement. Some managers also choose to have their companies described in terms of GAAP, even if there are no external users of their statements. Chapter 6 describes the standards overload problem that can arise when these smaller nonpublic companies are required to prepare financial statements under GAAP that are primarily designed to deal with public companies.

EXHIBIT 1–2 The Structure of the FASB

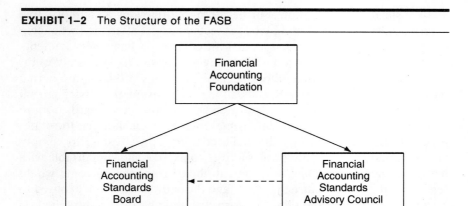

WHAT IS THE BASIC STRUCTURE OF THE FASB?

The Financial Accounting Standards Board is the operating arm of the three-part organizational structure represented in Exhibit 1–2.

The *Financial Accounting Foundation* (FAF) is the parent organization, and its trustees constitute the governing body. The Foundation is recognized as a nonprofit organization under the Internal Revenue Code. The Foundation has an executive vice president and is administered by 16 trustees. The two primary tasks of the trustees are to raise funds for the operation of the organization and to appoint members of the FASB.[6] Under the Foundation's bylaws, the trustees are not to interfere in any way with the standards-setting work of the FASB. Of course, their power to appoint and reappoint members provides the opportunity for the trustees to have indirect influence over the process in the long run just as the president of the United States can influence future decisions of the Supreme Court through appointments of the justices.

The *Financial Accounting Standards Advisory Council* (FASAC) is a group of approximately 30 influential persons. The number actually serving on FASAC varies from year to year; the bylaws merely call for at least 20 members to be appointed. The actual number serving has grown larger to obtain representation of more groups of interested parties. The purpose of the Council is to advise the FASB, particularly on financial accounting issues and on the priorities that should be placed on resolving them. FASAC also advises the FASB on the suitability of its tentative resolutions of the issues that it is addressing. The members of the Council are appointed by the trustees of the Foundation.

---

[6] The trustees also raise funds for and appoint the members of the Governmental Accounting Standards Board (GASB), which develops standards to be used in preparing financial statements for state and local government entities.

EXHIBIT 1–3 The Sources of the FASB's Authority

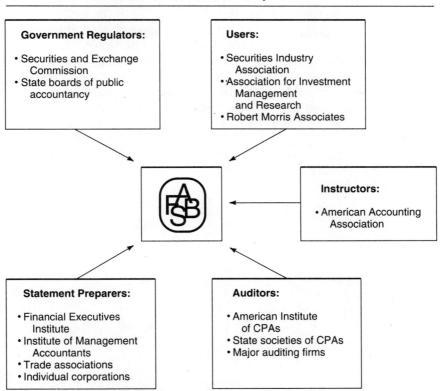

FROM WHERE DOES THE FASB DERIVE ITS AUTHORITY?

From the articles in the Prologue, it is clear that the Financial Accounting Standards Board has authority for setting standards; because of this authority, some people mistakenly assume that the FASB is actually a government agency.[7] The previous discussion has shown that it is a privately funded, nongovernmental entity. Nonetheless, the FASB's authority does depend largely on its endorsement by governmental bodies, particularly the federal Securities and Exchange Commission and state-level regulatory agencies. It derives additional authority from other nongovernmental sources. The relationships between these organizations and the FASB are depicted in Exhibit 1–3. In particular, the reader should note how the different organizations represent the interests of the various constituent groups.

---

[7] Some think the "F" in FASB stands for "Federal."

The Securities and Exchange Commission

In its founding legislation (passed in 1933 and 1934), the Securities and Exchange Commission was given authority to establish accounting principles for its registrants, which is the name given to those corporations that must comply with its reporting requirements. These companies must meet certain size tests and have shareholders in more than one state. Normally, a company must comply with the SEC's registration requirements if it has at least $5 million in assets and/or 500 stockholders. Such companies must register their securities (stocks and bonds) before they are issued to the public and must subsequently file regular periodic and special reports with the SEC. The Commission's statutory authority over its registrants can be represented with this diagram:

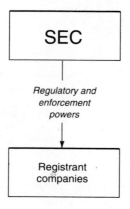

The early Commissioners of the SEC decided against developing a new set of accounting standards to be used by registrants; instead, they adopted the policy of relying on existing principles for which there was "substantial authoritative support." This policy was established in 1938 in the SEC's Accounting Series Release No. 4. In effect, this action shifted the authority for rule-making to the *American Institute of Accounting* (AIA), now the *American Institute of Certified Public Accountants* (AICPA), which shortly thereafter empowered the *Committee on Accounting Procedure* (CAP) to resolve controversial issues. The Committee was succeeded in 1959 by the AICPA's *Accounting Principles Board* (APB). Both of these organizations are described in the appendix to Chapter 2.

Largely because giving authority to a committee composed primarily of independent auditors did not appear to provide an equal opportunity for all interested groups to participate in (and to affect the outcome of) the standards-setting process, the FASB was formed in 1972 and began operating in 1973. Shortly thereafter, the SEC specifically recognized the Board as the official source of generally accepted accounting principles. The following endorsement was first published in Accounting Series Release No. 150 and was incorporated into the SEC's Financial Reporting Release No. 1 in 1982:

> . . . the Commission intends to continue its policy of looking to the private sector for leadership in establishing and improving accounting principles and standards. . . . [Consequently,] principles, standards and practices promulgated by the FASB in its Statements and Interpretations will be considered by the Commission as having substantial authoritative support, and those contrary to such FASB promulgations will be considered to have no such support.

Thus, this diagram is more descriptive of the relationship among the SEC, the FASB, and the SEC's registrants:

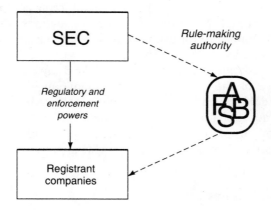

The dotted line represents the fact that the FASB has authority only for the setting of accounting principles—the SEC remains the sole authority for regulating other aspects of corporate governance, such as the solicitation of stockholder proxies and the trading of securities by insiders, who include managers and major stockholders. It must be emphasized that the FASB has not been delegated any enforcement authority by the SEC. Furthermore, the FASB has only limited authority for establishing accounting principles because the SEC can adopt its own rules where the FASB is silent or when the Commission thinks that other practices will provide more useful information. These powers of the Commission have rarely been exercised. Notable situations in which they have been used include the SEC's decision in 1978 to reject the FASB's answer to the question of how oil and gas producing companies should measure their income and the FASB's issuance of Statement of Financial Accounting Standards No. 33 in 1979 requiring the presentation of supplemental information about the effects of changing prices.

In addition, as shown in the articles in the Prologue, the SEC can act to encourage the FASB to resolve an issue. Typically, the Commission does not apply pressure to the Board; rather, the SEC and the FASB operate within an atmosphere of "mutual nonsurprise."[8]

State Regulatory Authorities

Another governmental source of authority for the FASB is the endorsement of its pronouncements by state-level agencies that license public accountants. The task of these agencies (usually called *state boards of public accountancy*) is to control certified public accountants' professional activities, primarily through two channels. A state board is authorized first to identify sources of GAAP for individuals practicing under its jurisdiction, and second to establish means of enforcing compliance with GAAP. Usually through some type of ethics regulations, the FASB is recognized as the authority for establishing GAAP, but the enforcement authority is retained by the State Board.[9]

Additional credibility is given to the FASB by state authorities through their use of the Uniform CPA Examination in their licensing process. Because this exam (which is compiled by the AICPA) includes a large number of questions about FASB pronouncements, the state authorities are essentially establishing the fact that a competent public accountant must have a thorough knowledge of FASB matters.

Nongovernmental Bodies

Nongovernmental support has also proven to be vital in establishing the authority of the FASB. For example, the AICPA has endorsed FASB standards in its ethics rules for its members since 1973. Essentially, Rule 203 of the Institute's Code of Professional Conduct does not allow an auditor to state that a client's financial statements are prepared in accordance with GAAP when they do not comply with FASB pronouncements.

---

[8] This expression was used in testimony by former FASB Chairman Don Kirk before the Subcommittee on Oversight and Investigations, Committee on Energy and Commerce, U.S. House of Representatives, February 20, 1985. Mr. Kirk attributes its first use to Dr. John C. Burton, who was the SEC's chief accountant from 1972 to 1976.

[9] This arrangement also requires FASB rules to be used in the financial statements of companies that are *not* SEC registrants. Because the FASB must shape its requirements to meet the needs of the SEC, complaints often arise that the FASB is not sensitive to the needs of smaller companies. This standards overload problem is discussed in Chapter 6.

Rule 203 does allow an exception for circumstances in which compliance with GAAP will produce misleading information if the exception is clearly and completely described in the auditor's opinion. (In practice, this exception is virtually never invoked.) Because the Institute has no governmental authority, its strongest sanction for unethical behavior is merely to expel a CPA from its membership. However, this action can diminish the individual's reputation and ability to practice and can motivate AICPA members to comply with GAAP developed by the FASB.

The same effect is accomplished for members of *state professional societies* of CPAs that adopt an ethics rule similar to the AICPA's Rule 203. These societies are voluntary associations separate from the state boards that grant licenses. Those CPAs who join a society are seeking some additional benefits, such as continuing education programs and access to life and disability insurance. The societies have their own ethics rules that usually correspond to those of the AICPA and that may or may not be different from the regulations established by the state boards.

Other nongovernmental organizations have increased the influence of the FASB without adding to its authority in the same way as the SEC, the state boards, and the AICPA. These other organizations' primary means of support for FASB is their participation in the standards-setting process. The most significant national organizations of this kind (and the typical orientation of their members) are:

- Securities Industry Association (SIA)
  —investment bankers.
- Association for Investment Management and Research (AIMR)
  —investment advisers.
- Financial Executives Institute (FEI)
  —corporate accounting officers at highest levels.
- Institute of Management Accountants (IMA)
  —corporate accountants at all levels.
- American Accounting Association (AAA)
  —accountants from various fields, but predominantly professors.

Together with the AICPA, these groups comprise six of the eight sponsoring organizations that have special powers in the governance of the Financial Accounting Foundation.[10]

Additional credibility is attributed to FASB pronouncements through extensive participation in the Board's due process activities by individuals, corporations, trade associations, and public accounting firms. One particularly active users' group is Robert Morris Associates, which is composed of bank lending officers. Examples of trade associations that

---

[10] The other two sponsoring organizations are the Government Finance Officers Association and the National Association of State Auditors, Comptrollers, and Treasurers.

have participated are the American Petroleum Institute and the Edison Electric Institute.

The complexity of the Board's position should be clear from this discussion. Specifically, it derives its legal authority from its endorsement by governmental bodies but depends on nongovernmental bodies for its funding and its governance. This arrangement inevitably produces ambiguities and controversy. Various dimensions of these issues are discussed throughout this book, especially in Chapter 6.

WHAT PROCEDURES DOES THE FASB FOLLOW IN SETTING STANDARDS?

To accomplish its duties, the FASB must mobilize members of the business community[11] to participate in its procedures. Through their participation, the FASB is more capable of: (1) identifying unresolved financial accounting questions, (2) ranking those questions in importance, (3) identifying the alternative answers, and (4) evaluating the answers to find the most suitable one for the present circumstances. Furthermore, by involving the community in extensive and thorough *due process procedures,* the Board can develop a more broadly based consensus in support of its conclusions than it could if it operated in a vacuum. The detailed steps in the due process are described in Chapter 3.

In going about its work, the FASB must focus on controversial issues. In the words of former Board Chairman Don Kirk,

> There are no easy, universally popular answers to most of the questions facing the FASB. Problems that are amenable to clear-cut solutions never reach the Board. The problems it is asked to deal with generally are those on which reasonable and informed people differ.[12]

Although the Board listens to the entire business community in identifying which issues to try to resolve, its members determine which projects are admitted to its agenda. However, they are closely advised on this point by FASAC and are not likely to be able to avoid an issue because it promises to be difficult to resolve. The actual steps used to create a project are discussed in Chapter 3.

Chapter 5 describes a series of controversial issues that the FASB, its predecessors, and the accounting profession have faced over a number of

---

[11] In an unpublished report forwarded to the trustees of the Financial Accounting Foundation in 1985, a committee of the Financial Executives Institute identified the financial preparer constituency of the FASB as the "business community." The authors believe that this extremely narrow usage of the phrase is inappropriate because auditors, users, regulators, academicians, and the FASB are all part of the business community. Consequently, the phrase is used in this book in the more well-established sense to mean all who participate in business activity, rather than just corporate management.

[12] Testimony before the Subcommittee on Oversight and Investigations, Committee on Energy and Commerce, U.S. House of Representatives, February 20, 1985.

years. As Don Kirk suggested, without controversy there is no need for the FASB, but with controversy there is need for debate and change. As a consequence, members of the profession need to be prepared to cope with changes in practice. In order to deal with such changes, it is helpful to understand the changes that have occurred in the past.

The Conceptual Framework

When the FASB faces controversial issues, particularly in a public arena, it is understandable that its members would want to deal with the questions one at a time rather than as parts of a larger whole. If a one-at-a-time (or ad hoc) approach is adopted, compromises and resolutions tend to take on customized forms to deal with the needs of specific constituents. Because different groups are affected differently by different issues, the standards setters can drift into this ad hoc approach under which each issue is resolved without regard to previously developed resolutions of others. For example, similar transactions may occur in two different industry settings and create what appear to be two separate problems, with the result that the standards setters would have to deal with two different constituent groups. If the ad hoc approach were to be used, the standards setters could compromise and reach a different consensus solution for the seemingly different problems. The likelihood of inconsistency is even greater if several years intervene between two projects and new appointees are serving on the authoritative body. These situations are generally undesirable because they may introduce inconsistencies and contradictions among standards that can rob the financial statements of comparability and other attributes of usefulness.

The ad hoc approach is also undesirable because it tends to create redundancy in discussions when the same basic issues are debated over and over again with the different constituents involved in different specific projects. For example, the Board and the affected constituents could come to an agreement as to the meaning of the term *asset* in the discussion of an issue in the utilities industry. Then, when a problem arose in the software industry and different people were involved in the deliberations, it would be necessary to debate once again what *asset* means.

To help avoid these problems, the FASB undertook the development of its own *Conceptual Framework* that attempts to establish a more global view of accounting and defines basic terms. As the result of a number of practical considerations, the nature of the FASB and its processes do not allow these types of problems to be eliminated or avoided.

Because the Framework is important for understanding how the FASB works, Chapter 4 explains its fundamental components and the difficulties that the FASB faced in building it and continues to face in using it.

IS THE FASB A POLITICAL INSTITUTION?

The answer to the question of whether the FASB is a political institution depends, of course, on the definition of the term *political* that one chooses to adopt. There are two common definitions that need to be distinguished before going on to the answer. One holds that the term *political* (or *politics*) merely refers to the processes of governing an entity or activity. The second definition includes a connotation of manipulation of that system for the purpose of promoting one's self-interest to the detriment of others.

In applying the first definition, it can be seen that the FASB and any other organization (such as a company, a school, a church, a club, or even a family) is indeed political. In carrying out its tasks, the Board will inevitably make decisions that benefit some more than others. If it were possible for all participants to be better off as a result of an accounting standard, there would be no need for the standard because there would be no controversy. In all likelihood, everyone would be using the practice without having to be told to do so.

In making those decisions, it is equally inevitable that compromises among the constituents will be made in order to develop the necessary consensus to establish the standard as "generally accepted." A compromise may involve accepting less than the full amount of information that a particular group might like to see presented, or it may involve one party getting what it wants on one issue in exchange for giving up what it wanted on another. While the process of reaching the compromise is inevitably political, there is no necessity that the process must involve any of the unsavory practices that are often connoted by the term *politics*.

However, as indicated by the reference to "lobbying" in one of the articles in the Prologue, it is readily apparent that many of the constituents in the Board's processes act out of self-interest. Indeed, it is the opportunity to seek favorable solutions from the Board that brings such great vitality and thoroughness to the standards-setting process.

For those who would disparage the presence of *any* politics in standards setting, it may be instructive to consider what alternative system could be implemented. In lieu of a deliberative body, a single autocrat of accounting might be appointed to derive solutions from the logical analysis and extension of a few basic fundamental truths. However appealing that system might be, it is too simplistic because unambiguous principles have not yet been uncovered. Furthermore, it is inevitable that the autocrat would impose some costs on some parties in excess of their benefits. In the same sense that taxation without representation is inherently unfair, something is lacking in a standards-setting system that does not call for participation by those affected by the standards.

The FASB's structure is designed to capture some of the advantages of both the participative and the autocrat approaches. The due process procedures are established in order to give everyone an opportunity to

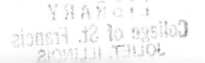

protect their interests; however, the issues are not resolved by counting the votes of all those who participate. Rather, the Board members have the powers of a collective autocrat in the sense that they are given the authority to choose the final answer. But they are constrained by the need to obtain continuing support from the participants, particularly the SEC and influential leaders in the profession and the business community. It is important to note that constraints are also created by the integrity of the individuals appointed to the FASB, the Board of Trustees, and FASAC, as well as those who donate funds to the Foundation and those who participate in the FASB's activities. If that integrity were to be lost or too severely compromised, the system would probably not function very well.

Three Levels of Politics

In fulfilling its mission, the FASB encounters the need for political activity on at least three levels:

- Among its seven members.
- Between itself and its constituencies.
- Between itself and the SEC.

On the first level, negotiation and compromise are essential to the development of a consensus on the issues related to a proposed accounting standard. Seldom do even two people agree on what the question is, much less its best answer. Because passage of a new standard requires an agreement among five Board members, it is virtually always necessary that they give up something that they would otherwise prefer to be part of the answer. Thus, each Board member must enter deliberations on a project with an idea of which points are most important and least important; then, as the debate ensues, the struggle becomes one of attempting to preserve the most important, even if it means letting the others fall aside. This compromising is a critical part of politics.

On the second level, the Board must be responsive to the apparent positions of its constituent groups of the public, statement users, statement preparers, and auditors. If the steps in the due process reveal that these groups do not agree with the Board's assessment of the situation, then it behooves the Board to find a compromise that is more likely to be acceptable. Although the independence of the Board allows it to act like an autocrat, it would not be prudent to push that power to its limits except in very limited circumstances. The articles in the Prologue show how the FASB reacted to the input from the affected companies and others in the mark-to-market project.

On the third level, the Board has to acknowledge that the SEC has more power than the other groups, with the consequence that careful attention must be paid to the Commission's needs. After all, it would not be worth the effort to establish a standard that would be unacceptable to the SEC. Thus, as described earlier in the chapter, it is important for the FASB to establish and maintain close communications with the SEC and to be responsive to the demands placed on the commissioners in their own environment.

In summary, the answer to the question of whether the FASB is a political institution is a clear "yes." This answer should be understood to mean that the FASB governs by negotiation and compromise rather than by manipulative means. On the other hand, it would be naive to believe that manipulative methods and motives never enter into the activities of the Board and its constituents.

The Implications of a Political Process

At this point, it is appropriate to observe four implications of the fact that accounting standards setting is a political process.

First, politics tend to make generally accepted accounting principles logically inconsistent because the consensus needed to resolve an issue will be shaped by those in power and how important the issues are to them. Thus, inconsistencies will appear between standards issued at different times, under different standards setters, and in different industry settings. One example of this type of inconsistency can be seen in the differences between Statement of Financial Accounting Standards No. 2 (SFAS 2), which requires all research and development costs to be expensed, and SFAS 86, which was issued 11 years later and requires capitalization of certain costs of developing computer software.

Because the FASB derives its authority from the SEC, and because the SEC derives its authority from the Congress and the president, there can be inconsistencies between standards issued under different national administrations. For example, disclosures of information about the effects of changing prices were required by SFAS 33, which was issued during the populist Carter administration. On the other hand, these provisions were rescinded by SFAS 82 and SFAS 89, which were issued during the deregulatory Reagan administration. Of course, other factors also contributed to the elimination of these requirements.

A second major implication of politics is found in the attitudes of constituents toward GAAP. Given the different interests and the need to compromise to reach a consensus, it is virtually certain that at least someone will be unhappy with any rule. It may even be true that everyone will be unhappy because so many compromises will have been reached. Because of this condition, the FASB (or any standards setter) must expect opposition on any issue that it attempts to resolve. Furthermore, it must have the institutional will to stand up to the opposition, or it will lose its capacity to bring about meaningful reform.

A third implication concerns the occurrence of change in GAAP. Given the dynamics of politics with its shifts in power and priorities, it is inevitable that GAAP will change. No one can count on a rule remaining in effect forever. On the other hand, a fourth implication is that GAAP cannot be changed quickly. Those who want to bring about change must muster their forces to get a project on an agenda and then keep it moving ahead to a satisfactory resolution against a stubborn opposition that will want to keep the change from taking place. In effect, change will happen, but not sudden change. This inertia is frustrating to those who would seek to reform practice, but it has the positive feature of creating stability in the social order of accounting.

As a result of these last two implications of the political process, students and practitioners will always have to continue studying in order to stay informed about new generally accepted principles. The status quo will always be changing, and those who don't keep up with the change will be left behind.

SELECTED READINGS

AICPA. *Objectives of Financial Statements*. Report of the Study Group on the Objectives of Financial Statements. New York, 1973.

CARMICHAEL, DOUGLAS R., AND JAMES L. CRAIG. "The FASB at Work." *CPA Journal*, January 1992, p. 42.

CYERT, RICHARD M., AND YUJI IJIRI. "Problems of Implementing the Trueblood Objective Report." *Studies on Financial Accounting Objectives*, supplement to *Journal of Accounting Research*, 1974, pp. 29–32.

DEAKIN, EDWARD B. "Rational Economic Behavior and Lobbying on Accounting Issues: Evidence from the Oil and Gas Industry." *Accounting Review*, January 1989, pp. 137–51.

GERBOTH, DALE L. "Research, Intuition, and Politics in Accounting Inquiry." *Journal of Accountancy*, July 1973, pp. 475–82.

JOHNSON, STEVEN B., AND DAVID SOLOMONS. "Institutional Legitimacy and the FASB." *Journal of Accounting and Public Policy* 3 (1984), pp. 165–83.

SOLOMONS, DAVID. "The Politicization of Accounting." *Journal of Accountancy*, November 1978, pp. 65–72.

WYATT, ARTHUR R. "Accounting Standards and the Professional Auditor." *Accounting Horizons*, June 1989, pp. 96–102.

————. "Professionalism in Standard Setting." *CPA Journal*, July 1988, pp. 20–28.

ZEFF, STEPHEN A. "The Rise of Economic Consequences." *Journal of Accountancy*, December 1978, pp. 56–63.

2

The People and the Structure of the FASB

The structure of any organization should reflect its purpose. The FASB is no different in this respect, and its structure is intended to allow it to meet its responsibility for resolving controversial issues while providing for participation by a large number of interested parties. However, the FASB's structure must be unusual to cope with a difficult paradox. On one hand, the Board must be independent of any *particular* constituent group in order to be relieved from pressure to provide standards that promote the interest of that group. On the other hand, the Board must remain dependent on *all* the groups in order to derive sufficient power from their endorsements to allow it to create authoritative answers. This dependence also encourages the members of the groups to participate in the FASB's due process procedures. The fine balance between independence and dependence is not easy to maintain; however, many observers feel that the FASB has been successful because it has balanced these opposing forces.

As described briefly in Chapter 1, the organization has these three components:

- Financial Accounting Foundation
- Financial Accounting Standards Board
- Financial Accounting Standards Advisory Council

Each component has its own duties and responsibilities for performance; each is also subject to constraints that limit its ability to interfere with the others. By subdividing the responsibilities and limiting the powers, the designers produced a system that achieves the balance considered essential to the Board's success.[1]

Because so much of the FASB's activity involves the work of the *Research and Technical Activities (RTA)* staff, this chapter also describes its structure, personnel, and duties.

FINANCIAL ACCOUNTING FOUNDATION

The Foundation is the parent organization in the FASB's structure. Incorporated under the laws of Delaware as a nonprofit corporation, it qualifies as an institution "organized to operate exclusively for charitable, educational, scientific and literary purposes" under Section 501(c)(3) of the federal Internal Revenue Code. Because of the Foundation's nonprofit status, its income is exempt from taxation and donations are deductible as charitable contributions on donors' tax returns. As justification for this tax treatment, the Foundation's certificate of incorporation includes this language:

> . . . the purposes of the Corporation shall be to advance and to contribute to the education of the public, investors, creditors, preparers and suppliers of financial information, reporting entities and certified public accountants in regard to standards of financial accounting and reporting; to establish and improve the standards of financial accounting and reporting by defining, issuing and promoting such standards; to conduct and commission research, statistical compilations and other studies and surveys; and to sponsor meetings, conferences, hearings and seminars, in respect of financial accounting and reporting.[2]

The overall responsibility for these activities rests with the Foundation's 16-member Board of Trustees.

One major task of the trustees is raising the funds needed to finance the operations of the three-part organization. It follows that the trustees are accountable to donors and the public at large for the appropriate use of these funds.

A second major duty is the appointment of the members of the Financial Accounting Standards Board and the Financial Accounting Standards Advisory Council. The procedures used for this task and the qualifications of the appointees are discussed later in this chapter.

A third activity of the trustees is reviewing the performance of the FASB. As a result of such administrative reviews by the trustees' Struc-

---

[1] The basic structure was designated by a special study group of the AICPA headed by Mr. Francis M. Wheat. The 1972 proposal of the Wheat Study Group was endorsed by the AICPA and other organizations, and implemented within a year.

[2] *Restated Certificate of Incorporation of the Financial Accounting Foundation*, as amended through June 29, 1984, section 3.

ture Committee, a number of changes in Board procedures have been implemented. The following items are examples of these changes:

- Expanded use of task forces and scheduling of public hearings outside New York City. (Chapter 3 describes the nature and purposes of these steps in the due process procedures.)
- Broadened membership of the board of trustees, the FASB, and FASAC to be more representative of the constituent groups.[3]
- Expansion of the size of the RTA staff and the delegation of greater responsibilities to staff members.
- Reduction (in 1977) of the number of assenting members needed to approve a standard for publication from a two-thirds majority (five Board members) to a simple majority (four members). This change was reversed in 1990 when the two-thirds majority voting rule was reinstated by the trustees.
- Elimination of closed-door meetings of the FASB.[4]
- Expanded use of special meetings with constituents for the purpose of educating Board members about highly specialized areas of practice.
- Distribution of prospectuses prior to adding a major project to the Board's agenda.
- Assignment of Board members as chairmen of task forces created for major projects (task forces are described in Chapter 3).

None of these changes can be considered a radical reform of the basic structure created in 1973.

To maintain the Board's independence, the Foundation's review is supposed to be limited to examining the FASB's efficiency and its ability to respond to the views of its constituencies. The trustees are not supposed to interfere in or even attempt to influence the outcome of the standards-setting process. The Foundation's bylaws specifically state:

> . . . the Trustees shall not, by or in connection with the exercise of their power of approval over annual budgets or their periodic review of such operating and project plans, direct the FASB or GASB to undertake or to omit to undertake any particular project or activity or otherwise affect the

---

[3] Under the structure initially established in response to the Wheat Study Group report, four of the seven FASB members had to be CPAs. This provision may have reflected the concerns of the AICPA about relinquishing its 35 years of control over the establishment of accounting principles. The major factor that triggered the elimination of this rule was the investigation of the accounting profession by congressional subcommittees in the mid-1970s. A report prepared by one of the subcommittees expressed concerns that auditors had too much influence on standards setting and that statement preparers had too much influence on auditors.

[4] Prior to this change, virtually all deliberations among the Board members were closed to the public, with the consequence that the constituencies were not as involved in the process. This change was also a result of the congressional hearings described in footnote 3.

exercise by the FASB or GASB of their authority, functions and powers in respect of standards of financial accounting and reporting.[5]

By this limitation, the separation of powers is nominally maintained. While this provision makes it difficult for trustees to exert direct influence on Board members concerning accounting issues, the fact remains that trustees control reappointment to the Board. Thus, it is at least theoretically possible that a Board member might modify a position on an issue to ensure reappointment; however, there is no evidence that such a result has ever occurred.

It is also possible that the Board's independence could be endangered if a particular constituency group were to gain control of the Foundation's Board of Trustees who would then select new Board members who in turn would advocate the group's interests over the interests of others. Clearly, the greatest threat to the FASB would arise if this control were to rest with financial statement preparers because they are the group being regulated. This issue of whether preparers dominate the Board is discussed in more detail in Chapter 6. At this point, it is sufficient to say that a number of events and conditions indicate that the Board is close to being dominated by preparers.

The Trustees

The 16 trustees of the Foundation meet at least four times each year, usually in New York City. The agenda for the meeting is announced publicly, and the meetings are open to the public, except for deliberations on particularly sensitive matters, including the evaluation of candidates for appointment and reappointment to the FASB and FASAC.

The trustees can serve no more than two terms of three years each. They select their own president, but the day-to-day administration is performed by a salaried executive vice president and chief administrative officer. In 1993, the president was Dennis D. Dammerman, senior vice president of finance for General Electric Company. The executive vice president was Joseph S. LaGambina.

Exhibit 2–1 describes the relationship of the trustees to the FASB and the sponsoring organizations that were identified in Chapter 1. Thirteen of the sixteen trustees are elected to their positions by electors who represent the eight sponsoring organizations. The electors are the official members of the nonprofit corporation as required by Delaware laws. Each of the eight electors is selected by the governing board of one of the organizations, and is either its senior elected official or full-time executive director. Although the electors technically have the power to vote for any

---

[5] *Bylaws of the Financial Accounting Foundation*, as amended through May 1, 1991, chapter A, article 1–A, section 1.

EXHIBIT 2–1   Relationships and Activities of the Sponsoring Organizations, Electors, Trustees, and FASB Members

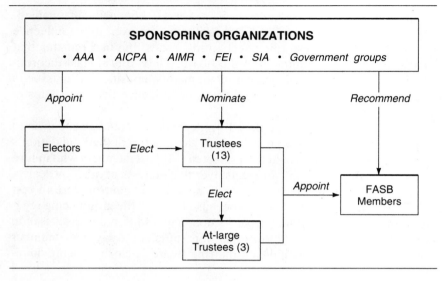

candidate for a trustee's position, history shows that they have merely approved the candidates nominated by the sponsoring organizations.

Exhibit 2–2 shows how the trustees' positions are allocated among the sponsoring organizations. As indicated in Exhibit 2–1, the 3 at-large positions are filled by individuals chosen by the other 13 trustees. In 1993, these trustees included Dennis Dammerman, senior vice president of finance for General Electric and also the president of the Foundation; Philip Searle, a retired banker; and Kathryn Wriston, an independent director of several corporations. Exhibit 2–2 also classifies the 16 trustees according to the constituencies that they represent. It shows that two of the trustees from the government-sponsoring organizations are preparers of financial statements presented to the public. One is a city manager and the other is a comptroller of a state treasurer's office. In addition, the trustee from the Securities Industry Association is a chief financial officer of a major brokerage company. Because Philip Searle was the chairman of the bank that he used to work for, he is more appropriately classified as a preparer than a user. This analysis shows that half of the trustees represent the preparer constituency. This composition is unfortunate and undesirable because of the influence that the trustees exert on the Board and because of the power it gives the preparer constituency to shape the membership of the Board. Instead, the authors believe that the Board's independence and credibility would be substantially enhanced by trustees who are nationally prominent leaders from outside business, such as

EXHIBIT 2–2 Financial Accounting Foundation Trustees and Their Constituencies (as of 1993)

Trustees Appointed by	Number	Constituency Represented			
		Auditors	Preparers	Users	Public
AAA	1				1
AICPA	4	4			
AIMR.	1			1	
FEI.	2		2		
IMA	1		1		
SIA	1		1		
Government groups.	3		2		1
At-large	3		2		1
Totals	16	4	8	1	3
Percentages		25%	50%	6%	19%

former cabinet officers, a retired elected national official, or a president of a major university. The trustees' collective understanding of the Board's mission and activities would also be enhanced by appointing one or more former Board members as trustees.

A Financial Perspective

To grasp the magnitude of the operations of the Foundation and the responsibilities of the trustees for raising funds, it is helpful to see these amounts from the financial statements included in the FAF's annual report for 1992:

	FASB	GASB	Total
Operating revenues:			
Net contributions	$ 5,367,000	$1,957,000	$ 7,324,000
Net sales of publications	9,738,000	937,000	10,675,000
Total operating revenues	15,105,000	2,894,000	17,999,000
Operating expenses:			
Salaries, wages, and benefits	10,906,000	1,960,000	12,866,000
Other operating costs	3,462,000	848,000	4,310,000
Total operating costs.	14,368,000	2,808,000	17,176,000
Excess of revenues over costs . . .	$ 737,000	$ 86,000	823,000
Investment income.			771,000
Combined revenues in excess of costs			$ 1,594,000

The report shows that 41 percent of the total operating revenues come from contributions, but that contributors constitute only 36 percent of the FASB's operating revenues.

Of the funds contributed to the FASB, 40 percent came from public accountants and 60 percent from groups that the Foundation identifies as "industrial companies, banks, and financial institutions." According to the executive vice president, amounts contributed by individuals and organizations from the statement user constituency were negligible. As with the mix of the trustees, these measures again raise the issue of whether the FASB is dominated by statement preparers.

The expenditures section of the financial statements shows that the FASB is clearly a labor-intensive operation because salaries, wages, and benefits consumed $10.9 million, or about 76 percent of the total operating expenses.

The statement of financial position as of the end of 1992 reports working capital of $3.9 million, with an additional $2.6 million invested in fixed assets. In addition, there were $11.8 million of investments in the Foundation's reserve fund. With this much set aside, the Foundation could manage to operate for several years at a decreased level of contributions if any major contributors decided to reduce their donations.

THE FINANCIAL ACCOUNTING STANDARDS BOARD

In the three-part structure, the FASB is the action arm in the sense that it is responsible for setting accounting standards. Its structure (and the staff's) is directed toward the achievement of these three tasks:

- Serving as the focal point for *research*.
- *Communicating* with constituents.
- *Resolving* financial accounting issues.

Board Members

The primary purpose for making the trustees responsible for fund-raising is to insulate the seven Board members from the pressures associated with that task. This arrangement allows them to work full time on the issues and, importantly, to deal with them without concern for the effect of a standard on the constituents' willingness to contribute funds. Whether the system actually accomplishes that goal is a significant question; however, there is no systematic evidence that a Board member has taken a position on a proposed standard because of the threat of withheld funds. (As an item of anecdotal evidence of a related phenomenon, one of the authors participated in a conference in which the controller of Texaco stated that his company would withhold its donation to the Foundation if the FASB implemented its proposed accounting for pensions.)

Other steps have been taken to help Board members preserve their independence in fact and in appearance. In particular, they sever their relationship with their previous employers and become full-time employees of the Foundation. Their independence is also bolstered by the size of their annual salaries, which (in 1993) were $305,000, with the chairman receiving an additional $70,000. This arrangement makes their situation far different from the one faced by members of the Accounting Principles Board, who received no compensation and remained affiliated with (and presumably under the influence of) their employers. To protect Board members against one form of lobbying, they can accept only token gifts as a result of a speech or other public appearance, and any cash honoraria are turned over to the Financial Accounting Foundation. They must file a quarterly statement that discloses the nature and size of investments they hold. They are required to disqualify themselves from voting on issues in which there could be a conflict of interest concerning their investments or other conditions; however, no Board member has ever done so.

Generally, a Board member is appointed for a five-year term, with the possibility of reappointment for one additional term. If the initial appointment is for a partial term as a replacement for a member who resigned, the individual is still eligible for two complete five-year terms.[6]

In selecting Board members, the trustees attempt to find individuals who possess a number of qualifying characteristics. For example, according to a report prepared by the Foundation's Special Committee, Board members should have the following qualifications:[7]

1. Knowledge of financial accounting and reporting.
2. High level of intellect applied with integrity and discipline.
3. Judicial temperament.
4. Ability to work in a collegial atmosphere.
5. Communication skills.
6. Awareness of the financial reporting environment.
7. Commitment to the FASB's mission.

The Special Committee also considered whether there is a need for a formal requirement for maintaining a rigid balance among the Board members in terms of the constituencies from which they come. Basically, the members of the committee determined that the background should be "secondary" to the qualities listed above, but they also recognized that

---

[6] In 1990, the ending date of Board members' terms was changed from December 31 to June 30, reportedly to facilitate the transition of new members with children in school. This arrangement is also less likely to take new members away from their companies during the busy end-of-year reporting or auditing season. The change gave an extra six months of service to each of the Board members who were serving in 1990.

[7] Financial Accounting Foundation, "Report of the Special Committee to the Board of Trustees," December 4, 1986, pp. 15–18.

> . . . a reasonable mix of backgrounds should be an important consideration
> in selecting members so as to ensure a realistic range of viewpoints and/or
> perspectives on the Board. It was recommended by the Review Committee
> and approved by the Board of Trustees in July 1985 that the trustees continue
> to seek a Board make-up which includes a mix of backgrounds of members
> who have had major experience in public accounting, in business or industry,
> as a user of financial information, and as an accounting educator. (p. 4)

Essentially, the committee acknowledged that it is politically prudent to
balance the membership for the Board to remain broadly supported and
viable. Consequently, even before this recommendation, the trustees usually attempted to replace a retiring Board member with another individual
with a similar background. In 1985, this practice came under attack from
some members of the statement preparer constituency who suggested
very strongly that at least two and preferably three members of the Board
should be preparers. This sort of criticism is to be expected from this
group because its members are most constrained by the FASB's standards. However, it should be apparent that this pressure is directly contrary to the earlier quoted bylaw that restricts the Trustees from using
their power to "affect the exercise by the FASB or GASB of their authority, functions, and powers in respect of standards of financial accounting
and reporting." Events in the ensuing years since 1985 suggest that this
pressure has affected the Board's membership, trustee appointments, the
pace of the Board's output of standards, and even the nature of its standards. The authors believe that these developments are inappropriate and
contrary to the public's interest in useful financial statements and efficient
capital markets. Chapter 6 describes the events in more detail and explains these conclusions.

Throughout this section of the chapter, there are short biographies of
the Board members who were serving in 1993.

The Chairman of the Board

The chairman of the FASB is selected by the board of trustees and is
given special responsibilities beyond those of other Board members.
Denny Beresford was serving as the chairman in 1993. In return for this
designation and duties, the chairman receives additional compensation.
His most visible additional duty is to serve as the moderator of regular
Board meetings and other sessions, such as public hearings. His less
visible duties include the development and supervision of a number of
administrative policies for members of the Board and staff. The chairman
also works with the trustees in developing the operating budget for the
Board. In addition, he is the primary contact point between the FASB and
its constituencies and the public. As such, he is called on to make many
speeches and to appear before congressional committees or in other settings in which the Board is to be officially represented.

The report by the Foundation's Special Committee identified these leadership qualities that the chairman should possess:

1. Ability to set a sensible course toward a reasonable objective (or multiple objectives) and to direct an organization in following that course.
2. Ability to inspire colleagues and subordinates to maximum effort.
3. Ability to mediate among conflicting claims on resources.
4. Ability to represent the organization effectively.
5. Ability to deal with the unique character of the FASB:
    a. To steer a diverse group of strong-minded individuals toward consensus.
    b. To be politically sensitive to current and potential problems and conflicting needs with regard to the SEC, Congress, other governmental units, and to the private sector constituencies.

Thus, the committee recognized that it takes more than mere technical or executive ability to be a successful chairman.

Dennis R. Beresford

Age in 1994: 54
Education: B.S., University of Southern California
Appointed to FASB: January 1, 1987
Term Expires: June 30, 1997
Eligible for Reappointment: No

Denny graduated from USC in 1961 with a B.S. in public accounting and then joined the staff of the Los Angeles office of Ernst & Ernst (now Ernst & Young). His next 10 years of experience exposed him to a wide variety of clients, including companies in the electronics, aerospace, publishing, and banking industries. He especially enjoyed auditing the L.A. Rams and California Angels. In 1971, Denny was transferred to the firm's national office in Cleveland, and was shortly made a partner. In 1986, he was named the Accountant of the Year by Beta Alpha Psi. When he was appointed to the Board, he was serving as national director of Accounting Standards and drafted the firm's responses to FASB documents. He was no stranger to the Board's activities because he had served on FASAC for four years, was a member of the income tax project's task force, and was a charter member of the Emerging Issues Task Force (EITF). He considers the chairmanship to be the "culmination of everything I've been doing in my professional career." Denny is married and has two grown children. His wife is an accomplished artist and photographer. In his limited time away from the office, he enjoys golf, mystery and spy novels, and the noncomplaining companionship of his golden retriever.

James J. Leisenring

Age in 1994: 53

Education: B.S., Albion College; M.B.A., Western Michigan

Appointed to FASB: October 1, 1987

Term Expires: June 30, 1995

Eligible for Reappointment: Yes, for one term ending June 30, 2000

A native of Michigan (and always an avid Tigers fan), Jim brings an unusually diverse background to the FASB. After earning his master's degree, he taught finance at Western Michigan University for several years. He then joined a regional public accounting firm, where he was later made a partner, and served as the director of accounting and auditing. He was identified as the Accountant of the Year by Beta Alpha Psi in 1981. Jim's first experience with standards setting came with the AICPA's Auditing Standards Board, where he eventually served as chairman. Jim came to the FASB in 1982 as the director of the FASB's Research and Technical Activities staff, and served in that position until he was appointed to the Board. His humor, intellect, energy, and infectious enthusiasm have made him an effective and popular Board member and vice chairman, a position that calls upon him to represent the Board in a variety of settings, ranging from college classrooms to congressional hearings. Jim is often seen playing racquetball with fellow Board member Bob Swieringa. His excitement about the opportunities in public accounting must have showed because one of his two daughters is working in the New York office of a Big Six firm.

When the authors asked Denny Beresford whether being the chairman affects his ability to reach or express a stance on an issue, he stated that he prefers to "put his position on the table" in order to "try to influence other Board members." Unlike his predecessor, who preferred to meet with the staff team after its members had talked with other Board members in small group sessions, Denny said that he likes meeting with the other members to understand more about their positions. With respect to his approach to running public Board meetings, it is his goal to have "real debate" instead of careful expression of predetermined points. By having more discussion, he says, some of the Board's "inefficiency can be eliminated."

FINANCIAL ACCOUNTING STANDARDS ADVISORY COUNCIL

The principal mission of the Financial Accounting Standards Advisory Council is to provide advice to the Board. This advice is generally directed along two lines. First, it concerns the priorities of projects that are either before the Board or that could come before it. Thus, FASAC can

Robert J. Swieringa

Age in 1994: 51

Education: A.B., Augustana College; M.B.A., University of Denver; Ph.D., University of Illinois

Appointed to FASB: January 1, 1986

Term Expires: June 30, 1996

Eligible for Reappointment: No

After receiving his Ph.D., Bob joined the faculty of Stanford University, where he took over the courses that had been taught by Dr. Robert Sprouse. By coincidence, his appointment to the Board again made him the successor to Dr. Sprouse, who served on the FASB from 1973 through 1985. By the time Bob was appointed to the FASB, he had become professor of accounting at Cornell University in Ithaca, New York. When pushed to answer, he said that he believes the most important reason for his selection to the Board was his research record. His colleagues have suggested that his honest and forthright friendliness and his analytical abilities probably had something to do with it, too. When he isn't working, Bob is active in his local church, where he heads up (what else?) the finance committee. With a twinkle in his eye, he admits that he was very close to being a music major as an undergraduate. In fact, summer weekends often find him in the bandstand playing the euphonium (a brass instrument like a small tuba) for the New Canaan Community Band. Bob enjoys reading nonfiction and hiking in the Adirondacks with his family. He often plays racquetball with Board member Jim Leisenring but modestly encouraged us to ask Jim who was winning. Bob expects to return to university teaching after completing his second term. His students will be doubly fortunate to have him.

suggest that the Board move more quickly to get certain issues resolved or that it move more slowly on less pressing ones. FASAC can also suggest that new issues be added to the Board's agenda.

The second area in which advice is offered concerns the suitability of the preliminary positions that the Board has developed in the projects on its agenda. The positions can be those that have been drawn only tentatively, or they can be those that have been expressed in an Exposure Draft (discussed in Chapter 3). In this capacity, FASAC serves as a sounding board to let the FASB know more about how it is doing and how it is perceived by the community at large.

It might be seen, then, that FASAC fills the void left by the restriction that is supposed to keep the trustees from advising the Board on its tentative resolutions of the issues. However, FASAC has no responsibility for raising funds or being involved in any way in the administration of the FASB's activities.

There are approximately 30 members of FASAC, each of whom may be appointed by the Board of Trustees for as many as four consecutive

Joseph V. Anania

Age in 1994: 62
Education: B.B.A., University of Pittsburgh
Appointed to FASB: May 16, 1991
Term Expires: June 30, 1994
Eligible for Reappointment: Yes, for terms ending June 30, 1999 and June 30, 2004

Joe began his public accounting career in 1956 with Price Waterhouse in Pittsburgh, and spent 35 years with the firm in various capacities before his appointment to the Board in 1991. While he was with PW, Joe dealt extensively with acquisitions and sales of divisions by several multinational clients. For a while, he also worked with smaller private companies when he headed up the Pittsburgh office's specialized services department. He also helped the firm resolve technical accounting issues and indirectly participated in standards setting in a variety of ways, including a Pennsylvania state society committee that reviewed issues and wrote comment letters to the Accounting Principles Board. He was also on a PW committee that dealt with accounting issues and served on a task force that assisted the firm's national office in developing a position on accounting for postretirement benefits other than pensions. Joe feels that these experiences and his diverse client practice experience in the manufacturing, banking, utility, not-for-profit, and international sectors have helped him as a Board member. When he can find the time, Joe reads a lot of nonfiction books, pursues a physical fitness regimen, and plays a little golf. He is very involved with his family, which includes two grandchildren and several accountants. His oldest son and his daughter-in-law both work for Big Six firms and his son-in-law is a tax accountant for a public corporation.

one-year terms. Originally, it was thought that 20 members would be sufficient to attain the balance that was essential to providing well-rounded advice from all quarters; however, practice showed that more people wanted to serve and that their views could be heard efficiently. Consequently, the actual number has been higher than the minimum of 20 called for in the Rules of Procedure [Section III (C)]. Except for the chairman, Council members receive no compensation for their services and their employers are generally expected to pay their travel and other expenses. In 1993, the chairman was E. Virgil Conway, a financial consultant and former chairman and chief executive officer of The Seaman's Bank for Savings. His duties include arranging for the four quarterly meetings of the Council (which requires providing all members with adequate information about the Board's agenda), moderating the meetings, preparing plans and budgets for Council activities, preparing reports on those activities, and advising the trustees on the appointment of Council members. He is assisted by Jane Adams, who is also a project manager on the FASB's staff.

Robert Northcutt

Age in 1994: 59

Education: B.B.A., Emory University; M.B.A., Georgia State University

Appointed to FASB: March 1, 1992

Term Expires: June 30, 1996

Eligible for Reappointment: Yes, for one term ending June 30, 2001

Upon graduating from Emory University in 1956, Bob spent several years in the air force as a pilot trainee on B–25 light bombers as well as an accounting and finance officer. Afterward, he worked for a local public accounting firm in Atlanta for four years. While there, Bob not only passed all sections of the CPA exam on the first sitting but also won the Georgia state gold medal for his high scores and received an honorable mention for the AICPA Sells Award. After starting with Lockheed in Marietta, Georgia, in 1963, he went on to spend three fourths of his 28-year career with the company in Los Angeles. Just before joining the FASB, he was Lockheed's vice president and controller. Bob was first involved in standards setting in the FASB's early years when the Board was studying the issues related to accounting for research and development costs. At the time, Lockheed had more than $500 million of capitalized R&D for the L–1011 commercial airplane. Later in his career, Bob became active in the Financial Executives Institute and served on the Committee on Corporate Reporting. He was a member of FASAC when he was asked to accept Board membership. Bob feels that he brings a practical background to the Board because he lived with the issues as a preparer and may be able to see them from a different viewpoint than other members. Bob relaxes with mystery novels and some computer hacking, but doesn't find as much time for it as he would like. During our visit with Bob at the Board offices, he and Paul Miller found a common interest and could have spent the entire day talking about famous Lockheed aircraft ranging from the legendary P–38 up through the F–117 Stealth.

Like Board members, Council members are selected with the objective of balancing views. In effect, the goal in appointing members is to obtain a "microcosm" of the business community that will be likely to keep the Board from failing to consider some significant constituent's views when it resolves an issue. The 1993 Council members represent the following constituencies:

Constituent Group	Number	Percent
Users	3	10%
Public	5	17
Auditors	6	20
Preparers	16	53
Total	30	100%

Anthony T. Cope

Age in 1994: 56

Education: B.A., M.A., Cambridge University

Appointed to FASB: July 1, 1993

Term Expires: June 30, 1998

Eligible for Reappointment: Yes, for term ending June 30, 2003

A native of England, Tony earned his degrees in English from Cambridge and began his career with three years in television production in London. After coming to the United States in 1963 to get married, he and his wife decided to settle in the Boston area and Tony began working in trust management with the New England Merchants Bank. In 1969, he accepted a position with the Wellington Management Company as an equity research analyst and became a chartered financial analyst the next year. When appointed to the FASB in 1993, Tony was still affiliated with Wellington as a senior vice president and partner. Only the second Board member to be selected from the user constituency, he was very active in policymaking for much of his career, as shown by his service on a number of national committees of the Association for Investment Management and Research that developed position papers, comment letters, and public hearing presentations on financial accounting and reporting issues. These efforts not only allowed him to be very familiar and comfortable with the Board and its process but also led to his being recognized in 1992 with the AIMR's Distinguished Service Award. Tony and his wife have four children and a variety of interests. When he was appointed, his wife was serving as the chair of the Board of Selectmen in Sudbury, Massachusetts, which is roughly equivalent to being the mayor. Tony obviously approaches life enthusiastically, as shown by his hobbies of skiing and golf. He was also playing midfield for a Sudbury soccer team before joining the FASB and hopes that he can find a team in Connecticut that needs his experience.

Again, the numbers show that the preparer constituency representation is disproportionate.

Council Meetings

The Council meets once each quarter, usually in New York City. Each meeting is attended by most members of the Council as well as all Board members. Council meetings are also attended by the chief accountant of the Securities and Exchange Commission, who (in 1993) is Walter P. Schuetze, one of the original members of the FASB when it began operating in 1973. Although he is not a member, the chief accountant participates in the discussions and informs the FASAC of the SEC's views on

John M. (Neel) Foster **Age in 1994:** 44

Education: B.A., Colorado College, with additional courses at the University of Colorado at Colorado Springs

Appointed to FASB: July 1, 1993

Term Expires: June 30, 1998

Eligible for Reappointment: Yes, for term ending June 30, 2003

After he received an economics degree with honors from Colorado College, Neel (a shortened form of his middle name of McNeely) began working as an administrative officer for a stock brokerage in Colorado Springs, but soon decided to return to school. Upon completing six accounting courses at the University of Colorado at Colorado Springs, he began working for Price Waterhouse in Houston in 1973. When Neel left public accounting eight years later, he took a position with a company in the oil and gas industry. In 1983, a lunch with a PW partner led to an interview and a job with a virtually unknown start-up high-tech company that wanted to go public. By the time Neel left Compaq Computer Corporation late in 1992, he was vice president and treasurer, and its annual sales had grown from $100 million to over $4 billion! Also in 1992, he began serving on FASAC, which was his first personal experience with the standards-setting process. When asked what he planned to do as a Board member to make a special contribution, Neel told the authors that he hopes to be able to speak to many different groups to help them understand the FASB's mission and why it has proposed changes in practice. His obvious energy, intelligence, and sense of humor make it clear to us that he will be a very effective representative for the Board wherever he goes. While he plans to pursue his interest in golf in Connecticut, he expects to return to his home state of Colorado once or twice a year to enjoy a life-long passion for fly fishing in the Frying Pan and Roaring Fork rivers, and a special place back in the mountains that he would rather not talk about.

the issues. Staff members are present to answer questions about their projects. Occasionally, one or more FAF Trustees may attend.

Before the meeting, Council members respond to a lengthy questionnaire concerning the Board's activities and potential activities. No votes are taken on any issues because the Council has no power to establish any policies. Rather, its purpose is to ensure that the Board at least hears all possible views on the questions it is trying to answer.

RESEARCH AND TECHNICAL ACTIVITIES STAFF

In the simplest terms, the duty of the 40 to 50 members of the Research and Technical Activities (RTA) staff is to do whatever is needed to facilitate the work of the FASB and its members. Among the specific tasks of the staff are:

- Researching the issues at all stages in a project.
- Communicating with constituents.
- Facilitating communication among Board members.
- Preparing preliminary proposals for Board deliberations.
- Preparing summaries of Board meetings.
- Drafting publications, including discussion documents and final pronouncements (described in Chapter 3).
- Analyzing written and oral comments from the constituencies.
- Distributing informal implementation guidance.
- Speaking and otherwise representing the FASB.
- Other public relations activities.

Like Board members, staff members are full-time employees of the FASB. With the exception of those participating in the various "fellow" programs to be discussed below, staff members must sever their relationships with their previous employers to provide at least the appearance of independence, if not independence in fact. All staff members must file a quarterly statement of their investments and are subject to the same prohibitions on their investment activity that apply to Board members. Furthermore, staff members generally do not serve on committees of professional organizations to avoid an appearance of conflict of interest.

Organizational Structure of the Staff

The nature of the Board's work has caused the staff to operate without a traditional hierarchical structure. Specifically, the key element in the Board's activity is the project, and the staff is assigned to project teams under the direction of a project manager. Included among the team members might be those from higher, equal, and lower levels. For example, project manager A might work for project manager B on one project as a consultant, but project manager B might work for project manager A on another. Each project team is assigned a senior technical adviser and a variety of professional and clerical personnel, including an assistant project manager, a technical associate, and a project administrative assistant.

Because of the nature of the work and its pressures, staff members tend to be high-energy individuals who are also highly mobile. Resignations are common but the vacant positions are usually filled relatively quickly. This high turnover rate is not a sign of instability but rather of the qualifications of the staff members and the nature of the FASB. Continuity is provided by a group of long-term staff members, while special expertise and injections of energy are provided by members who stay for fairly short periods of time.

Timothy S. Lucas

Age in 1994: 47

Education: B.A., B.S., M.A., Rice University

Appointed Director of RTA: November 30, 1987

Immediately after graduating from Rice, Tim served several years as an officer in the Navy Supply Corps. He began his public accounting career in 1972 with Haskins & Sells (now Deloitte & Touche) in Houston. While he was working, he also taught graduate-level financial accounting at Rice for three years. He had risen to the manager level at Deloitte when he was recruited as a FASB project manager in 1979. Tim's main efforts were focused on the very difficult and significant pension accounting and conceptual framework projects. He left the staff after SFAS 87 was issued to be a consultant, but returned to become the director of RTA in 1987. In that position, Tim takes an active part in all Board discussions and he is especially interested in the challenges created by the need for international accounting standards. He believes that progress has been made in developing the necessary communication channels between the FASB and the rest of the world's accounting communities. Tim spends at least 10 to 15 percent of his effort as RTA director as the chair of the Emerging Issues Task Force. Tim is the father of five children and relaxes from his busy workday by sailing and jogging. Lately, he has become something of a computer hacker and modestly admits that his interest in database applications eventually led to the Board's *Financial Accounting Research System*™ that puts essentially all the authoritative accounting literature at the user's fingertips.

The Director of Research and Technical Activities

The RTA staff is headed by a director who (at the suggestion of the trustees' Structure Committee in the late 1970s) holds equal status with Board members. Specifically, the director has the same salary as a Board member, is seated at the Board meeting table, and participates in the discussions of the issues. In 1993, the director was Tim Lucas.

The director is selected by the chairman of the FASB and is given the responsibility for seeing that the staff carries out its duties. Included with the responsibility is the authority to hire and fire other staff members. The director often helps staff members in selecting strategies for developing a consensus on a project and occasionally participates in the private staff meetings that take place with Board members before a public meeting.

Dr. J. T. Ball, one of two assistant directors of RTA, has primary responsibility for the general supervision of *Implementation and Practice Problem* projects. These projects involve more narrow issues that can be resolved with less due process and more quickly than *major projects*.[8] Prior to joining the FASB at its founding in 1973, J. T. was a research associate at the AICPA, where he produced more than 200 Interpretations of Accounting Principles Board Opinions. The other assistant director in 1993 is David Mosso, who brings special insights and experiences to the staff, having served 10 years as a member of the Board.

There are two senior technical advisers, Jules Cassell and Dr. Reed K. Storey. Reed was director of research at the AICPA until 1974 and played a key role in the operation of the Accounting Principles Board. One or the other serves as a consultant for every major project team and is called on for advice about technical, theoretical, or political considerations. Another special position is the research manager, who is Dr. L. Todd Johnson. Before taking this position, he was a professor of accounting and a dean of a college of business, as well as a project manager for the FASB in the early 1980s.

Project Managers

In many respects, the project managers are the main workhorses of the FASB staff. In a sense, they are analogous to middle-level management in typical corporate structures. Their compensation is comparable to the amount received by managers or new partners in public accounting firms. In 1993, their annual salaries ranged from $85,000 to $125,000.

One of their important responsibilities is to serve as go-betweens in several relationships. First, they serve as the main contact between the Board members and the staff. Second, as seen in the Prologue, they serve as the primary contact between the Board and the business community, particularly the press.

Perhaps the project manager's most difficult task is serving as the interface between Board members in the process of developing a consensus on the issues. Specifically, the project manager attempts to find the compromises that will develop a sufficiently large consensus to allow a pronouncement to be issued. In doing so, the project manager goes between different Board members, attempting to negotiate an acceptable position for as many of them as possible. This arrangement is generally preferable to having the Board members deal with each other directly because they do not have to reveal what concessions they are willing to make. On the other hand, it often makes the project manager's job more like diplomacy than accounting and is frequently frustrating.

---

[8] Examples of major projects include financial instruments, stock compensation, and marketable securities.

Robert C. Wilkins

Age in 1994: 51
Education: B.S., M.B.A., Xavier University
Appointed Project Manager: 1978

Right out of Xavier, Bob served several years as an officer in the U.S. Army Finance Corps. After that experience, he worked with Haskins & Sells (now Deloitte & Touche) in the Cincinnati office. Five years later, his abilities were acknowledged by his transfer to the executive offices in New York from 1972 to 1975. During this assignment, Bob worked in the firm's accounting research department, which allowed him to further develop his interest in technical issues and the standards-setting process. He returned to the Cincinnati office of H&S in 1975 but only stayed until 1978, when he gave up his position as an audit manager and joined the FASB as a project manager. He has managed a large number of projects while at the FASB, including the difficult mark-to-market project that is described in the Prologue. Bob is the father of four children, who are all in their 20s. They still get together often, and Bob and his wife enjoy sharing family activities with them. He plays a lot of tennis but most of his reading material is technical. He is active in his parish's administration and has served as a leader in its youth program. He also sings in the "Fairfield Ambassadors of Song," a group of 35 male singers from Fairfield, Connecticut, that gives about six concerts every year.

The backgrounds of project managers are varied. Many of them come from public accounting; however, it is risky for them to interrupt their careers because of the difficulty of returning to their previous positions. Others have come from private accounting or from teaching positions, and several have been promoted from lower staff levels. As an insight into the types of people who fill this position, additional information is provided above and on the next page about two project managers, Bob Wilkins and Jane Adams.

Fellow Positions

The FASB also has a fellow program to bring in staff members for relatively short appointments for fixed terms. These programs provide the Board with special expertise and some fresh energy. Furthermore, the various programs lay a foundation for a network of leaders in the profession who have an intimate and useful knowledge of the Board and how it works.

Jane B. Adams

Age in 1994: 39

Education: B.A., Vassar College, M.B.A., Pace University

Appointed Project Manager: 1991

Perhaps unexpectedly for a FASB project manager, Jane's degree from Vassar was in Latin-American Studies and Developmental Economics. After graduating, she worked several years in the not-for-profit sector in a museum. She enrolled in a graduate business program because of the demand for business skills in her work. After getting her MBA from Pace, Jane took the CPA exam and won the gold medal for New York state and received the AICPA Sells Award with high distinction. From 1984 to 1987, she worked for Main Hurdman (now KPMG Peat Marwick) in its Stamford office. One of her clients turned out to be the FASB. She must have made a good impression because she was asked to join the staff as an assistant project manager. She was promoted to project manager in 1991. Jane has worked on the projects associated with postretirement benefits other than pensions, not-for-profit issues (not surprisingly), and accounting for investments with prepayment risk. She also served on a rotating assignment as the executive director of FASAC. She believes that the greatest challenge of being a project manager is the demand for effective communication in articulating an issue and its alternative solutions. She told us that it is a great experience to take an issue and then be put in the middle of the Board to attempt to build a consensus. For relaxation, Jane enjoys white-water rafting, and has gone down major rivers in Arizona, Oregon, and northern California. She also has stayed active in the not-for-profit sector by serving as the treasurer and a director for a shelter in Westport, Connecticut.

Each year, several *practice fellows* from CPA firms come to the FASB for two-year terms. Most of them are on leave from the so-called Big Six firms.[9] This dominance is not planned, but merely reflects the fact that a larger firm is more capable of absorbing the loss of the fellow's services for two years and of using the special knowledge that he or she gains at the FASB. To use their practical experience and to allow them to see a project through to its conclusion, practice fellows are typically assigned to Implementation and Practice Problem projects. Virtually all fellows have been promoted to partner after their service, and some have continued to work with the Board as representatives for their firms.

---

[9] The Big Six include these six largest firms in the United States: Arthur Andersen & Co.; Coopers & Lybrand; Deloitte & Touche; Ernst & Young; KPMG Peat Marwick; and Price Waterhouse. The firms were called the Big Eight for many years until the mergers in the mid-1980s of Deloitte Haskins & Sells with Touche Ross & Co. and of Ernst & Whinney with Arthur Young & Company.

Teri List

Age in 1994: 30

Education: B.A. Northern Michigan University

Practice Fellow Term: September 1991 through August 1993

Before becoming a practice fellow, Teri worked for Deloitte & Touche, first for five years in Saginaw, Michigan, and then for two years in the firm's national office in Wilton, Connecticut. Her work there involved researching and resolving technical accounting issues raised by partners and employees in the various practice offices of the firm. Her work also required her to follow the activities of the FASB's Emerging Issues Task Force and to work with the firm's representative on the EITF. These efforts put her in direct contact with the FASB and its staff. During her two-year term at the Board, she has worked on a number of projects, with her greatest attention concentrated on the many complicated implementation issues associated with SFAS No. 109, the Board's latest income tax accounting standard. In addition, her fellowship gave her the opportunity of working with a variety of constituents as she was called on to handle written and telephone inquiries regarding the highly controversial and politically charged stock compensation issues. This challenge helped her develop her communication skills and her patience in dealing with people who have strongly held views. Teri is married and has a two-year-old daughter. In her spare time, she began antiquing in Connecticut, and has put together a collection that she will use to furnish her new home. She also enjoys reading and outdoor activities. She will rejoin Deloitte & Touche in St. Louis after her fellowship at the Board is completed in 1993.

Occasionally, an *industry fellow* will come to the FASB from a corporate setting to provide some specific expertise. The presence on the staff of a person with this background helps assure members of the preparer constituency that the staff has some balance in its experience that should lead to balance in its deliberations and pronouncements.

Faculty fellows come from university teaching positions, usually with sufficient prior development to justify the interruption of their academic career paths. Because of their training and interests, faculty fellows have typically been associated with the Conceptual Framework project or with projects requiring extensive research, such as the Accounting for Changing Prices project. Paul Miller, one of the authors of this book, was a faculty fellow in 1982–83.

Graduate interns serve one year and come directly to the FASB after earning a degree but before beginning their professional careers. The individuals selected may have either a bachelor's degree or a master's degree. Approximately four interns are selected each year from nominees

Carl Bass

Age in 1994: 33

Education: B.B.A., University of Texas at Austin

Practice Fellow Term: June 1992 through June 1994

As is apparent by his open friendliness and smile, Carl is a native Texan who is just as comfortable working for the FASB in Connecticut as he was in the Houston office of Arthur Andersen & Co. Like a lot of people, Carl started his university studies with one major and ended up with another. His initial plan was to major in history and then go on to attend law school and become an attorney. Along the way, he found himself attracted to the different challenges and opportunities of the accounting profession. He also found it attractive because he could start working at the professional level without having to complete an additional three years of formal education. He has never regretted the change, and is definitely enthused about his current work with the Board. Unlike other professional fellows, Carl had no contact with the FASB prior to his appointment. He was encouraged to apply and did so without knowing exactly what would happen. When asked how his experiences were different from his initial expectations, he said that he did not anticipate that the people on the staff would have such diverse backgrounds. During his time at the FASB, he has worked on a variety of projects, with the greatest emphasis on the projects involving issues in accounting for business combinations and classifications of equity. In addition, like most practice fellows, he has been responsible for working with the Emerging Issues Task Force to ensure that Board and task force members are well informed about the issues on the agenda for each meeting. Carl is married and has two small children. He relaxes by running and stays in touch with his initial interests by reading history and biographies of political leaders.

provided in response to invitations. Interns have been appointed from the following schools:

- Alabama
- Albion College
- Auburn
- Bucknell
- California at Berkeley
- Case Western Reserve
- Central Michigan
- Central Washington
- Clemson
- Colorado at Boulder
- Connecticut at Storrs

- Louisiana State
- Nebraska at Lincoln
- North Carolina at Chapel Hill
- Northeast Missouri State
- Northern Illinois
- Notre Dame
- Ohio State
- San Diego State
- Seattle
- Southern California

Ann Perry

Age in 1994: 23
Education: B.S., College of the Holy Cross
Appointed Graduate Intern: 1992

Ann graduated from Holy Cross in 1992 as an accounting major. One of her professors, J. D. O'Connell, interested her in the possibility of becoming a graduate intern and then successfully nominated her. She had previous experience in public accounting as a summer intern with Ernst & Young in 1991. Ann has worked on several different projects and feels that she has made a variety of contributions. For example, she helped analyze the comment letters on the loan impairment project and worked with a PC version of a database program to help the project team organize and summarize the information in the letters in a variety of ways. She also has worked on a project to review and catalog differences among U.S., Canadian, and Mexican accounting standards in anticipation of the North American Free Trade Agreement (NAFTA). She believes that the FASB intern experience has provided her with a background that will help her in any career that she might choose. She has found it interesting and educational to see how policies are made at the highest level and has especially enjoyed observing how the Board and staff members deliberate the issues. When asked how she had grown from the intern experience, Ann indicated that she has developed a lot of respect for the responsibilities and achievements of the Board members. Their careful treatment of the issues has provided a good model for her future. In her free time, Ann enjoys aerobics and skiing. After completing her year at the FASB, Ann plans to attend Chicago-Kent Law School at the Illinois Institute of Technology.

- Denver
- Florida State
- Georgia
- Holy Cross
- Illinois at Champaign/Urbana
- Indiana at Bloomington
- Kent State
- Texas A & M
- Texas at Austin
- Utah
- Virginia
- Wisconsin at Eau Claire
- Wisconsin at Madison

Upon completing their terms, interns have typically taken positions with public accounting firms or continued their schooling. Paul Bahnson, another of this book's authors, was an intern while he was a Ph.D. student at the University of Utah.

The accompanying sidebars provide short biographies of Teri List and Carl Bass, who were practice fellows in 1993, and Ann Perry, who was an intern in 1993.

APPENDIX
Predecessors of the FASB

The Committee on Accounting Procedure

In 1934, the Committee on Accounting Procedure (CAP) was formed by the American Institute of Accountants (now the American Institute of Certified Public Accountants). Its power was upgraded significantly in response to the SEC's issuance of Accounting Series Release No. 4, which established that accounting principles used in filings with the SEC had to have "substantial authoritative support" in order to be considered generally accepted.[10]

During its existence, the committee generally had about 20 members, all of whom were members of the Institute. They all served on a part-time basis, and none of them were paid for their services.

The CAP did not have the broadly based authority that has been granted to the FASB. In fact, its pronouncements were not even binding on members of the Institute, who could consider alternative practices to be acceptable in some circumstances. Nonetheless, its publications were considered helpful guidance.

During its 21-year life, the CAP issued 51 Accounting Research Bulletins on a variety of subjects. ARB 43 was issued in 1953 as a codification of the preceding bulletins with some modifications. To the extent that it has not been amended or superseded by subsequent pronouncements, ARB 43 is still widely influential.

Because it lacked authority, the CAP generally was unable to be definitive in its pronouncements. In dealing with inventories, for example, ARB 43 says only that "A major objective of accounting for inventories is the proper determination of income through the process of matching appropriate costs against revenues." This statement lacks operational guidance without a specification of what constitutes "proper determination" or "appropriate costs." Similarly, ARB 43 says that "it is perhaps in some circumstances permissible to show stock of a corporation held in its own treasury as an asset" but does not describe what those circumstances are or the rationale that supports this treatment.

Despite these weaknesses, Accounting Research Bulletins are recognized by the FASB as GAAP in its Rules of Procedure [Section III(B)] except when they have been specifically superseded. SEC Accounting Series Release No. 150, which endorsed the FASB's pronouncements,

---

[10] The CAP had its own predecessor body, dating back to 1917, when the AIA cooperated with the Federal Reserve Board in developing a booklet called *Approved Methods for the Presentation of Balance Sheet Statements,* which described basic accounting principles.

also acknowledges that Accounting Research Bulletins are acceptable for filings.

Because the CAP was entirely within the AICPA and consisted solely of individuals who belonged to the Institute, it lacked the broad power base that the FASB has developed. Moreover, locating the rule-making authority (however limited) within the auditing profession may have led to solutions that tended to address auditors' needs to the detriment of the interests of others. For example, because auditors need to reduce the risks of making incorrect judgments, they generally prefer such common practices as the use of cost-based measures, the application of systematic allocations, and reliance on transactions as events critical to the recognition of income (unless income is to be reduced). It is legitimate to debate whether such conservative practices help or hinder users and preparers of financial statements; however, that question cannot be resolved in this setting.

The CAP was dissolved in 1959 and replaced by another AICPA committee, the Accounting Principles Board.

The Accounting Principles Board

Like its predecessor, the CAP, the Accounting Principles Board (APB) was a committee of the AICPA. It was established in 1959 and existed until 1973. The APB was created as a result of a general concern within the Institute that the CAP was simply not working well. One frequently cited reason was the lack of systematic research assistance for the CAP's members because the CAP shared its staff with a large number of other AICPA committees. There was also concern about the CAP's authority because none of its members were authorized by their employers to describe their official positions on the issues; rather, each member was supposed to describe a more-or-less personal view.

The APB was created to deal with these apparent weaknesses. It was given a full-time research staff of six individuals and a director of accounting research. This position was initially filled by Dr. Maurice Moonitz, who was succeeded by Paul Grady, who in turn was followed by Dr. Reed K. Storey, now senior technical adviser on the FASB staff.

In its first few years, members of the APB were predominantly the most senior partners of major accounting firms (the Board always included a representative from each of the Big Eight public accounting firms). The strategy in having such high-level members was to derive authority for the Board's pronouncements from the authority of its members. However, most of these members did not commit as much time as the Board's work demanded, and a different solution was implemented. The chosen answer was to use slightly less senior personnel and have the AICPA governing council give authority to the Board's pronouncements by requiring AICPA members to specifically identify the effects of any departure from APB pronouncements in the auditor's opinion accompanying the client's financial statements.[11]

In response to a complaint that the CAP did not have a consistent approach to solving accounting problems, the APB was initially given the task of developing a set of "postulates" (or basic concepts) to provide guidance for the settling of issues. This project led to the publication of Accounting Research Studies Nos. 1 and 3 (the former was written by Maurice Moonitz and the latter by Moonitz and Robert Sprouse, who was a member of the FASB from 1973 through 1985). Both studies were rejected in APB Statement No. 1 as "too radically different from present generally accepted accounting principles to be acceptable at this time." Subsequently, other attempts to develop such underlying postulates were published, including the AICPA's Accounting Research Study No. 7 by Paul Grady in 1965 and APB Statement No. 4 in 1970. None of these efforts produced results that were particularly helpful to the APB. Despite the struggles in this area, similar goals were established for the FASB's Conceptual Framework project, which is discussed in Chapter 4.

During its 14-year life, the APB issued 31 authoritative *opinions,* which the FASB also acknowledges in its Rules of Procedure as creating GAAP to the extent that they are not superseded or amended. The opinions were generally more definitive than the CAP's Accounting Research Bulletins, largely because of the authority passed to the APB by the AICPA Council. It also issued four nonauthoritative *statements.*

The APB was dissolved in 1973, several months after the FASB was created. While there were many causes for its demise, perhaps the most significant was the lack of a broadly based mandate for authority. It is important to note that the SEC never did formally endorse the APB as a source of authority while it existed, although its pronouncements were eventually endorsed in ASR 150 in 1973.

The APB also had a number of structural weaknesses, particularly its relatively large size (it started with 20 members, increased to 21, fell back to 18, and had only 17 in 1973) and the fact that its members served part-time. Furthermore, the members were not perceived as being independent of their firms or, in the case of the auditor members, the clients of their firms. In order to avoid these weaknesses, the FASB was given a smaller size and its members were made independent of their previous employers.

---

[11] Accounting Principles Board, *Status of Accounting Research Bulletins* (Opinion No. 6), (New York, 1965) Appendix A.

SELECTED READINGS

AICPA. "The FASB's Second Decade." *Journal of Accountancy,* November 1983, pp. 86–96; December 1983, pp. 94–102.

DEITSCH, MIMI. "From One Firing Line to Another." *Financial Executive,* January/February 1992, p. 59.

FASB. "Facts about FASB." [New edition released each year.]

KIRK, DONALD J. "Looking Back on Fourteen Years at the FASB: The Education of a Standard Setter." *Accounting Horizons,* March 1988, pp. 8–17.

MEYER, P. E. "The APB's Independence and Its Implications for the FASB." *Journal of Accounting Research,* Spring 1974, pp. 188–96.

ZEFF, STEPHEN A. "A Chronology of Significant Developments in the Establishment of Accounting Principles in the United States, 1926–1972." *Journal of Accounting Research,* Spring 1972, pp. 217–27.

————. "Some Junctures in the Evolution of the Process of Establishing Accounting Principles in the USA: 1917–1972." *Accounting Review,* July 1984, pp. 447–68.

3

The FASB's Due Process

The term *due process* is used in several different settings to describe the steps taken to ensure that an administrative matter is given the careful consideration needed to adequately protect the interests of those involved. Thus, individuals accused of crimes cannot be convicted without having the allegations heard through a series of due process procedures. Similar concepts are applied in labor relations disputes and in legislative activities.

The Financial Accounting Standards Board (FASB) also uses a set of due process procedures to ensure that the interests of its constituents are considered in the development of accounting standards and other pronouncements. In carrying out these procedures, the FASB attempts to accomplish the following five broad goals:

- Discovery of an accounting problem.
- Identification of the accounting issues underlying the problem.
- Identification of alternative positions on those issues.
- Evaluation of those alternatives.
- Selection of the preferred alternative.

These goals are achieved through a set of procedures described later in the chapter.

Due process is considered essential, not only because it produces a systematic approach to problem solving, but also because it creates an environment in which the constituents and other members of the business community can feel that they have had an opportunity to affect the out-

come. Even though a group may not agree with the FASB pronouncement, its members can have confidence that their needs were at least
addressed and not completely disregarded.

This chapter contains the following sections on the FASB's procedures:

- The final pronouncements issued by the FASB.
- The steps in the overall process.
- The FASB's public relations activities.
- Participating in the FASB's due process.

THE FINAL PRONOUNCEMENTS ISSUED BY THE FASB

The first step toward the FASB's goal of establishing generally accepted
accounting principles (GAAP) was taken soon after its founding with its
endorsement of the pronouncements of its predecessor bodies.[1] It has
continued to establish GAAP by using its own pronouncements, including
many revisions of earlier documents. The following four types of documents have been issued:

- Statements of Financial Accounting Standards.
- Interpretations.
- Statements of Financial Accounting Concepts.
- Technical Bulletins.

Before discussing each of these types of pronouncements, it will be useful
to understand the unique role that each of them plays in establishing
GAAP.

Hierarchy of Generally Accepted Accounting Principles

For various reasons, including the increased complexity of financial markets and greater levels of professional liability for accountants, a bewil-
dering array of published guidance describes practices that ought to be
used in preparing financial statements. Thus, accounting practitioners,
whether auditors or preparers, need to know which guidance must be
applied in financial statements that are claimed to be prepared in accordance with GAAP. If they publish financial statements that are not prepared in accordance with GAAP, or if they present an unqualified opinion
on noncomplying statements, the accountants violate at least ethics Rule
203 of the AICPA's Code of Professional Conduct, and possibly state and
federal accountancy and securities laws.

To provide auditors with this important guidance, the AICPA's Auditing Standards Board issued Statement of Auditing Standards No. 69 in

---

[1] FASB Rules of Procedure (as amended in 1991), Section III(B).

December 1991. This statement identifies five levels of pronouncements that describe GAAP. These levels are listed in Exhibit 3-1, which also classifies the pronouncements of the FASB, the AICPA, and others into those five categories. Exhibit 3-1 identifies the categories by the number and letter of the paragraphs in SAS 69 that describe them.

Category 10a. The principles at the highest level are issued by those organizations designated by the AICPA as authoritative. These entities include the FASB, the Governmental Accounting Standards Board (GASB), the Auditing Standards Board, and others that have jurisdiction over specialized practice areas. The FASB's Statements of Financial Accounting Standards and Interpretations fall into this category. Also included are the following pronouncements issued by FASB's predecessors: Accounting Principles Board Opinions and Accounting Research Bulletins published by the Committee on Accounting Procedure. The SEC's reporting requirements are not included in this category because they apply only to financial statements issued by companies who fall under its jurisdiction. Thus, non-SEC companies do not need to apply them.

Category 10b. At the second level, and thus secondary to any items in Category 10a, are pronouncements of entities composed of expert accountants that deliberate accounting issues in a public process that includes not only an opportunity for public comment, but also approval of an authoritative body identified in Category 10a (this process of approval is called *clearing* in SAS 69). The only FASB pronouncements that fall in this category are its Technical Bulletins (TB), which are described later in this chapter.

Category 10c. The third level also consists of pronouncements of entities composed of expert accountants. Like the documents at the second level, they have been cleared by an authoritative body; however, the pronouncements at the 10c level are not exposed for public comment. For the FASB, this category includes only the consensuses reached by its Emerging Issues Task Force (EITF). This group, which is described in more detail in Chapter 6, deliberates relatively narrow accounting issues in public meetings but does not seek comments from the public on the suitability of its conclusions. However, a consensus solution that is objected to by FASB members is not considered to be cleared and cannot be identified as generally accepted.

Category 10d. At the fourth level are various descriptions of common practices that are not included in any of the three prior levels but that can be identified by well-informed accountants as describing prevalent and useful accounting methods. Virtually any body of experts can create pronouncements in this area, but practitioners should carefully determine whether a particular publication is issued by a dependable source. The FASB is involved at this level by issuing implementation guidance for some of its standards, usually in a "questions and answers" form (called

EXHIBIT 3–1 Hierarchy of Generally Accepted Accounting Principles According to Statement of Auditing Standards No. 69—December 1991

Level (paragraph in SAS 69)	FASB Pronouncements	AICPA Documents	Others
10a—Principles issued by a body designated by AICPA Council.	Statements of Financial Accounting Standards. Interpretations.	Accounting Principles Board Opinions. Accounting Research Bulletins.	
10b—Pronouncements of expert accountant bodies that deliberate issues in a public forum, provided they have been exposed for public comment and cleared by FASB and/or AICPA.	Technical Bulletins.	Industry Audit and Accounting Guides. Statements of Position.	
10c—Pronouncements of expert accountant bodies that deliberate issues in a public forum for the purpose of describing, establishing, or interpreting accepted accounting principles, provided they have been cleared by FASB and/or AICPA.	EITF Consensuses.	Practice Bulletins.	
10d—Prevalent practice in a particular industry or knowledgeable applications of generally accepted pronouncements to specific circumstances.	Implementation guidance issued by staff ("Qs and As").	Interpretations.	
11—Literature that provides guidance without being one of the four above categories; does not fall under AICPA Ethics Rule 203.	Statements of Financial Accounting Concepts.	APB Statements. Issues Papers. Technical Practice Aids.	International Accounting Standards. Accounting textbooks and handbooks. Journal articles.

Qs and As in SAS 69). These documents are published by the FASB staff in conjunction with a task force or a special committee without public comment or specific approval by any Board members, although the members are given the opportunity to object to any answer they find to be deficient. This level includes the Interpretations that were formerly issued by the Research Division of the AICPA to help accountants understand and apply APB Opinions.

Category 11. At the fifth and least influential level are all other descriptions of practices that are or might be generally accepted. The only FASB pronouncements that fall in this category are the Statements of Financial Accounting Concepts issued through the Conceptual Framework project (this project is described in Chapter 4). Although the concepts statements were voted on by the FASB after an extended process that included extensive public comment, they were never intended by the Board to establish or describe GAAP. Therefore, they do not fall under the requirements of ethics Rule 203. Also included in this category are standards issued by the International Accounting Standards Committee (IASC), which is composed of representatives from approximately 80 countries. (The IASC and its relationship to the FASB are described in more detail in Chapter 6.) Finally, the category includes accounting textbooks and journal articles written by individual experts without any public deliberations or public comments. Although their contents may be persuasive presentations of acceptable or desirable practices, the lack of due process means that they are not authoritative.

Statements of Financial Accounting Standards

Because of the AICPA's ethics Rule 203, the GAAP hierarchy, and similar regulations of state societies and state boards of public accountancy, a Statement of Financial Accounting Standards (SFAS) unambiguously creates generally accepted principles that must be complied with. Specifically, a CPA cannot state in an auditor's opinion that a client's financial statements are in compliance with GAAP if they are not in compliance with all SFASs. As mentioned in Chapter 1, a rarely invoked exception to this rule applies if compliance would produce misleading information in the financial statements. According to the SEC's Financial Reporting Release No. 1 (as originally stated in Accounting Series Release No. 150, issued in 1973), a SFAS must be applied by all preparers registering their securities with the SEC and their auditors. As of June 1993, 117 standards had been issued.

Establishing an accounting principle in a SFAS does not necessarily mean that the underlying problem was pervasive among most (or even several) sectors of the economy. Although many standards have affected a large number of companies in different industries (such as the standards that govern accounting for research and development expenditures, segments, contingencies, leases, and pensions), many others have been highly specialized in the sense that they have attempted to solve narrow problems or problems arising in only a specific industry (such as the standards that govern accounting for the tax effects of United Kingdom stock relief, railroad track structures, and motion-picture companies). The length of standards has also varied substantially, ranging from only a few pages to over a hundred pages.

The extent of the due process procedures applied to a standard varies significantly from situation to situation. Some projects go through many steps and others fewer. However, all final standards must be preceded by the issuance of an exposure draft, which is described in the next major section of the chapter. According to the FASB's Rules of Procedure, a standard can be issued only after a two-thirds majority of Board members votes in favor of its issuance.

Interpretations

Under the hierarchy of pronouncements described in Statement of Auditing Standards No. 69, FASB Interpretations create GAAP. According to the Board's Rules of Procedure [Section IV(H)(3)], the purpose of Interpretations is "to clarify, explain, or elaborate on" an existing SFAS, an APB opinion, or a CAP Accounting Research Bulletin "as an aid to its understanding." Because of their limited nature, Interpretations pass through a less extensive set of due process procedures than the one used for a SFAS. Specifically, an exposure draft of a proposed Interpretation is distributed to all subscribers of the FASB's publications with the invitation to comment over a period of at least 30 days. Like a SFAS, an Interpretation is issued only after a two-thirds majority of Board members votes in favor of its issuance.

As of June 1993, 40 Interpretations had been issued. Evidence of their rarity is provided by the fact that Interpretation No. 36 was issued in October 1981, No. 37 in July 1983, No. 38 in August 1984, and No. 39 in March 1992.

Examples of Interpretations include the following:

- No. 16: "Clarification of Definitions and Accounting for Marketable Equity Securities That Become Nonmarketable" (an Interpretation of SFAS 12).
- No. 27: "Accounting for a Loss on a Sublease" (an Interpretation of APB Opinion No. 30 and SFAS 13).
- No. 34: "Disclosure of Indirect Guarantees of Indebtedness of Others" (an Interpretation of SFAS 5).
- No. 39: "Offsetting of Amounts Related to Certain Contracts: An Interpretation of APB Opinion No. 10 and FASB Statement No. 105."

Although allowed by the Rules of Procedure, no Interpretation of a Statement of Financial Accounting Concepts has ever been issued.

Statements of Financial Accounting Concepts

Unlike Statements of Financial Accounting Standards, Statements of Financial Accounting Concepts (SFAC) are not intended to create GAAP and are not included under the SEC's Financial Reporting Release 1, the AICPA's ethics Rule 203, or similar rules issued by state societies of CPAs or state boards of public accountancy.

According to the Rules of Procedures [Section IV(H)(2)], there are three purposes for issuing a SFAC: (1) to guide the FASB in its standards-setting work, (2) to guide practicing accountants in dealing with issues not resolved in the authoritative literature, and (3) to help educate nonaccountants. As discussed in Chapter 4, it is not clear whether these goals have been served by the Conceptual Framework or whether they even could have been.

Despite their non-GAAP status, SFACs were taken through extensive due process procedures because of their significant implications on the development of GAAP in the future. The steps included discussion memoranda, public hearings, and exposure drafts, as well as others.

The titles of the six existing statements are:

No. 1 Objectives of Financial Reporting for Business Enterprises
No. 2 Qualitative Characteristics of Accounting Information
No. 3 Elements of Financial Statements of Business Enterprises
No. 4 Objectives of Financial Reporting by Nonbusiness Organizations
No. 5 Recognition and Measurement in Financial Statements of Business Enterprises
No. 6 Elements of Financial Statements—a replacement of FASB Concepts Statement No. 3 (incorporating an amendment of FASB Concepts Statement No. 2)

The six concepts statements and the Conceptual Framework project are discussed in more detail in Chapter 4.

Technical Bulletins

As described earlier, the GAAP hierarchy places a FASB Technical Bulletin (TB) at the second level below a SFAS or an Interpretation. This ranking arises from the fact that a TB is not formally voted on by the FASB; instead, a TB is actually issued by the Research and Technical Activities staff after public comment. This simpler process is appropriate because the issues addressed in TBs are neither pervasive nor particularly controversial; rather, they are usually troublesome to only a relatively small number of accountants.

According to the policies of the FASB, a TB is issued when:

- The guidance in the TB is not expected to cause a major change in accounting practice for a significant number of entities.
- The cost of implementing the guidance is not expected to be significant to most affected entities.
- The guidance does not conflict with a broad fundamental principle or create a novel accounting practice.[2]

Because of this restricted nature, only limited due process procedures are applied to proposed TBs. Like proposed interpretations, they are distributed to the subscribers to the FASB's publications for comments. The comment period cannot be less than 15 days.

Unlike the situation for other types of pronouncements, Board members do not formally vote for or against the contents of a Technical Bulletin. However, if the discussion of the TB at a public Board meeting reveals that more than two members object to its issuance, it will not be issued. The objections can be based on a disagreement with the proposed solution to the problem, an opinion that the problem should be covered by another type of pronouncement, or any other reason that a Board member cares to raise.

The practice of issuing TBs began in 1979 as a result of concern with informal implementation advice requested in telephone or written inquiries from individuals who were trying to apply standards and Interpretations. Because similar problems were raised in many inquiries, it was decided to make the advice more formal so that it could be indexed in the authoritative literature and thus be more widely applied. Nineteen TBs were issued in 1979 as the staff dealt with a backlog of problems that had been addressed over the preceding years. After that date, TBs were relatively infrequent. However, as a result of recommendations from a Timely Guidance Task Force of business leaders, the FASB decided in 1983 to use the TB as a way of getting guidance to financial accountants quickly and cheaply. Briefly, the task force determined that a number of problems deserved authoritative answers but were not sufficiently widespread or urgent to justify the cost and effort of producing a SFAS or an Interpretation. In response to the recommendation, the Board adopted the procedures described above. Under the prior policy, a TB was issued by the staff, with little or no involvement by the Board and with little or no public comment.

---

[2] FASB Technical Bulletin 79-1 (revised), "Purpose and Scope of FASB Technical Bulletins and Procedures for Issuance," par. 4.

As of June 1993, 48 Technical Bulletins had been issued. Examples include the following:

No. 79–7 Recoveries of a Previous Write-Down under a Troubled Debt Restructuring Involving a Modification of Terms

No. 81–2 Accounting for Unused Investment Tax Credits Acquired in a Business Combination Accounted for by the Purchase Method

No. 86–2 Accounting for an Interest in the Residual Value of a Leased Asset

No. 90–1 Accounting for Separately Priced Extended Warranty and Product Maintenance Contracts

It can be seen from the titles that the issues are narrow in scope compared to those addressed in other FASB pronouncements.

Other Publications

In addition to the four types of pronouncements described above, the FASB also publishes a number of other documents as part of its due process procedures and its public relations activities. These procedures and activities are described and discussed in the rest of this chapter.

THE STEPS IN THE OVERALL PROCESS

The diversity of problems facing the FASB makes it appropriate for the Board to tailor the due process for the unique needs of each project; nonetheless, similar steps must be applied for most individual projects in order to achieve the goals of the process.

The basic process is shown in the flowchart in Exhibit 3–2, which shows that up to six steps can take place. More information on each phase is also provided in Exhibit 3–2, and this section of the chapter examines them in more detail.

Preliminary Evaluation of the Problem

A common question addressed to FASB members and staff members concerns the procedures for uncovering the problems the Board attempts to solve. The answer is not easily given because there are many ways in which the problems come to the FASB's attention.

One source is the Emerging Issues Task Force that was formed in 1984 to deal quickly with new problems. If the task force can reach a consensus about the solution to a narrow problem, no further action is taken. On the other hand, if the task force reaches a consensus that a problem is important and agrees that its solution is unclear, it will recom-

EXHIBIT 3–2 Activities and Publications in the FASB's Due Process

Step in the process	Activities	Possible publications
1. Preliminary evaluation of the problem	Emerging Issues Task Force recommendations Press monitoring Constituent communications SEC recommendations	Research studies Project prospectus
2. Admission to agenda	Board meetings	None
3. Early deliberations	Staff literature search Project task force Project advisory group Public hearings Board meetings	Discussion memorandum Invitation to comment
4. Tentative resolution	Board meetings Balloting	Tentative conclusions Preliminary views Exposure draft
5. Further deliberations	Board meetings Public hearings Field tests	Revised exposure draft
6. Final resolution	Board meetings Balloting	Statements Interpretations

mend that the Board undertake the development of a more careful resolution of the issues.

A key duty of the Research and Technical Activities staff is to closely monitor the newspapers and periodicals in the business press for stories about unusual transactions, events, or conditions that create financial accounting issues. When a possible issue is identified, a staff member may make preliminary inquiries to determine the details and the potential for its occurrence in other settings. If it appears that the problem could be pervasive, the staff will begin to work toward determining whether the Board should add a project to its agenda.

Another task of the staff is responding to technical inquiries received from preparers and auditors by telephone and in writing. Although many of these inquiries can be handled on an ad hoc basis, some may lead to the development of a Technical Bulletin or another type of pronouncement.

The Board also remains in communication with professional groups, such as the AICPA and the Financial Executives Institute (FEI), and is thus informed of emerging problems reported by their members. One particularly notable source of this kind is the AICPA's Accounting Standards Executive Committee (AcSEC).

In maintaining the relationship of "mutual nonsurprise" described in Chapter 1, the Board and the staff communicate frequently with the Securities and Exchange Commission and its staff. Because the SEC staff examines the financial statements included with filings from all public companies, it is quickly informed about new problems. If the SEC's chief accountant and staff members cannot resolve a problem using the existing authoritative literature, they may suggest to the FASB that it conduct a study of the issues. For example, the SEC placed a moratorium on the capitalization of software development costs in 1983 and strongly encouraged the FASB to undertake a project to establish a standard in this area.

Occasionally, the FASB will seek to learn more about a problem before pursuing the possibility of putting it on the agenda as a project; in doing so, the FASB may commission a *Research Study* to examine it in detail. Studies are also executed at other stages in the process. In addition, the staff may prepare and distribute a project prospectus that describes the proposed project and its issues in order to solicit responses from the public before the Board formally votes to add it to the agenda.

The articles in the Prologue show that the issues in the mark-to-market project were first addressed by the Accounting Standards Executive Committee (AcSEC), a rule-making body of the AICPA. The scope of the project included accounting for debt securities by financial institutions. As part of its normal contact with the various bodies that provide accounting guidance, the FASB was well aware of the problems that AcSEC was having with the mark-to-market issues. By October 1990, it had become clear that AcSEC would not be able to resolve the issue to the satisfaction of the SEC. As a result, AcSEC sent a letter to the FASB requesting that the Board assume responsibility for the project. Additional input was also received by the FASB at about the same time in a joint letter from the Big Six accounting firms that also encouraged the Board to resolve the issues. With this urging and support from the SEC, the staff began its efforts to define an appropriate scope that the project would assume if it were to be added to the agenda.

Admission to the Agenda

The mere discovery of a problem is not sufficient to ensure that the FASB will undertake its solution. Other conditions must exist, and the Board must agree to admit the problem to the agenda. In doing so, it deliberates the question in one or more public meetings, following the usual meeting process described on page 70.

A decision by the Board to create an agenda project not only commits its own resources but also mobilizes the entire financial reporting community by inviting its participation in the due process. As a consequence of this involvement, substantial deliberation takes place before this decision is made. A number of factors must enter into the decision. The following three points are always considered:

- The problem must be *sufficiently significant* in terms of its effect on the financial statements and its pervasiveness throughout the economy—if the problem does not create significant difficulties, the cost of the due process may not be justifiable.
- The alternative solutions to the problem must be sufficiently different to be *controversial*—if there is no serious disagreement about the answer (or no significant difference in the financial statements from applying the alternatives), an authoritative resolution is not necessary.
- There must be a suitably *high likelihood that the Board can resolve the issues* in a manner that will be acceptable to the constituency—without some prior sense of the likelihood that the Board members will be able to reach a consensus, it is generally not advisable to undertake a formal project.

If the Board cannot determine whether a particular problem merits a project, it often instructs the staff to carry out further study rather than completely rejecting the possibility of creating a project.

One important dimension of the agenda decision is the determination of the type of pronouncement to be issued at the completion of the project. For the major issues related to the Conceptual Framework, there was simply no debate—a Statement of Financial Accounting Concepts was needed. In other specific situations, it is clear that a Statement of Financial Accounting Standards is needed because the transactions, events, or conditions to be accounted for have not occurred or existed previously or have not been addressed in the authoritative literature. In less certain situations, the decision may be made to proceed as if a SFAS will be issued in order to ensure that the due process procedures are complete, even though another type of pronouncement may eventually emerge. Only when a problem is narrow or similar to others that have been previously resolved will the Board decide to issue an Interpretation or Technical Bulletin.

The FASB staff invested a substantial amount of time researching the mark-to-market issues before recommending that the project be added to the agenda. The staff met with various experts in the financial reporting community and gave special attention to the question how inclusive the project should be. Included among the alternatives was a broad project

FASB MEETING PROCEDURES

Frequency. Typically, the Board meets on Wednesday of each week in its meeting room in its offices in Norwalk, Connecticut.

Announcement. Each meeting is announced in a weekly newsletter called *Action Alert*. The announcement briefly describes the specific issues to be discussed for each project that has been scheduled.

Public attendance. The general public is admitted to the meeting up to the seating capacity of the room, which is determined by local ordinances to be only 85 persons, including the Board and staff members. Typically, the number attending is much smaller than the capacity. The audience is not allowed to participate in the discussion, although (on rare occasions) a specific person may be called on by the chairman to illuminate a particular point. Copies of the documents being discussed by the Board and staff members are not available to the public as a matter of economy and to prevent preliminary positions from being perceived as final. However, a brief summary handout is provided. The audience usually includes representatives of public accounting firms, the SEC, and others especially interested in the particular issues under consideration.

Preliminary sessions. At least two weeks before each meeting, the staff gives Board members memoranda that identify the specific issues and other questions that are to be addressed and resolved in the public meeting. Then (usually on Monday and Tuesday), the project team holds private meetings with all Board members (in groups of four or less) to gauge their reactions and understand their preliminary positions, as well as to brief them on the thoughts of the other Board members.

The meeting. When the Board meeting actually begins, a staff member summarizes the points under consideration, primarily for the benefit of the audience. The ensuing discussion usually repeats the results of the preliminary meetings, although the dynamics of the session may generate movement toward a consensus.

Minutes. No transcripts or other detailed minutes are prepared for the meeting; rather, the staff members involved in the project are responsible for preparing an unpublished summary document that is available to the public for examination and duplication. A shorter summary (only a few sentences in length) is published in the *Action Alert* printed during the following week.

that would examine the use of fair values for a wide range of investments held by all companies. Another much narrower project would have focused on using fair values only for those types of investments that had been susceptible to management manipulation through gains trading. After considering the choices, the Board members agreed in June 1991 to undertake the mark-to-market project with an even broader scope, including the possibility of using fair value to measure and report a company's liabilities that are associated with its investments. (For example, an insurance company might choose to fund a pension liability with investments

Financial Accounting Standards Board meeting room

in long-term bonds. If market interest rates increased, both the liability and bonds would decrease in value. The financial statements would be incomplete if only the change in the assets were to be recognized.)

Early Deliberations

To the extent that it was not done in the prior stages, adding a project to the agenda triggers staff effort to carefully identify the underlying issues and the alternative positions on them. This phase generally includes a review of the authoritative and other professional literature on the topic, and may produce additional research studies. The staff also may conduct surveys of statement users and other groups to define the nature and extent of the problem.

In some situations, the staff will formalize its contact with the constituencies by creating a *task force* or an *advisory group* composed of individuals whose experiences provide them with special insights on the issues. For major projects, a task force is chaired by a Board member and typically has about 20 members (some have as few as 10, and others as many as 30). For Implementation and Practice Problem projects, a smaller advisory group may be created, typically with 6 to 10 members. In some cases, the advisory group may actually be formed in the agenda decision phase to assist the staff in making its recommendation to the Board. Many projects do not have any formal groups; in these cases, the project manager merely maintains contact with a few knowledgeable people.

In some major projects (but certainly not all), the task force assists the staff in publishing a discussion document that solicits responses from the constituencies to help identify the important issues and to help assess the merits of the different positions on previously identified issues. The document may be called a *discussion memorandum* (DM) or an *invitation to comment* (ITC). A DM is typically drafted by the staff and is fairly broad in its scope. An ITC is often partially drafted by an external consultant and is more narrowly focused. After the document has been published, the task force or advisory group may have no further official function; however, the project manager may keep it intact so that he or she can call on some or all of its members for advice as the due process continues. Task force members are also encouraged to remain actively involved in later phases of the process.

When the project is sufficiently significant, or when the Board members want to become more completely informed, the staff will arrange a round of *public hearings* subsequent to the publication of the discussion document. Through announcements in *Action Alert* and in the discussion document itself, as well as by other means, potential respondents are invited to present their views to the Board and staff. Those who wish to present their positions at the hearing must first submit a written comment so that Board members can get the most out of the process. After a brief oral testimony, the participants then respond to questions from the Board members. A hearing may last only one day, or it may go on for longer periods. For example, four separate rounds of public hearings on the Pension project took more than 10 days to complete. Altogether, 175 presentations were made.

Throughout this early stage in the due process, responses to discussion documents are analyzed by the staff and sent to Board members together with summaries. The issues are also discussed at Board meetings, and in private sessions between the staff and individual Board members. No formal votes are compiled, although a straw poll may be taken to establish the extent of the consensus on particular questions. Of course, the staff project team develops an idea of Board members' positions through the course of the deliberations.

For the mark-to-market project, the Board and staff determined that no preliminary discussion documents would be released and that no task force would be created. One factor in this decision was the need to move relatively fast to the resolution of the issues. Another consideration was the fact that the staff already had a source of useful input from the existing task force for the Financial Instruments project. The early deliberations addressed these three major issues: (*a*) that specific categories of investments should be marked to market; (*b*) which liabilities, if any, should also be marked to market; and (*c*) how to account for the holding gains and losses resulting from adjusting the assets and liabilities to reflect their market values. As reported in the articles in the Prologue, much time was spent in these deliberations because of the midstream introduction of a new Board member and because of changes in the views of other Board members.

Tentative Resolution

After the early deliberations are completed, the Board moves on to the next stage of the due process, which involves a more formal description of the members' positions on the issues and any consensus that may have developed. Although abstract discussions are informative, they do not generate the public interest that a concrete proposal can create. To focus this interest and to "test the waters," as well as to solicit responses from constituency members who have not participated in the earlier stages, the Board publishes documents that describe a proposed solution to the problem.

For two especially complex and controversial projects, the Board issued special documents that outlined its position. In 1976, it issued a *Tentative Conclusions* document on the Conceptual Framework project as part of a Discussion Memorandum. In 1982, it issued a *Preliminary Views* document on the Pensions project.

An *exposure draft* (ED) must be published for all projects that lead to a Statement of Financial Accounting Standards or a Statement of Financial Accounting Concepts. A draft may be published for an Interpretation, but not necessarily. This document is essentially a pro forma final document, including a discussion of the problem, a presentation of the proposed solution, a proposed effective date, and a discussion of the reasons underlying the Board's decision. An exposure draft is prepared and distributed only if a two-thirds majority of the Board members votes in favor of its publication. Board members who do not agree with the majority can cause the draft to include their "alternative views," but their names are not identified. Of course, the identity of the dissenters is quite obvious to those who have followed the project closely.

The exposure draft for the mark-to-market project was issued in September 1992, 15 months after the project was added to the agenda. The proposal in the exposure draft reflected a major change from the original broad scope of the project. Although the original scope had included all investments and possibly some liabilities, the inability to find enough common ground among five Board members caused the project to become much narrower. In effect, the Board decided that the most that it could do was eliminate inconsistencies across industries and diminish the possibility of gains trading. Under the exposure draft's proposed requirements, a company's investments in debt securities would be divided into three portfolios: (*a*) those intended to be held to maturity, (*b*) those available for sale, and (*c*) securities held only temporarily by financial institutions for trading purposes. Both the securities available for sale and those held for trading would be marked to market, while those intended to be held to maturity would still be carried at amortized cost. The holding gains or losses on the trading securities would be added to or charged directly against net income. As a compromise, the holding gains or losses on the investment securities would be added to or subtracted from a separate unrealized component of owners' equity instead of being recognized on the income statement as part of annual earnings.

Approximately 26,000 copies of the mark-to-market exposure draft were distributed, and 572 comment letters were received in response. According to the staff's analysis, the responses came from the following groups: banking (369), insurance (65), public accounting (45), industry (37), securities industry (14), utilities (12), government (9), academe (6), law (4), actuary (2), and other (9). The heavy response from banks and insurance companies (76 percent) and the nature of the comments (see the sample letters in Exhibit 3–3) reflect the efforts of the American Banking Association (ABA) and other industry groups to encourage their members to flood the FASB with negative letters. This campaign was mounted despite the Board's major compromises in excluding debt securities expected to be held to maturity and using the unrealized equity account. The ABA continued its strong resistance to the proposal, even after it became apparent that the Board would not back down from its position (see the April 14, 1993, article in the Prologue). Three days of public hearings were also held during December 1992 and January 1993. As might be expected from the comment letters, most of the testimony at the hearings expressed dissatisfaction with the proposed requirements.

Further Deliberations

Following the return and analysis of the responses to the exposure draft, the Board again discusses the issues to determine if any evidence has been uncovered that has led to the reversal of a member's previous position. In some circumstances, more public hearings may be held. For example, hearings were held in the fall of 1991 subsequent to the issuance of the exposure draft on accounting for income taxes that eventually was issued as SFAS 109.

In some projects, the Board members instruct the staff to perform field tests of the proposed accounting measurements and procedures in order to assess both the difficulty of developing the information and its potential effects on the reported income and financial position of complying companies. These tests are usually conducted in cooperation with a relatively small number of corporations and their auditors and reported to the Board in a special report. Some members of the preparer constituency have called for field tests not only for the information they might provide but also to prolong the Board's due processes and thereby delay the implementation of the proposed standard. Despite this weakness, most field tests have proven to be useful to the Board for translating its theories into concrete procedures and will probably be used more frequently in the future than in the past.

There are three possible outcomes of this stage of the due process:

- The project may be terminated.
- Another exposure draft may be issued.
- The Board may move on to a final pronouncement.

A project will be terminated if the responses indicate that the problem is not significant or that the Board will be unable to resolve the problem in a manner acceptable to the constituents, or if it appears that the Board will not be able to reach a consensus. Only a few projects have been completely dropped from the agenda. For example, the Board decided in 1975 that it would not issue a standard on reporting price-level adjusted financial statement information based on a 1974 exposure draft. It reached similar conclusions for two projects in 1983 that involved very narrow income tax-related issues, and for a project in 1985 on joint mailing costs incurred by not-for-profit entities. It also dropped a project on investments with prepayment risks in 1992. Another example was the Board's decision in 1982 not to press ahead with a final concepts statement on reporting income, cash flows, and financial position because the responses to the exposure draft revealed substantial misgivings among the constituencies and because it became apparent that the Board members were more divided on the issues than they had been when the draft was published. Some of the material in the exposure draft was finally included in SFAC 5, but it was only a small portion of the original.

Small changes can usually be incorporated into the final statement without difficulty or controversy; however a second exposure draft will be issued at this stage if a significantly different solution is preferred by a majority of the Board. Although this step of issuing a second draft has been taken more often than completely dropping a project, it is relatively uncommon.

After considering the comments offered in response to the exposure draft for the mark-to-market project, the Board determined to issue the final pronouncement in essentially the same form as the proposed version. Because there were no substantive changes, there was no need to solicit additional input through a second exposure draft.

Final Resolution

After further discussions among Board members in small groups and public meetings, the staff prepares an internal *ballot draft* of the final pronouncement for distribution to the Board. If a two-thirds majority votes for its approval, it is published as a statement or interpretation. Those members who voted against its issuance are identified, and the nature of their dissent is described in the document.

For the mark-to-market project, the Board issued SFAS 115 in June

1993. There were 5 assenting and 2 dissenting votes. This quotation from the standard illustrates the content and style of a dissent:

> Messrs. Sampson and Swieringa disagree with the accounting treatment prescribed in paragraphs 6–18 of this Statement because it does not resolve two of the most important problems that caused the Board to address the accounting for certain investments in debt and equity securities—namely, accounting based on intent, and gains trading. They believe that those problems can only be resolved by reporting all securities that are within the scope of the Statement at fair value and by including unrealized changes in fair value in earnings. . . .
>
> Reporting all securities that are within the scope of this Statement at fair value and including unrealized changes in fair value in earnings would result in reflecting the consequences of economic events (price changes) in the periods in which they occur rather than when managers wish to selectively recognize those consequences in earnings. Messrs. Sampson and Swieringa believe that this reporting is the only way to resolve the problems of accounting based on intent and gains trading that have raised concerns about the relevance and credibility of accounting for certain investments in debt and equity securities.

On occasion, the Board may decide to issue a final pronouncement in a form different from the one that was originally contemplated. This action occurred when the responses to a 1982 exposure draft of a standard on accounting for the investment tax credit indicated that the problem was too narrow to justify issuing a statement. Consequently, the final decision was to issue Technical Bulletin 83–1, "Accounting for the Reduction in the Tax Basis of an Asset Caused by the Investment Tax Credit."

Subsequent Review

The due process does not always stop after the issuance of the final pronouncement, particularly for controversial projects. The Board attempts to monitor the acceptance of a pronouncement informally through communications with the constituents, in much the same way that it attempts to locate new problems. On occasion, the Board has also formally solicited comments from its constituents concerning standards that are in place. Additionally, one function of FASAC members is to report to the Board any problems that have been created or left unsolved by a pronouncement.

As a result of these processes, the Board may decide to issue a Technical Bulletin or an Interpretation to resolve a minor problem. In other cases, an additional standard may be needed to expand the applicability of the earlier solution or to solve a related problem that was not addressed in the initial document. As an extreme example, the Board found that SFAS 13 on accounting for leases needed to be supplemented by a series of later Standards, Interpretations, and Technical Bulletins to deal with a number of related problems (included are SFAS 17, 22, 23, 26, 27, 28, 29, and 98, as well as Interpretations 19, 21, 23, 24, 26, and 27, and Technical Bulletins 79–10, 79–11, 79–12, 79–13, 79–14, 79–15, 79–16, 79–17, 79–18, 85–3, 86–2, and 88–1.

In a few cases, the Board has issued a subsequent pronouncement that drastically altered an earlier one. For example, SFAS 25 (on oil and gas accounting) was issued to indicate that the requirements of SFAS 19 were not to be imposed; it was needed because the SEC did not accept the solution provided in SFAS 19. SFAS 52 (on translation of foreign currency) was issued to replace SFAS 8, which proved extremely unpopular among financial statement preparers. SFAS 82 and SFAS 89 were issued to rescind the mandatory disclosures of SFAS 33 because their continued use was not supported by research, the Board members, or the constituencies. More recently, the FASB issued SFAS 109 in 1992 to supersede SFAS 96, which was originally issued in 1988.

For the mark-to-market project, SFAS 115 represented the outcome of the subsequent review of SFAS 12, which was originally issued in 1975. That standard applied only to marketable equity securities and required the use of the lower-of-cost-or-market method.

THE FASB's PUBLIC RELATIONS ACTIVITIES

In addition to all the preceding due process procedures, the FASB communicates with the business world in other ways because it is sensitive to its role as the focal point of a political process. On the basis that a better informed constituency is more likely to participate in the due process, support specific pronouncements, and provide financial support, the Board carries on a number of public relations activities, which are coordinated through Debbie Harrington, a full-time public relations counsel. These activities include the publication of several newsletters.

Action Alert was mentioned earlier. This weekly summary of future and recent Board meetings is distributed to approximately 2,500 subscribers.

Status Report is issued irregularly, but about 15 issues are published each year. It describes other events relating to the Board, and summarizes new and proposed pronouncements. The first issue of each quarter includes the "Technical Plan," which describes the status of each project on the agenda and the schedule of expected events, such as the publication of an exposure draft or the convening of a public hearing. *Status Report* is distributed to approximately 40,000 subscribers.

Viewpoints provides a forum for the expression of unofficial or personal opinions of Board and staff members, and others. It has been used to report the results of research projects that are not published as separate

Research Studies and to obtain wider circulation of speeches. It is distributed to subscribers of *Status Report*.

The Public Relations Office also prepares an annual version of *Facts about FASB* for free distribution to any interested individuals or groups. This publication includes a mission statement for the Board and short biographies of the Board members and the director and assistant director of the Research and Technical Activities staff. A large number of copies are printed and distributed each year.[3]

The FASB has sponsored several special conferences on significant and controversial topics. Their purpose is to provide a forum for the discussion of the issues and evidence relating to their solutions without the political (and possibly confrontational) nature of a public hearing or a Board meeting. For example, the Board has sponsored conferences on the Conceptual Framework, the economic consequences of accounting standards, and research related to accounting for changing prices. To help practitioners learn about the intricacies of two key standards (SFAS 106 on other postemployment benefits and SFAS 109 on income taxes), the FASB developed training courses and seminars that were marketed in conjunction with the FEI, the IMA, and various state CPA societies.

In addition, Board members, the director of RTA, and staff members are encouraged to accept speaking engagements in which they can explain the activities of the Board and receive comments and questions from significant constituent bodies. Thus, many speeches are delivered to major professional groups in national, regional, and local meetings. They are also given to college and university groups, including Beta Alpha Psi chapters and student accounting clubs. In 1992, 268 speeches were presented; 103 of these were delivered by Board members, 15 by the director of RTA, and 150 by members of the staff and others.

The Board also maintains an ongoing relationship with the press, particularly with publications that focus on business affairs. To help ensure that reporters have access to accurate explanations of all new pronouncements, press releases are distributed to about 500 major newspapers and other periodicals. In special circumstances, news conferences are held to allow reporters to obtain clarification from Board and staff members. Press conferences have been held on such occasions as the release of the exposure draft on foreign currency translation (eventually issued as SFAS 52) and the publication of the Board's Preliminary Views on pensions. In other cases, special background briefings have been provided in Washington for government personnel, and the press was invited to attend and participate. One of these briefings was held in December 1988 to describe SFAS 96 on accounting for income taxes.

---

[3] In response to requests, *Facts about FASB* can be mailed out to accounting instructors for distribution to their classes.

In dealing with the FASB, press representatives generally do not seek interviews with Board members for their positions on issues; instead, they usually deal with the project manager. Although this practice is not the result of a deliberate policy, it is useful to the Board because it allows Board members more flexibility in changing from a preliminary position on the issues. For example, if the press had quoted a specific member as being against the recognition of investments at historical cost, it would have been more difficult for him to change his position, regardless of how persuasive the arguments were.

PARTICIPATING IN THE FASB's DUE PROCESS

It may be apparent from the preceding discussion that the nature and contents of FASB pronouncements are shaped at least in part by communications from the Board's constituents. This section is provided for the guidance of those readers who would like to affect the outcome of the process by participating directly in it.

In interviews with the authors, Board and key staff members asserted that comment letters and testimony at public hearings do indeed affect their positions on the issues. However, they also agreed that all communications are not equally effective in accomplishing the senders' goals. To help readers understand more about the process and participate in it more effectively, the authors asked Board and staff members to identify the qualities of effective and ineffective communications. Some of those comments are presented:

- Articulate, well-presented arguments are effective. Presentations that dismiss opposing views out of hand as simply wrong or "stupid" are very unconvincing.
- Persuasive communications are neither too long nor too short. Letters with many single-spaced pages are likely to be overlooked because the writer does not focus on the critical points. On the other hand, very short letters merely demonstrate that the respondents do not understand the controversies.
- Responses that include clear examples are well received, if they provide insight into the effects of a proposed treatment on common transactions in a nonmainstream industry (such as software development).
- In general, letters that merely promote the respondent's self-interest are not considered effective. One Board member said that he finds such letters to be interesting, but asserted that they are helpful only if the respondents clearly know that their position is self-serving and do not try to stretch logic beyond its limits.
- Comment letters are not used to "count noses" on the popularity of a preliminary position. Accordingly, multiple copies of the same

letter from different members of the same constituency are particularly unpersuasive. One Board member said that he seldom finds such letter-writing "campaigns" to be convincing but he does consider them useful for gauging how deeply the issues affect respondents' emotions.

- Threatening letters are extremely unsuccessful.
- Speaking independently of each other, three Board members said that they learn nothing from letters that simply say, "I don't like what the Board has proposed." In fact, one member said that he found these letters to be "almost useless." Instead, compelling letters identify specific implementation problems that are not addressed in the document or specific implementation situations where the proposed accounting will not work well.
- One Board member indicated that it is usually ineffective for a respondent to attempt to address the issues at the same conceptual level that the Board uses. He explained that the Board and staff members have substantially more familiarity and expertise with the Conceptual Framework than others, with the result that comment letters seldom use the concepts appropriately.
- Especially appreciated are letters that describe the results of actually trying to apply the proposed requirements to a company's situation, even if the writer is against the change.
- Board members are also influenced by negative letters that go beyond criticizing the proposed solution to offer some other specific new approach that will improve existing requirements.

One Board member said that presentations at public hearings varied significantly in their effectiveness. He pointed out that presentations that follow up on a previously submitted comment letter are particularly useful. He also indicated that interesting and lively presentations are more likely to get points across whereas presentations read from prepared scripts are "duds." Finally, he cautioned that arrogance or overaggressiveness is likely to be counterproductive.

In order for the reader to see examples of responses received by the FASB, Exhibit 3–3 reproduces several unedited comment letters that were submitted in the mark-to-market project.

EXHIBIT 3–3 Sample Comment Letters

UNIVERSITY OF SOUTH DAKOTA
Vermillion, South Dakota

Gentlemen:

Subject: ED "Accounting for Certain Investments. . ."

After attempting to explain the current exposure draft to my Intermediate Accounting students, I became convinced that the proposed standard (1) increases (not reduces) management's manipulative power—Issue 1, and (2) lacks specificity as to how it is to be administered.

Paragraphs 6 and 7 of the ED attempt to provide a structure for determining if "held to maturity" is appropriate. Since most of the conditions are subjective, it is possible that two otherwise similar companies could account for debt securities differently—Paragraph 57 recognizes that this could be true for the same securities. Further, introduction of "ability to hold to maturity" forces all callable securities into the "held for sale" category. However, the call provisions usually exceeds the holder's cost and seems (by itself) to cause little need for fair value accounting.

Did the Board consider having all debt securities classified as current assets reflected at lower-of-cost-or-market and apply the proposed standard to debt securities classified as noncurrent assets?

If the Board is going to edict a change in existing practice, it should (by its own standards) make the change within the context of the Conceptual Framework. Not only does the Board admit that the recommendation results from pressure groups—Paragraph 2—but it admits that a workable approach to providing the desired matching was unattainable—Paragraph 43.

I recognize the frailty of historical cost in financial reporting but cannot support *partial* fair value accounting based on intent of management and subjective (if not flawed) evaluations of the ability to hold securities to maturity.

Thank you for your attention.

Sincerely,

Richard W. Metcalf, Professor

EXHIBIT 3–3 *(continued)*

DAVID SOLOMONS
Swarthmore, Pennsylvania

September 22, 1992

Dear Sir:

File Reference No. 119-A
Accounting for Certain Investments in Debt and Equity Securities

The above exposure draft, dated September 9, 1992, asks for comments on the use of intent as the basis of accounting for debt and equity securities and, by implication, perhaps for other assets and liabilities. If this issue could be resolved, most of the other questions raised by the ED can be easily answered.

I am substantially in agreement with the alternative view expressed in paragraphs 86-90 of the ED. Intent is *not* an appropriate basis of accounting for several reasons:

1. Even the firmest intent at the time an investment is made may, for any number of reasons, be changed. An initial intention to hold a debt security to maturity may look foolhardy in the light of subsequent changes in interest rates or credit risk.
2. Intent is too subjective a concept to serve as a basis of accounting, and opens up opportunities for "managing" earnings by the judicious timing of sales and transfers. This is particularly relevant when considering the proposed distinction between "trading securities" and those "available for sale." As is pointed out in paragraph 87, the use of intent can result in the use of different bases of accounting for precisely the same security in the same circumstances. This is not the way to make like things look alike, one of the Board's declared purposes.
3. My fundamental reason for objecting to the use of intent as a basis for accounting is that it puts the cart before the horse. Management intent should be formed *on the basis of accounting information*, not the other way round. If accounting numbers do not guide management's and investors' intentions and decision making, what purpose do they serve? Accounting information cannot be useful if it *depends* on the intentions that it ought to help management to form.

These arguments lead me to the conclusion that all securities for which fair values can be established with reasonable reliability ought to be carried on that basis, regardless of the purpose for which they are said to be held.

I am also entirely in agreement with the arguments put forward in paragraphs 89 and 90. All gains and losses on securities, realized and unrealized, should be shown in the income statement as components of comprehensive income. As for volatility, concern about it points to a "bottom line" mentality, a mentality that thinks that massaging the bottom line can change volatility into stability. Volatility in security prices, and therefore in enterprise results, is determined by the market, not by what accountants do. They may choose to recognize it or not to recognize it. To favor an accounting policy because it cloaks "economic

EXHIBIT 3–3 *(continued)*

reality" instead of illuminating it is not the way to better accounting. However, so long as gains and losses are disclosed, it does not much matter whether they go into income or owners' equity. Users can rearrange them as they think fit. But why put them to that trouble if comparability is the goal?

Sincerely,

David Solomons
Ernst & Young Professor Emeritus
University of Pennsylvania
Former member of FASAC

AMERICAN MUTUAL LIFE INSURANCE COMPANY
Des Moines, Iowa

November 24, 1992

Dear Sir:

As Chairman of the Board and Chief Executive Officer of American Mutual Life Insurance Company, I would like to express my opposition to your proposed accounting standard for valuing debt and equity securities, the mark-to-market proposal.

First of all, marking to market assets and not liabilities will result in a distorted and misleading financial picture and would also result in very erratic measures of net worth or surplus.

As a life insurance company, we purchase assets that we feel will match our liabilities as closely as possible. Since these liabilities are long term in nature, it is only prudent to invest in long term assets. Your proposal would force companies to shorten their assets in order to reduce the impact of fluctuating asset prices on surplus.

The National Association of Insurance Commissioners (NAIC) has recently implemented new reserve requirements for insurance companies. These changes require that we establish reserves for all assets including mortgage loans and real estate which were previously excluded. The new Asset Valuation Reserve (AVR) along with the new Interest Maintenance Reserve (IMR) will reflect a much better picture of a company's financial strength and stability than will mark-to-market accounting for one side of the balance sheet.

Sincerely,

Sam C. Kalainov
Chairman
Chief Executive Officer

EXHIBIT 3–3 *(continued)*

THE BANK OF REESEVILLE
Reeseville, Wisconsin

December 10, 1992

Dear Mr. Lucas:

I have been a small town community banker for 30 years serving a community of 1,000. We have a current loan to deposit ratio of 78% but with more needless regulation like (FASB) it's becoming increasingly clear we can no longer serve our customer's with endless rules & regulations. The FASB proposal will in no way provide better information to the users of our financial statements when the average citizen of our community does not take the time to comprehend financial accounting of unrealized gains or losses in the banks investment portfolio. Possibly useful only to financial experts.

As a banker, I am not stupid since I will be forced to shorten the maturity of my investment portfolio and compromise long-term profitability of the security portfolio to retain the flexibility to respond to changing rate environments. The added cost of more high price accountants reviewing more complex accounting information and the added expense of bank personnel formulating & compiling the information with valuations that may still be questioned or unavailable will have a detrimental effect on earnings for a small institution such as ours. CONGRESS needs to know that Government regulation is SUCKING billions of dollars out of our local economies and they Fail to see the Impact of these regulations. (FASB) loan treatment proposal will be the load that breaks the Camel's back. Don't blame bankers for the so-called credit crunch created by CONGRESS.

The Congress of the United States is trying to take the risk out of a business that is a risk management business. IMPOSSIBLE to do! A doctor can't provide the same medication to cure all the ills of individuals, but the CONGRESS believes it can provide medication to cure all the ills of Financial Institutions. What a mistake to regulate us to death! Hope government will soon pay attention to "SMALL TOWN AMERICA," the backbone of U.S.A. Get off our backs, Allow us to be Bankers, Cut the Government Red Tape and the economy will improve. That's the type of medication we need and it will cost nothing! Enough is Enough.

Sincerely,

G.W. Yerges
President

EXHIBIT 3–3 *(concluded)*

KENTLAND BANK
Kentland, Indiana

December 11, 1992

Dear Sir:

PLEASE BE REASONABLE! Why must you punish the masses for a few. Mark-to-market is a giant overkill. What is so difficult about setting up a standard or minimum amount of gains that could be taken in the bond account in relation to the losses carried on the books at the same time. Aren't you really trying to prevent distortion in the balance sheet and earnings?

Why oh why must you make everybody jump through the hoops with a tremendous amount of energy and expense to accomplish so little. For those violators, do whatever is necessary to reprimand them or change their balance sheet or earnings statement but please, please don't put all of the innocent people through these hoops for the sins of a few.

PLEASE BE REASONABLE!

Sincerely,

Ronald L. Humphrey
President

APPENDIX
Obtaining FASB Publications

To participate effectively in the FASB's due process, respondents must be well informed on the issues and the preliminary deliberations that have taken place prior to the Board's solicitation of comments. To be informed, the respondents need to have access to facts about what has already happened. Although public accounting firms and other organizations publish summaries (such as those contained in the *Deloitte & Touche Review*), they are seldom as complete or as timely as the materials provided by the FASB to those who subscribe to its publications. The following subscription packages were available in 1993:

- The Comprehensive Plan includes all publications of the FASB, except for *Action Alert*; its cost is $205 for one year or $370 for two years. A 20 percent discount applies to all educators and to members of the Financial Accounting Foundation.

- The Basic Plan includes only final documents (and thus omits exposure drafts and discussion memoranda) and *Status Report*; its cost is $100 for 12 months or $175 for 24 months, with the same 20 percent discount to members and educators.
- *Action Alert* is distributed only by separate subscription, which costs $63 per year; no discounts are offered.

Single copies of discussion memoranda and exposure drafts are available without charge during the comment period. Multiple copies of these documents and any copies of final pronouncements must be purchased through the Board's Publication Office. The Board also markets volumes that combine the pronouncements of the Committee on Accounting Procedure, the Accounting Principles Board, and the FASB. The *Original Pronouncements* volumes present the material in chronological order and indicate which sections have been amended or superseded; the *Current Text* volume takes the material out of the original format and recombines it by subject matter for easier reference when dealing with a specific topic, such as executive compensation or treasury stock.

For additional information or to order materials, inquiries should be addressed to:

> Publications Office
> Financial Accounting Standards Board
> 401 Merritt 7
> P.O. Box 5116
> Norwalk, CT 06856-5116

SELECTED READINGS

BERTON, LEE. "FASB, Which Decides Accounting Questions, Sparks Much Criticism." *The Wall Street Journal*, April 30, 1984, p. 1.

FOGLIASSO, CHRISTINE E.; GUY W. OWINGS; AND JEAN STRADER. "Conflict in Accounting Standards." *Accountants Journal*, Fall 1992, pp. 36–43.

KELLY-NEWTON, LAUREN. *Accounting Policy Formulation: The Role of Corporate Management*. Reading, Mass.: Addison-Wesley Publishing, 1980.

KIRK, DONALD J. "Concepts, Consensus, and Compromise: Their Roles in Standard Setting." *Journal of Accountancy*, April 1981, pp. 83–86.

NAKAYAMA, M.; S. LIEBEN; AND M. BENIS. "Due Process and FASB No. 13." *Management Accounting*, April 1981, pp. 49–53.

RODDA, ARLEEN K. "The AICPA's Role in Standard Setting." *Journal of Accountancy*, February 1993, pp. 67–70.

4

The Conceptual Framework Project

This chapter provides a closer examination of the Conceptual Framework, which is widely considered the single most important project in the FASB's history. Its importance is indicated by several facts. First, it was placed on the Board's initial agenda in 1973 with high expectations for its accomplishments. Second, it led to the publication of six Statements of Financial Accounting Concepts. Third, it involved a long and complex set of due process procedures, including five discussion memoranda, a tentative conclusions document, seven exposure drafts, a series of eight research studies, and six public hearings. Fourth, it generated substantial controversy among Board members, staff members, and the FASB's constituencies. Finally, and most significantly, the project was given the goal of laying the foundation for future directions in setting standards. A critical evaluation of the project is included in this book because many observers have argued that the Framework has not met the expectations that were established at its inception. Some have asserted that it is a failure, and some have called it a disappointment. Still others consider it a success.

In dealing with the Conceptual Framework, this chapter presents three sections:

- The reasons for having a conceptual framework and approaches to developing one.
- The FASB's experience.
- A summary and evaluation of the contents of the concepts statements.

THE REASONS FOR HAVING A CONCEPTUAL FRAMEWORK AND APPROACHES TO DEVELOPING ONE

In any field of study or activity, including financial accounting, there are a number of reasons for developing a *conceptual framework*, which is a collection of broad rules, guidelines, accepted truths, and other basic ideas. These three reasons for creating a conceptual framework for accounting are discussed in this section:

- Description of existing practice.
- Prescription of future practices.
- Definition of commonly used terms.

Description of Existing Practice

One main goal of developing a conceptual framework is to describe existing practice in order to make it easier to *educate* nonaccountants about what it is that accountants do. This education may occur for the purpose of training new accountants or simply for helping nonaccountants understand how to use accounting information. Another goal of the description may be to help standards setters solve new problems by stating general rules that are followed for existing similar transactions, events, or conditions. By relating the new problems to previously encountered ones and then reasoning by analogy, it may be possible to come up with solutions that are acceptable because they appear to be consistent with those that are already in use.

The basic approach to developing a *descriptive* framework starts by examining what is being done in practice and then moves to higher level abstractions. As symbolized in Exhibit 4–1, the approach can be called *bottom-up*; a more technical term that is used to describe it is *inductive*.

Advantages and disadvantages. One advantage of the descriptive approach is its tendency to produce practical concepts that take into consideration the real-world problems leading to existing practices. For example, a descriptive framework might include the concept that a corporation should not recognize its internally generated goodwill as an asset because there are no reliable measures of its value; thus, other intangible assets can be recognized because they can be measured.

As briefly discussed in Chapter 1, many accountants want existing practices to be kept intact because, among other things, if there are no changes, they will not have to learn any new techniques and they will not lose control over the information reported to their corporations' stockholders. When this attitude is combined with the fact that a descriptive conceptual framework captures the essence of the status quo, the descriptive approach is widely preferred because it protects practice against changes. For example, if a descriptive concept is established that assets are recognized at cost, it will be fairly difficult to argue persuasively that a

---

EXHIBIT 4–1 Bottom-Up Approach

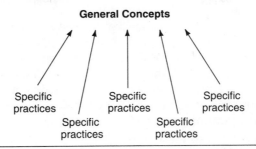

new standard should require a new type of asset to be reported at market value. Whether this protective effect is really an advantage depends, of course, on one's belief about the status quo. To those who want the status quo to be maintained, the approach is advantageous; to those who favor change, the approach is not advantageous. As described later in the chapter, the conflict over the suitability of the status quo had a very significant effect on the FASB's efforts to establish its Conceptual Framework.

Regardless of one's position on the desirability of change, a major disadvantage of the descriptive approach is that it depends on observations of what is actually happening. Two problems arise from this dependence. First, an assumption must be made that the practice being observed is the right thing to do. That is, the observer has to conclude that a technique used in practice is the best that can ever be used. In fact, all that can be legitimately concluded is that the technique is merely *used*; it is not valid to conclude that it is the *most useful* technique or even that it is *useful at all*. Second, the development of a descriptive framework depends on obtaining agreement among a number of observers not only about *what* is actually happening but also (and more important) about *why* it is happening. In a sense, developing a descriptive framework is like giving several people an answer and then telling them to guess what the question is. It does not take much experience to know that there will be significant differences of opinion among them. For example, a number of people may agree that accountants initially recognize an asset at the amount paid for it. However, that agreement does not necessarily extend to the reason for using that amount. Some might argue that the accountants are interested in the original *cost* as a measure of the amount invested in the asset; on the other hand, others might assert that the amount paid is merely a reliable estimate of the asset's *fair market value* on the purchase date. It may be impossible to determine why accountants do what they do, but it is precisely the reason why it is done that is important for the conceptual framework.

For another example, it can be observed from practice that inventories are commonly presented in the statement of financial position at cost, except for agricultural products, which are presented at market value. Without making an assumption, it is not possible to determine whether the general rule is to use cost or market. If cost is the desired goal, then the treatment of agricultural products is the exception and cost should be used for new types of inventories. Alternatively, if market is the desired goal, but cost is substituted when market is not reliably measured, then the treatment of agricultural products is not an exception and accountants should pursue the use of value for all inventories.

Descriptive accounting frameworks. Because of these problems, widely accepted and useful descriptive frameworks for financial accounting have proven difficult to develop. Three examples of efforts to compile such frameworks are:

- *An Introduction to Corporate Accounting Standards*, written by William A. Paton and A. C. Littleton and published in 1940 by the American Accounting Association.
- *Accounting Research Study No. 7: An Inventory of Generally Accepted Accounting Principles*, written by Paul Grady and published by the AICPA in 1965.
- *Accounting Principles Board Statement No. 4: Basic Concepts and Accounting Principles Underlying Financial Statements of Business Enterprises*, developed by the APB and published by the AICPA in 1970.

Because these documents were descriptive, the concepts they contain often do not help a standards-setting body accomplish its mission; instead, a different type of framework is needed.

Prescription of Future Practices

In contrast to description, an important reason for developing an accounting conceptual framework is to provide guidance to help resolve old and new unsettled questions. There are at least two ways in which such a *prescriptive* framework can be helpful.

First, the guidance in its concepts can be for the benefit of a formal standards-setting body such as the APB or the FASB. Toward this end, the Accounting Principles Board made several attempts to develop a set of concepts, but it did not succeed in obtaining the guidance it sought.[1] Second, that guidance can help individual practicing accountants resolve reporting problems that are not covered by authoritative pronouncements.

---

[1] For a description of these efforts and their effect on the FASB's project, see Paul A. Pacter, "The Conceptual Framework: Make No Mystique about It," *Journal of Accountancy*, July 1983, pp. 76–88.

EXHIBIT 4–2   Top-Down Approach

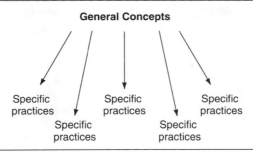

General Concepts

Specific
practices

Specific
practices

Specific
practices

Specific
practices

Specific
practices

A prescriptive framework is developed by starting with a few general concepts and working down through their implications to statements of what ought to be done in practice. As shown by the direction of the arrows in Exhibit 4–2, this approach is often called *top-down*; more technical terms that are used to describe this approach are *deductive* and *normative*.

A prescriptive approach assumes a clean slate, in the sense that it attempts to define the objectives of and limits on an activity without being constrained to include what is already being done or to exclude what is not being done.

Advantages and disadvantages.   Because a prescriptive framework is not based on the assumption that what is being done is right, it offers the advantage of uncovering areas in existing practice that can be improved. To many accountants, of course, this feature is not an advantage because they want to keep the status quo in place without major changes.

A second advantage of a prescriptive framework is that it tends to produce simpler concepts that do not attempt to include all the intricacies of existing practice. For example, a prescriptive concept might state that all inventories should be carried at the most reliably estimated measure of their market value (one of which might be its cost). If both the cost and market of a new type of inventory are available (and they are different), there is no confusion as to how it should be accounted for. This concept is far different from a descriptive rule that says inventories are *usually* reported at their cost but are *sometimes* reported at their market value.

Another advantage of the top-down approach is that the developer of the framework does not have to carry any preexisting theories into it. At any point, the relevant question to be answered is whether the suggested lower level practice is consistent with the higher level concepts, and the developer does not need to be concerned about what *is* being done in practice. This approach tends to bring more rigor to standards setting because the usefulness of any procedure (new *or* old) should be proven before it is accepted as useful. In short, there is no presumption of usefulness simply because a practice is used.

Yet another advantage of a prescriptive framework is that its lack of ties to the status quo means that prescriptive rules can be more easily applied to new situations. In other words, reasoning by analogy is used less extensively when a prescriptive framework is applied than when a descriptive framework is applied. Additionally, a prescriptive framework is not made obsolete as soon as a new situation arises, whereas a descriptive framework must be modified to include the new practices that stem from that situation.

Of course, there are disadvantages to prescriptive frameworks. For one, they are difficult to compile because it is necessary to construct a consensus on the question of what accounting *ought* to accomplish. In effect, the top-down approach forces the resolution of all problems at the same time instead of providing the luxury of dealing with them one at a time. For example, if a proposed concept suggested that all assets should be measured in terms of their market values, it would be necessary to deal with this concept's implications for receivables, investments, inventory, operating assets, and intangibles and in all industries. In contrast, if each area and industry were tackled more or less independently, the affected constituent groups would be smaller and more easily satisfied.

A second disadvantage of prescriptive frameworks is that their concepts may be perceived as being so abstract as to be inapplicable. A typical reaction of practitioners to such frameworks is that they come from an "ivory tower" that has an artificial view of the "real world."

Prescriptive accounting frameworks. Several prescriptive frameworks for financial accounting have been attempted; among them are:

- *Accounting Research Study No. 1: The Basic Postulates of Accounting*, written by Maurice Moonitz and published by the AICPA in 1961, and *Accounting Research Study No. 3: A Tentative Set of Broad Accounting Principles*, written by Robert T. Sprouse and Moonitz and published by the AICPA in 1962. (Both of these studies were discussed in the appendix to Chapter 2.)
- *A Statement of Basic Accounting Theory*, written by a committee of the American Accounting Association and published by the AAA in 1966.
- *Objectives of Financial Statements*, written by the Trueblood Study Group and published by the AICPA in 1973.

When this list is combined with the list of descriptive frameworks provided earlier on page 90, it can be seen that the APB and the AICPA had a particularly difficult time determining which approach was preferable for meeting their needs. Without a strong commitment to one of these approaches, there was only a small likelihood that success would be achieved.

Definition of Commonly Used Terms

A conceptual framework that defines commonly used terms is helpful to a standards-setting system (such as the FASB) that involves deliberations and due process. There are two main advantages. First, the process can become more efficient because all the participants have the same definitions for the words that they use in communicating with each other. Second, a fixed set of definitions is more likely to help new standards be consistent.

The main disadvantage of a framework that merely defines terms is that it will not eliminate debates. For example, Statement of Financial Accounting Concepts No. 3 defines assets as

> probable future economic benefits obtained or controlled by a particular entity as a result of past transactions or events. (par. 19)

Although the definition appears to be reasonable and straightforward, a more careful analysis shows that its meaning depends in turn on the meanings of such words as *probable*, *economic*, *benefits*, *obtained*, *controlled*, *entity*, *result*, *transactions*, and *events*. Because the definitions of these other terms can be debated, they will be used by participants in the due process to make their points or to attack the opponents' arguments. Although the definitions will not end the debates, they will at least focus them on a smaller set of issues. Eventually, as these issues are settled over and over again, common meanings will become established and the process will become more efficient.

In order to have wide acceptance, the definitions in this type of framework have to be developed through a political process that involves a number of parties. Thus, neither a strict prescriptive nor a pure descriptive approach is likely to be effective. Instead, some combination will have to be applied.

No accounting conceptual framework has been developed simply for the purpose of defining the terms to be used in setting standards. Although a number of publications provide definitions of accounting words, they are more like dictionaries than theoretical structures.[2] Furthermore, they have not been put together for the purpose of guiding a standards-setting body.

Summary

In general, there are three purposes for developing a conceptual framework: to *describe* existing practices, to *prescribe* future practices, and to *define* commonly used terms. The preceding discussion of these purposes

---

[2] For example, W. W. Cooper and Yuji Ijiri, eds., *Kohler's Dictionary for Accountants*, 6th ed. (Englewood Cliffs, N.J.: Prentice Hall, 1983).

and the approaches to developing frameworks that serve them has shown that they are very much in conflict. For example, a description of existing practice often does not provide a good prescription for dealing with new transactions. This point is especially important because it is very difficult (if not impossible) to obtain a consensus on the contents of a framework if its developers do not agree on which purpose is to be served. The next section describes what happened to the FASB's project and shows how this lack of agreement about its purpose played a significant role in the difficulties that were encountered and in shaping the compromise statements that were produced.

THE FASB'S EXPERIENCE

Section IV(H)(2) of the FASB's Rules of Procedure describes the goals of the Board's Conceptual Framework project by listing the following purposes for Statements of Financial Accounting Concepts:

- Establish objectives and concepts that the Standards Board will use in developing standards of financial accounting and reporting.
- Provide guidance in resolving problems of financial accounting and reporting that are not addressed in authoritative pronouncements.
- Enhance the assessment by users of the content and limitations of information provided by financial accounting and reporting and thereby further the ability to use that information effectively.

The first two purposes clearly establish that the FASB's Conceptual Framework was intended to be *prescriptive*, while the third purpose points out the *educational* goal. Nothing is said in this description about using a framework for *defining terms*.

In reflection of the priority on prescription, the Board's project was designed to be a top-down framework. It started with the identification of the highest level concept of what accounting ought to accomplish, and it was then to move down through lower levels.

Not surprisingly, the project proved to be very controversial. A large part of the controversy stemmed from the fact that many constituents prefer the status quo and do not want a prescriptive framework because it implies change. More controversy arose because of the need for the shapers of a prescriptive framework to resolve a lot of issues at the same time. Specifically, the Board found it difficult to resolve any issues because at least some constituents criticized the Board on every stand it took. Virtually every issue had a high priority for some influential group, and a vigorous defense of the status quo was mounted everywhere the Board turned. With opposition from so many different directions, the Board did not have much room for the compromising that is so essential to the development of a consensus on the issues.

As a result of this opposition, the Board had to move back and forth between the prescriptive and descriptive approaches, as demonstrated in Statement of Financial Accounting Concepts No. 1 (SFAC 1). First, paragraph 34 identifies the primary objective of financial accounting and reporting[3] as providing useful information to creditors, investors, and others for rational decision making. Paragraph 37 explains that such decision making involves the users' assessments of the amount, timing, and uncertainty of cash flows from the enterprise to them. Paragraph 39 explains that these assessments depend on assessments of the cash flows of the enterprise itself. This series of conclusions might suggest (on a *prescriptive* basis) that the most useful information to report would be based directly on the entity's cash flows. But a *descriptive* discussion in paragraphs 44–48 very carefully defends traditional accrual accounting on the basis that it provides better data for assessing the enterprise's future cash flows than does historical cash flow information. By including these comments, the Board alleviated fears that the prescriptive approach was going to produce a revolution in accounting practice.

Further into the project, the compromise between descriptive and prescriptive had advanced to the stage that the thrust of the project had become essentially descriptive. For example, paragraph 70 of SFAC 5 says:

> Rather than attempt to characterize present practice as being based on a single attribute with numerous exceptions for diverse reasons, this concept's statement characterizes present practice as based on different attributes.

If the project had been truly prescriptive, there would have been no need for the Board to attempt to characterize present practice in any way. The quote shows that the purpose of the framework had essentially become description of present practice rather than prescription of guidance for setting standards.

As a result of this compromising on the basic nature of the Conceptual Framework project, its output is neither very prescriptive nor descriptive but a combination that may be unsatisfactory for either purpose. Nonetheless, its output is useful because it defines a number of important terms that the Board can use in its internal and external communications. The terms also force constituents to be more rigorous in putting together their responses to discussion documents and exposure drafts. This accomplishment is somewhat ironic in light of the fact the Board never explicitly identified it as a goal for the project.

---

[3] The FASB decided to use the phrase "financial accounting and reporting" instead of only "financial accounting" because the Board members wanted to acknowledge that much of the information presented *with* the financial statements is as important as the information that is presented *in* them. For fear that the term *accounting* might be too narrowly interpreted, they chose to add the additional words *and reporting* to ensure that the wider scope of the Board's authority would be clearly stated.

The Basic Steps in the FASB's Conceptual Framework Project

As mentioned earlier, the Conceptual Framework project was on the early agenda of the FASB. The project's first discussion memorandum, published in 1974, concerned the Trueblood Study Group's *Report on the Objectives of Financial Statements*. A second discussion memorandum, on measurement and the elements (or components) of financial statements, was published in 1976. Hearings on these documents took place in 1974 and 1977. The first exposure draft for the project was distributed in 1977, and SFAC 1 was issued in 1978. As described later in this chapter, this statement put users' needs at the head of the list of those to be served by financial accounting. Although this idea does not seem particularly revolutionary in retrospect, it can be interpreted as an official recognition of the shift to user interests and away from the orientation toward auditors' needs that had dominated standards setting since 1938.

Over the next two years, the project progressed through two more exposure drafts, and SFAC 2 and SFAC 3 were issued in 1980. SFAC 2 describes the qualities of information that is useful to the decision makers identified in SFAC 1. These *qualitative characteristics* include relevance, reliability, and comparability, as well as several subcharacteristics. SFAC 3 identifies the *elements* of financial statements, which are the objects that the information should be about. They include such familiar items as assets, liabilities, owners' equity, revenues, and expenses. In 1980, the Board also issued SFAC 4, which adapted the objectives of SFAC 1 to nonbusiness entities, including universities, hospitals, charities, museums, and religious organizations, but not governmental organizations.

After this progress, the FASB ran into some difficulties in making the Conceptual Framework more specific. In particular, it ran up against opposition after issuing an exposure draft of a concepts statement concerned with the structure of the financial statements.[4] The primary trigger for the opposition was the Board's decision to focus on a broadly defined concept of income called *comprehensive income* instead of the more familiar concept of *earnings*. As a consequence of this focus, many constituents concluded that the FASB was proposing a revolutionary shift toward using many more current value measurements. This controversy put even more pressure on the "recognition and measurement" phase of the project.

Recognition and measurement. The goal of the recognition and measurement phase was to establish the very important concepts of *what* to put in the financial statements, *when* to put them there, and *what* amounts to associate with them. To many constituents, Board members, and others, these issues seemed to be merely another way of raising the

---

[4] "Reporting Income, Cash Flows, and Financial Position of Business Enterprises," FASB, *Proposed Statement of Financial Accounting Concepts,* November 16, 1981.

age-old (and surprisingly emotional) question of whether historical cost or current value should be the primary basis for measurement.

The phase started out with hopes for progress, although many constituents and at least some Board members had become wary of the direction in which it seemed to be heading. One consideration that seemed to concern many was the appointment of Robert R. Sterling to the staff for a two-year term as senior fellow. Sterling was a highly regarded academician with a reputation as a strong advocate of current values, particularly those representing the selling prices of assets.

The strategy adopted by the staff and Board was to submit a series of case studies to the Board members for discussion in meetings. Each case was designed to solicit an expression by each Board member of what he thought on the specific issues, with the intermediate goal of identifying his individual internal framework concerning recognition and measurement. Then, the staff would try to identify those areas in which there was a consensus and move forward to an exposure draft.

The first case concerned recognition and measurement issues related to a simple cash transaction, and the Board members all agreed on its treatment. However, difficulties arose in the next cases, which concerned receivables and payables. Those Board members who wanted to keep the status quo intact became reluctant to endorse any use of current values as preferable to original cost-based numbers in any circumstances. This reluctance progressed even to the point that Board member Robert Morgan said that he preferred the face value of a receivable in every circumstance, even if the interest rate was unrealistic. In effect, Board members were looking past the general concepts at the top to see what impact they would have on the specific practices that would be derived from them. This tendency (which became known as "*peeking at the answers*") was an example of the compromising between the prescriptive and descriptive approaches described earlier.

The deliberations became more and more difficult as the cases became more complex and closer to real issues in financial accounting. The peeking was clearly demonstrated in one case designed to have the Board members address some issues related to how a savings and loan institution should account for its mortgage loans receivable. Several Board members simply would not state their preference out of concern that the troubled savings and loan industry would interpret their hypothetical positions as an intent to modify practices then in use.

In the summer of 1982, it became clear that the Board members were deeply divided on the most basic question: three (David Mosso, Robert Sprouse, and Ralph Walters) favored more use of current values than under the status quo; three (Frank Block, John March, and Robert Morgan) favored less use; and Don Kirk was somewhere in between. Furthermore, the members of the two main subgroups did not always see eye to eye on the reasons for their positions. At the end of the summer, those

Board members who favored keeping the status quo publicly voiced a worry that the staff members were biased in favor of current values and were thus unable to offer legitimate assistance. In an effort to achieve some progress, two separate staff teams were created and the Board engaged Robert K. Mautz as a consultant. Because he was reputed to be an advocate for maintaining the status quo, his engagement was an attempt to counterbalance the presence of Sterling. Despite the ensuing efforts to seek a consensus, the Board remained at an impasse. The division held, even though there had been one change in the Board's membership when Vic Brown from Firestone replaced Morgan, formerly of Caterpillar Tractor.

Later in 1983, the Board abandoned its original goal for the recognition and measurement phase in favor of another strategy that would allow the Board members to agree on some issues and get a SFAC published. In order to do so, about the only choice was to draft a statement that would essentially endorse the previously published concepts and avoid coming to grips with the historical cost/current value question. Project managers Tim Lucas (see page 47) and Halsey Bullen were assigned to the project because Sterling's appointment was ending. Lucas was given the job because of the respect he had earned for his ability in forging a consensus on the difficult pensions project. Even though he was just appointed to the staff, Bullen's assignment was supported because he was untainted by the previous events.

An exposure draft incorporating the chosen strategy was issued in December 1983, just before Ray Lauver replaced Ralph Walters as a Board member. SFAC 5 was issued in December 1984, just before the replacement of Board member John March by Art Wyatt. Although SFAC 5 does open some doors for change by including a new additional statement of comprehensive income and by acknowledging that current value information might be useful in some circumstances, the movement toward a descriptive framework prevents SFAC 5 from providing much prescriptive guidance.

Not-for-profit concepts. The final step in the Conceptual Framework project was an effort to develop concepts that would guide the Board and its constituents in dealing with accounting for entities other than business enterprises. At the time that SFAC 4 was completed, these entities were called *nonbusiness*, but the term was resented by their managers because it seemed to imply that they were not "businesslike." As an accommodation, SFAC 6 uses the term *not-for-profit*.

There was substantial uncertainty in the project as to how to accomplish the extension of the Conceptual Framework to not-for-profit entities. SFAC 4 was comparable to SFAC 1, but did not repeat much of its content because the objectives of accounting for the two types of organizations are so different. However, there were no differences in the qualitative characteristics of useful information provided to statement users, and there were many similarities in the elements used in the financial statements issued by both types of entities. The process was further delayed by the stalemate in the recognition and measurement phase because of some similarities in the issues concerning the timing and amounts of revenues. Some fears also existed that opening SFAC 3 for amendment would bring about new debates from Board members and constituents who found the original version to be oriented too strongly toward current values. The final decision was to issue SFAC 6 as an amendment to SFAC 3 that would add new elements but leave the old ones intact. Once SFAC 5 was issued, the way was cleared for the amendment, which was issued in December 1985.

Some Observations on the Events

By 1993, enough time has passed to allow evaluations of the somewhat disappointing outcome of the recognition and measurement phase of the project, which was particularly meaningful in terms of the potential that existed for its contributions beyond the levels achieved by other authoritative efforts to define concepts. Four factors can be considered to be sources of the difficulties that were encountered.

The people. It is certainly possible that a different mix of Board and staff members might have led to different results. In any political process, it is inevitable that personality factors will enter into the deliberations and affect the outcome. Perhaps if different people had been involved (with different experience, emotional makeup, and knowledge of concepts and the mental processes of conceptualization), a different resolution could have been achieved. Of course, it is also possible that a different set of people might have produced a less useful framework.

The process. Over the long life of the Conceptual Framework project, the FASB's due process underwent substantial change. The project started when Board deliberations were private, with the result that the constituents did not have much information about the proceedings before the publication of a document. Later, particularly in the recognition and measurement phase, Board members felt that they were on public display and they found it very difficult to engage in open exchanges of ideas. They became cautious about even listening to another viewpoint or granting an assumption for the sake of argument because doing so might have been interpreted as a shift in their own position. Because the public discussion forced Board members into inflexible attitudes, it became very difficult for them to find the common ground that is so essential to forging compromises and consensus.

Constituents. Throughout the Conceptual Framework project, the FASB received a consistent message from many of its constituents that the status quo should be preserved. Accordingly, tension increased whenever the Board's discussions seemed to suggest a change in practice.

Because the constituents were so highly concerned, they became very active in the formal due process and in communicating informally through speeches and other media. For example, the proceedings in the project were the subject of discussions of the *Business Roundtable*, a group comprised of the chief operating executives of the very largest corporations. Unavoidably, tension in the constituencies added to the uncertainty and division felt among the Board and staff members and made compromise that much more difficult.

Balance of powers. Over the 12-year life of the project, some observers believe that there were some significant changes in how the Board obtains its authority, with the result that its ability to forge prescriptive concepts was constrained, eventually to the point that it could do nothing other than describe current practice.

The project began in 1973, when auditors (acting primarily through the AICPA) were the most influential constituent group. At this stage, the Board approached the Conceptual Framework project with the traditional strategy that reasonable people could come to intelligent conclusions through research and through careful and private deliberations.

The mid-1970s saw the profession and the Board facing new problems because of investigations conducted by Senator Lee Metcalf and Congressman John Moss. Even though legislation was not ever close to being enacted, the investigations and the publicity created by them did spur a number of reforms that reduced the AICPA's influence over the FASB and revived the SEC's use of the oversight powers it had been granted by the 1934 Securities Act.[5] Also at the time of the investigations, the chief accountant was John C. ("Sandy") Burton, an accounting professor who supported the presentation of more information based on current values. Evidence of the SEC's power over the FASB can be seen in its 1978 action rejecting the Board's carefully developed position in SFAS 19 on accounting by producers of oil and natural gas. This shift in power from auditors to users may have caused the Board to become more innovative, as characterized by the 1979 issuance of SFAS 33 that began the FASB's own requirements for current value disclosures. It was in this era that the groundwork was laid for the first three Statements of Financial Accounting Concepts.

The beginning of the 1980s saw another change in the power structure with the election of President Ronald Reagan in an atmosphere that favored less regulation. Among his appointments was a new chairman of the SEC, John S. R. Shad, who had a far less activist attitude than Harold Williams. After Burton's departure in 1976, the chief accountant's office was filled by Clarence Sampson, who had served on the SEC staff for a number of years prior to his appointment. He adopted a less visible profile

---

[5] See Mark Moran and Gary John Previts, "The SEC and the Profession, 1934–84: The Realities of Self-Regulation," *Journal of Accountancy*, July 1984, pp. 68–80.

than the one Burton established. (Sampson went on to serve as member of the FASB from 1988 through June 1993.)

In effect, these changes created a vacuum of power for the FASB because the auditors' influence had been diminished and the SEC's involvement on behalf of users was reduced. To a certain extent, this void was filled by statement preparers, as represented by the Financial Executives Institute (FEI) and individuals from specific corporations. They were able to use the FASB's due process effectively, as shown in their success in having SFAS 8 (on foreign currency translation) repealed and replaced by SFAS 52, which they generally consider preferable. Preparers also became more dominant in the due process. Some indication of their involvement is provided by the responses to the mark-to-market exposure draft (Chapter 3 showed that well over half of them came from preparers) and by the proportion of their donations to the Foundation (Chapter 2 showed that about 60 percent of the donations came from preparers). The potential problem created by such dominance by preparers is discussed at length in Chapter 6.

Without the clear mandate that it had in the second half of the 1970s to move ahead with a prescriptive framework that might imply major reforms, the Board apparently backed off in the 1980s to a less active stance and adopted a more defensive position on the question of whether it is an institution of reform. In 1983, for example, Paul Pacter, then the executive director of the Financial Accounting Foundation, included this statement in his article in the *Journal of Accountancy:*

> . . . all board members agree on one major point: if any significant change is ultimately concluded to be necessary, the change must be accomplished through a gradual, evolutionary process.[6]

SFAC 5 officially repeats the same defensive idea with this comment in paragraph 2:

> The recognition criteria and guidance in this Statement are generally consistent with current practice and do not imply radical change. Nor do they foreclose the possibility of future changes in practice. The Board intends future change to occur in the gradual, evolutionary way that has characterized past change.

This posture was also assumed in SFAS 87, which represented a significant withdrawal from the position expressed in the 1982 Preliminary Views discussion document. The following paragraph explained the Board's justification for the compromise that it reached:

> After considering the range of comments on *Preliminary Views* and the Exposure draft, the Board concluded that the changes required by this Statement

---

[6] Paul A. Pacter, "The Conceptual Framework: Make No Mystique about It," *Journal of Accountancy*, July 1983, p. 86.

represent a worthwhile improvement in financial reporting. Opinion 8 noted in 1966 that "accounting for pensions cost is in a transitional stage" (paragraph 17). The Board believes that is still true in 1985. FASB Concepts Statement No. 5, *Recognition and Measurements in Financial Statements of Business Enterprises*, indicates that "the board intends future change to occur in the gradual, evolutionary way that has characterized past change." The Board realizes that the evolutionary change in some areas may have to be slower than in others. The Board believes that it would be conceptually appropriate and preferable to recognize a net pension liability or asset measured as the difference between the projected benefit obligation and plan assets, either with no delay in recognition of gains or losses, or perhaps with gains and losses reported currently in comprehensive income but not in earnings. However, it concluded that that approach would be too great a change from current practice to be adopted at the present time. In light of the differences in respondents' views and the practical considerations noted, the Board concluded that the provisions of this Statement as a whole represent an improvement in financial reporting.[7]

A careful study of this rather lengthy quote shows a number of points; for the immediate purpose, attention should be focused on the declaration by the Board members that they *know* that the answer in the standard is not best but they are willing to require it because it is (1) a slight improvement and (2) acceptable to the constituents. In the authors' opinion, this position represents an unambiguous abandonment of the prescriptive nature of the Conceptual Framework.

Summary

The authors conclude that the FASB's Conceptual Framework project did not achieve its original goals. At least some Board members also acknowledged that the project would not accomplish all that it was thought it could achieve because these comments were included in the introduction to the exposure draft that eventually became SFAC 5:

> This process [of dealing with recognition and measurement questions] may have raised hopes that the Board's concepts Statements on recognition and measurement would produce instant, indisputable answers to questions about whether a particular event should be recognized and when, and what amount best measures it.
>
> If so, those were false hopes. . . . [because] concepts are tools for solving problems.

These comments can be interpreted to be the Board's denial of its ability to produce prescriptive concepts that would allow practicing accountants

---

[7] "Employers' Accounting for Pensions," *Statement of Financial Accounting Standards No. 87*, par. 103.

to solve problems without a published standard. In effect, this quote says that authoritative guidance will be necessary.

As an interesting anecdote, the authors of a journal article on financial reporting attempted to apply SFAC 5 to resolve an issue concerning a new type of financial instrument, but could only conclude that:

> Unfortunately, none of these [concepts] provide guidance in resolving [the issues at hand]. . . . It seems necessary for these [recognition and measurement conceptual] issues to be resolved, or at least addressed more fully, before the definitions of the elements of financial statements [in SFAC 3] can be made operational.[8]

In summary, as a result of the changes in the Conceptual Framework project (for whatever reasons they came about), the resulting framework is neither very prescriptive nor very descriptive. By the Board's own admission in the exposure draft and in the paragraph on the use of different measurement attributes in practice (see page 95), the Conceptual Framework does not provide operational guidance. Furthermore, it is not sufficiently descriptive to be useful for explaining to nonaccountants just exactly what it is that accountants do. For example, the statement of comprehensive income described in SFAC 5 is not presented by any corporations.

Although it is probably an overstatement to call the project a failure, it is certainly a disappointment. On the other hand, it makes a positive contribution to the accounting literature by establishing service to user needs as the primary objective of financial accounting. It also has contributed to the efficiency of the due process procedures by defining a number of key terms that are indeed used by the Board and its constituents. These accomplishments may bring more rigor and efficiency to the Board's deliberations, but that conclusion can be safely reached only in the long run, particularly when all Board members who created the framework have been replaced by others who had no part in its development.

Any conclusion as to whether the project was worth the effort is highly subjective and depends on what was wanted from the project and the assessment of what was obtained. In the authors' opinions, it seems to have been an appropriate use of resources and there are more benefits to be obtained from it.

A SUMMARY AND EVALUATION OF THE CONTENTS OF THE CONCEPTS STATEMENTS

This section briefly summarizes the basic points in the Statements of Financial Accounting Concepts issued by the FASB as part of its Concep-

---

[8] Richard L. Rogers and Krishnagopal Menon, "Accounting for Deferred-Payment Notes," *The Accounting Review,* July 1985, p. 555.

tual Framework project. More detailed descriptions are beyond the scope of this book; however, they can be found in most accounting theory textbooks. In addition to describing the contents of the statements, this section includes commentaries on the political nature of the Board and its activities.

Statement of Financial Accounting Concepts No. 1: Objectives of Financial Reporting by Business Enterprises

As mentioned briefly in an earlier part of the chapter, the foundation for SFAC 1 was the work of the AICPA's Trueblood Study Group on the Objectives of Financial Statements. Discussion memoranda related to the topic were published by the Board in 1974 and 1976, and its exposure draft was distributed in 1977. The statement was released in 1978.

The overall purpose of SFAC 1 is to state the highest level concepts in the prescriptive top-down structure adopted by the FASB. In doing so, the Board identified the primary objective for financial reporting and then clarified it with several others. The overriding primary objective was stated as follows:

> Financial reporting should provide information that is useful to present and potential investors and creditors and other users in making rational invest- ment, credit, and similar decisions. (par. 34)

By establishing this objective, the Statement elevates users to the highest level of priority among the Board's constituents. Pursuing this objective requires that all new and existing generally accepted accounting princi- ples be evaluated in terms of their contribution to the usefulness of the information provided to investors, creditors, and other decision makers who have limited access to financial data because of their position exter- nal to the firm.

To bring this very high-level objective down to a more applicable level, the Board went on to clarify it with these two subobjectives:

> Financial reporting should provide information to help present and potential investors and creditors and other users in assessing the amounts, timing, and uncertainty of prospective cash receipts from dividends or interest and the proceeds from the sale, redemption, or maturity of securities or loans. (par. 37)
>
> Financial reporting should provide information about the economic re- sources of an enterprise, the claims to those resources (obligations of the enterprise to transfer resources to other entities and owners' equity), and the effects of transactions, events, and circumstances that change resources and claims to those resources. (par. 40)

In effect, users are interested in information about cash flows to them- selves, which, in turn, are derived from the cash flows, resources, and obligations of the reporting company.

A notable additional feature of the Statement is its description of some of the qualities of the users that the Board said that it would be concerned with. Specifically, the Statement says:

> The information should be comprehensible to those who have a reasonable understanding of business and economic activities and are willing to study the information with reasonable diligence. (par. 34)

By creating this policy, the Board can usually disregard arguments that proposed information might not be understood by "typical" or "naive" investors. Although these people receive financial statements, the FASB does not intend to simplify the information to the point that it will be immediately comprehensible without training and effort. The policy is not designed to make the statements complex but it is an acknowledgment that the complexity of the financial statements arises from the complexity of the underlying economics.

Perhaps the greatest significance of SFAC 1 lies in its formalization on the conceptual level of the political fact that the Board has to put the public's interest first by promoting the decision usefulness of the information provided to the capital markets by the financial statements. This interest is the source of the SEC's own mandate for setting accounting standards and is crucial to its endorsement of the FASB as the primary standards-setting body.

Statement of Financial Accounting Concepts No. 2: Qualitative Characteristics of Accounting Information

Some material on the qualities of useful information was included in the 1976 discussion memorandum on the Conceptual Framework project and the 1977 exposure draft that led to SFAC 1; however, controversies caused the Board to omit that material from SFAC 1 to allow the objectives to be published without additional debate. A second exposure draft was released in 1979, and SFAC 2 was issued in 1980.

The overall purpose of the Statement is to identify criteria for determining whether information is useful for decisions to be made by users of financial statements. If the information at issue has the qualities, it should be reported; if it does not have them, it should not be reported. In accomplishing this goal, the Board identified a hierarchy of qualities of useful information.

Decision usefulness was selected as the most significant of these qualities because of the importance that the primary objective of SFAC 1 had assigned to users.

The Board went on to provide clarification by describing two primary qualities that produce decision usefulness. *Relevance* is defined in the

Glossary to the Statement as "the capacity of information to make a difference in a decision. . ." The discussion explains that, in turn, relevance is imparted to information when it is available to the user with *timeliness*, and has either *predictive value* or *feedback value*, or *both*. In other words, relevant information must be able to help the user make better forecasts of the future or better evaluations of the past.

The second primary quality of useful information is *reliability*, which is defined in the Statement's glossary to be "the quality . . . that assures that information is reasonably free from error and bias and faithfully represents what it purports to represent." In order to be reliable, the information must be subject to testing to ensure that its preparation is legitimate and must correspond to what it is thought to present. Additionally, the information is to be *neutral,* which is a quality imparted by standards setters. That is, they are not to use the system to achieve any goal other than better decisions by investors, creditors, and others. For example, a proposed standard for accounting by banks might more closely represent the risks in that industry, with the result that the amounts of their reported profits would be drastically changed. The possibility that the change might speed up the failure of some banks or cause others to succeed should not be a factor in the decision if neutrality is to be obtained. Thus, including neutrality in the hierarchy was another situation in which the political nature of standards setting was captured in the concepts.

The Statement identified *comparability* as a secondary qualitative characteristic of useful information and defined it as "the quality . . . that enables users to identify similarities in and differences between two sets of economic phenomena." Some confusion exists between the meanings of comparability and *consistency*, which SFAC 2 defines as "conformity from period to period with unchanging policies and procedures." SFAC 2 makes the point that consistency is necessary to achieve comparability but is not sufficient (par. 117). A similar quality, *uniformity*, was not defined in SFAC 2. It is commonly considered to be the use of the same policies and procedures by all reporting companies.

In addition to possessing these three qualities (relevance, reliability, and comparability), useful accounting information must pass a *materiality* threshold, such that the magnitude of the reported amount is large enough to affect decisions. Clearly, there is a relationship between materiality and relevance. In effect, the Board decided that relevance relates to the subject matter of the information, whereas materiality relates to the size of the amount reported. Drawing this distinction may create confusion because auditors and other accountants have tended to use the two terms synonymously.

Another test for decision usefulness described in SFAC 2 is the relationship between the *costs and benefits* of an item of information (pars. 133–44). In short, the Statement asserts that information must produce benefits in excess of its costs in order to be useful. While that concept is not likely to be challenged philosophically, an argument can certainly be made that it has only a small chance of ever helping the Board reach a decision. For one thing, there are no unambiguous techniques for measuring the costs and benefits of information. For another, costs may be borne by some groups and benefits may be gained by others, and the decision that must be made is who is going to get how much of each. In most comment letters that appeal to this test, it is apparent that the respondents are arguing that their costs of complying with the proposed standard will exceed their benefits. It seems self-evident that this condition will exist for someone in every controversial situation. If everyone's benefits must exceed their own costs, then no standards-setting system would be needed because all parties would adopt the practice voluntarily. Indeed, it is the need to impose costs on some parties to the benefit of others that causes a political system to be created; there is no reason to expect the FASB's situation to be any different.

As an overall evaluation of SFAC 2, it provides a set of definitions that the Board and its constituents can and do use to communicate with each other. The definitions should bring more rigor to the due process, and possibly to the thought processes of the participants. They certainly provide enough leeway to allow different interpretations by different people, but at least they lend direction to the deliberations, and can be considered worthwhile for that reason alone.

Statement of Financial Accounting Concepts No. 3: Elements of Financial Statements of Business Enterprises

Some material about the elements was included in the 1977 exposure draft that led to the SFAC 1, but, again because of controversy, it was carved out and placed in a different phase of the Conceptual Framework project. That work led to another exposure draft in 1979, with the final pronouncement coming out late in 1980.

The overall purpose of the statement is to identify and define the components from which financial statements are constructed. The term *elements* is defined in SFAC 3 as "the building blocks with which financial statements are constructed—the classes of items that financial statements comprise" (par. 5). Ten elements are defined, and a reference is made to the fact that the Board might define others later. The 10 elements are:

- Assets.
- Liabilities.
- Owners' equity.
- Investment by owners.
- Distributions to owners.
- Comprehensive income.
- Revenues.
- Expenses.
- Gains.
- Losses.

Assets and liabilities are the two most primary elements because the definitions of the other eight are based on them. For example, revenues are defined as "inflows or other enhancements of assets of an entity or settlements of its liabilities (or a combination of both) during a period" (par. 63).

Despite the familiarity of the terms and the simplicity of their definitions, SFAC 3 sparked controversy among some accountants, particularly those who wanted to preserve the status quo. Specifically, they saw the emphasis on assets and liabilities as an abandonment of the traditional preference for the income statement that has existed for decades. A familiar example of a preference for the income statement is the use of last-in, first-out (LIFO) inventory measures. In most cases, the preference for LIFO is justified on the basis that it produces a desirable measure of the cost of goods sold (and, thereby, net income), despite the fact that the number reported for the inventory on the statement of financial position does not reflect either the current value or the actual purchase price of the goods on hand. The apparent movement in SFAC 3 toward equalization of the income statement and the statement of financial position represented a change from current practice that particularly alarmed those who desired maintenance of the *status quo.*

As mentioned earlier, the use of the concepts of *comprehensive income* instead of earnings or net income also proved controversial because it seemed to portend a shift to more current value information.

The authors' evaluation of SFAC 3 is like their evaluation of SFAC 2. The Statement defines some commonly used terms, and thus has added to to the rigor and efficiency of the communications portion of the due process; however, the definitions are subject to interpretation and have not prevented all debates.

Statement of Financial Accounting Concepts No. 4: Objectives of Reporting by Nonbusiness Organizations

The Report of the Trueblood Study Group included some objectives for financial statements issued by nonbusiness organizations. Rather than include them in SFAC 1, the Board set them aside at the beginning of the Conceptual Framework project to focus on business situations. In 1977, efforts to include them began, and a discussion memorandum was published in 1978. It was followed by hearings, and an exposure draft was released in March 1980. The final Statement was issued in December 1980.

The scope of the Statement does not include governmental entities because of political difficulties in obtaining support from that constituency. As mentioned earlier, authority for setting standards in this area has been granted to the Governmental Accounting Standards Board.

Nonbusiness organizations are identified in paragraph 6 of the Statement as those entities that have these three qualities:

- Receipts of significant amounts of resources from resource providers who do not expect to receive either repayment or economic benefits proportionate to resources provided.
- Operating purposes that are primarily other than to provide goods or services at a profit or profit equivalent.
- Absence of defined ownership interests that can be sold, transferred, or redeemed, or that convey entitlement to a share of a residual distribution of resources in the event of liquidation of the organization.

In other words, there are no owners, no profits, and no owners' equity in the same sense as they exist for a business.

The Statement identifies seven objectives of different levels of importance that are similar to the objectives established in SFAC 1 for business enterprises. For example, the first one asserts that:

> Financial reporting by nonbusiness organizations should provide information that is useful to present and potential resource providers and other users in making rational decisions about the allocation of resources to those organizations. (par. 35)

As clarification of this objective, SFAC 4 goes on to say that financial reporting for these organizations should provide information that will help statement users in:

> . . . assessing the services that a nonbusiness organization provides and its ability to continue to provide those services. (par. 38)

> . . . assessing how managers of a nonbusiness organization have discharged their stewardship responsibilities and about other aspects of their performance. (par. 40)

In meeting these objectives, the financial statements should provide information:

> about the economic resources, obligations, and net resources of an organization, and the effects of transactions, events, and circumstances that change resources and interests in those resources. (par. 43)

The authors' evaluation of SFAC 4 is actually directed at the not-for-profit phase of the project, which has proven to be less controversial than the other phases. Nonetheless, the issues have been difficult to resolve, primarily because the Board lacks a clear-cut mandate from the SEC or any other authoritative group to actually resolve them. Because substantial benefits have not flowed from this phase of the project, it is quite possible that the Board would be better off if it had never undertaken it.

Statement of Financial Accounting Concepts No. 5: Recognition and Measurement in Financial Statements of Business Enterprises

The procedural history and many of the political considerations associated with the recognition and measurement phase of the project are described earlier in the chapter and will not be repeated here.

There were two conceptual goals for SFAC 5: the description of the basic set of financial statements and the description of *recognition criteria*, which are tests to determine whether and when information should be incorporated in the financial statements. The concepts of recognition are focused on the contents of the financial statements and do not apply to the additional disclosures included under the more inclusive area of financial reporting described in SFAC 1.

The section of SFAC 5 that describes the financial statements generally endorses the status quo, with the exception of its introduction of a second income statement. The five financial statements are listed below, together with a brief comment on each:

- *Statement of financial position.* The description suggests nothing particularly different from accepted practices.
- *Statement of earnings.* This statement would be essentially the same as the traditional income statement, except that it would *not* include cumulative effects of changes in accounting principles. The concept of this statement was created in order to alleviate concerns that the Board was going to discard traditional income measures based on matching.
- *Statement of comprehensive income.* No such statement currently exists in practice. It was included in SFAC 5 as a concession to those Board members and constituents who wanted the Conceptual Framework to endorse a greater use of current values. By its presence in the concepts statement, their position is acknowledged, but no effect is likely to be felt on practice for a long time, especially in light of the Board's decision in SFAS 89 to abandon the SFAS 33 experiment.
- *Statement of cash flows.* The statement of cash flows focuses on those events that caused cash and cash equivalents to come in and flow out of the enterprise, and categorizes them by their nature as either operating, financing, or investing. The goal is to provide a simple summary of what happened to the cash account. This information should allow statement users to more meaningfully assess their own cash flows from their investments. In 1987, the Board issued SFAS 95 in order to require the presentation of a statement of cash flows instead of the statement of changes in financial position that had been required by APB Opinion 19.
- *Statement of investments by and distributions to owners.* This statement also exists only in concept, but it corresponds to the

traditional statement of changes in owners' equity. It would differ from that statement because it would not include any changes from income events. This difference comes about because of the decision to create two concepts of reported income and because of the Board's inability to construct a consensus in favor of either earnings or comprehensive income.

From the discussion earlier in the chapter and from the above comments, it can be seen that SFAC 5 was so greatly affected by political difficulties that compromises had to enter even into otherwise straightforward ideas of what type of information should be reported in which financial statement.

In describing the recognition criteria, the Board merely restated what it had said in the previous concepts statements by identifying the following four criteria in paragraph 63:

- *Definitions*. The item [to be considered for recognition] meets the definition of an element of financial statements.
- *Measurability*. It has a relevant attribute measurable with sufficient reliability.
- *Relevance*. The information about it is capable of making a difference in user decisions.
- *Reliability*. The information is representationally faithful, verifiable, and neutral.

Thus, after abandoning the initial strategy of issuing a concepts statement that would resolve substantive recognition issues and adopting the new strategy of issuing a statement that a significant majority of Board members would endorse,[9] essentially all that could be accomplished was to repeat what had been said in SFAC 2 and SFAC 3. The entire content of the recognition criteria can be summarized as follows: If relevant and reliable quantitative financial information is available about an element, it should be included in the financial statements.

Furthermore, the last two criteria (relevance and reliability) are redundant—they merely repeat the meaning of the second (measurability). The explanation for this duplication lies in the simple fact that it was necessary in order to get the six assenting Board members to vote for SFAC 5.

The criteria also are too broad to provide helpful guidance either to standards setters or to individual accountants who are attempting to resolve a new issue. Again, the reason for this outcome is that the deep divisions among the Board members could be overcome only by returning to high-level and basically unarguable generalities.

---

[9] John March's dissent to SFAC 5 was the only negative vote cast by any Board member on any of the six concepts statements.

Statement of Financial Accounting Concepts No. 6: Elements of Financial Statements

SFAC 6 does not constitute a substantial modification of SFAC 3; rather, it is best viewed as an augmentation of the original pronouncement to make it applicable to not-for-profit entities.

One difference is the replacement of the term *owners' equity* by the more general terms *equity* and *net assets*. This change allows SFAC 6 to encompass both business and not-for-profit entities.

The biggest difference is the identification of what are called *classes* of net assets for not-for-profit organizations. These components are not at the same level as the elements, but are nonetheless basic. They are: restricted net assets, temporarily restricted net assets, and unrestricted net assets. The first class identifies amounts that cannot be spent or used for any purpose inconsistent with the stipulations implied or otherwise established by an agreement between the entity and the donor. For example, an endowment of a professorship will generally restrict the use of the donated and earned assets to compensation and other support of a faculty member. The second class encompasses those situations with a restriction on the use of the assets that will be removed by the passage of time or some other event. For example, a donor may endow a museum with a sum of money, with the understanding that the income will be used during the donor's lifetime to acquire certain types of art; at the donor's death, the restriction will be lifted, and the funds can be used as needed for any purpose. The third class refers to those funds that can be used for any purpose.

The Board has not had much opportunity to deal with these extensions of the elements, with the result that it is hard to determine whether they are indeed useful. In general, the effects of the amendments to SFAC 3 will not be felt by most accountants and users.

SELECTED READINGS

DOPUCH, NICHOLAS, AND SHYAM SUNDER. "FASB's Statement on Objectives and Elements of Financial Accounting: A Review." *The Accounting Review*, January 1980, pp. 1–21.

HEATH, LOYD C. "Commentary on Accounting Literature: The Conceptual Framework as Literature." *Accounting Horizons*, June 1988, pp. 100–104.

HINES, RUTH D. "The FASB's Conceptual Framework, Financial Accounting and the Maintenance of the Social World." *Accounting Organizations & Society*, 1991, pp. 313–31.

KIRK, DONALD J. "Completeness and Representational Faithfulness of Financial Statements." *Accounting Horizons,* December 1991, pp. 135–41.

KOEPPEN, DAVID R. "Using the FASB's Conceptual Framework: Fitting the Pieces Together." *Accounting Horizons*, June 1988, pp. 18–26.

MILLER, PAUL B. W. "The Conceptual Framework: Myths and Realities." *Journal of Accountancy*, March 1985, pp. 62–71.

_____. "The Conceptual Framework as Reformation and Counterreformation." *Accounting Horizons,* June 1990, pp. 23–32.

PACTER, PAUL A. "The Conceptual Framework: Make No Mystique about It." *Journal of Accountancy,* July 1983, pp. 76–88.

PATE, GWEN RICHARDSON, AND KEITH G. STANGA. "A Guide to the FASB's Concepts Statements." *Journal of Accountancy,* August 1989, pp. 28–31.

SOLOMONS, DAVID. "The FASB's Conceptual Framework: An Evaluation." *Journal of Accountancy,* June 1986, pp. 114–24.

SPROUSE, ROBERT T. "The Importance of Earnings in the Conceptual Framework." *Journal of Accountancy,* January 1978, pp. 64–71.

5

Some Recurring Accounting Controversies

This chapter reviews several of the most significant and controversial financial accounting issues that have been raised over the last 50 to 75 years and tackled by authoritative standards-setting bodies, including the FASB. The survey demonstrates several points.

First, it shows that major issues seldom go away. They may reappear in familiar forms as different people gain power and bring them up for reconsideration. They also may reappear in new forms when new types of transactions or other arrangements are developed. In either case, a resolution of an issue in an authoritative pronouncement is seldom the end of the debate.

Second, it demonstrates the implications of politics on GAAP that were drawn at the end of Chapter 1. Specifically, it is argued there that politics make GAAP logically inconsistent, that someone will be unhappy with any resolution of an issue, and that GAAP *will* change, although the process of change will probably be slow and arduous.

Third, the discussions will show how the FASB's Conceptual Framework has been used in the Board's approaches to these issues.

Most importantly, this review of the controversies demonstrates how the people, the process, and the politics of setting accounting standards

Note: The authors express special appreciation to Dr. J. T. Ball, assistant director of Research and Technical Activities, and Dr. Reed K. Storey, senior technical adviser at the FASB, for their assistance in providing background material for this chapter.

have come together in the past and will continue to come together in the future.

This chapter discusses the following specific controversies:

Capitalization versus expensing
  • Research and development costs
  • Interest costs
  • Software development costs
  • Oil and gas accounting
Off-balance-sheet financing
  • Leases
  • Unconsolidated finance subsidiaries
Employee compensation
  • Compensated absences
  • Pensions
  • Other post-employment benefits
  • Compensation paid with stock
Income taxes
  • Deferred taxes
  • The investment tax credit
Changing prices
  • Price-level adjustments
  • Current value

CAPITALIZATION VERSUS EXPENSING

The fundamental issue of *capitalization versus expensing* concerns the choice that arises after a cost has been incurred by giving up an asset, creating a liability, or creating equity. Specifically, the question is whether the debit for the transaction should be recognized as an *asset* that will appear on the statement of financial position or as an *expense* that will appear on the income statement.

In general, the interests of financial statement preparers are promoted by capitalizing costs and reporting them as assets on the statement of financial position. This approach reports higher income and equity, and improves the ratio of debt to equity. It also tends to produce a smoother reported income trend because amortizing the capitalized debit spreads the expense over a number of years instead of reporting its full amount as an expense when it is incurred. The primary disadvantage of capitalization for preparers is that future performance measures are depressed because the numerator (income) is reduced by the amortized expense while the denominator (assets or equity) is increased. Thus, different circumstances may produce different preferences for capitalizing or expensing a cost.

From another perspective, auditors may tend to favor expensing a cost because doing so eliminates the risk of overstating the reported income or assets.

In contrast, users may have no reason to prefer one method over the other as long as only real assets are capitalized and only real expenses are reported on the income statement. Of course, it is likely that merely providing adequate disclosures of the events and conditions will allow users to make appropriate assessments of future cash flows, regardless of management's decision to capitalize or expense the costs.

The public's interest in financial reporting is best served when the information provided in the financial statements helps the capital markets to be efficient in processing the information and allocating the resources. Thus, the best resolution for the public provides information that does not require a substantial amount of modification by users to make it useful.

It should be apparent that this issue reaches into all areas of accounting and into many transactions. In most cases, the issue is not controversial. For example, when the cost is incurred to purchase a physical asset or to pay managers' salaries, it is generally clear that the former is capitalized, while the latter is expensed. In many other situations, however, the question of whether to capitalize or expense a cost is controversial. As described in Chapter 4, the Conceptual Framework defines the elements of the financial statements by placing assets in the primary position. That is, assets are defined first and then expenses are defined as reductions in assets. This approach implies that costs should be capitalized only when it can be shown that they produced an asset. If there is insufficient proof that an asset exists, or if there are no reliable measures of an asset's initial value, the framework indicates that the cost is most usefully reported as an expense when it is incurred. Under the traditional matching approach, it is considered appropriate to capitalize costs simply in order to postpone recognizing them until future periods in which management expects to receive revenues. Under matching, the decision to postpone recognizing expenses may cause debit balances to appear on the balance sheet that do not meet the conceptual framework's definition of assets.

The following discussion deals with four types of costs that have been persistently troublesome: research and development costs, interest costs, software development costs, and oil and gas accounting.

Research and Development Costs

The capitalization issue for research and development costs is made controversial by the large amounts that some industries spend and by the difficulty of telling whether the expenditures produce any benefits. There is little disagreement that future benefits (and assets) are often generated from research and development activity. However, identifying which part of the costs produces the assets is difficult. An additional complicating factor is the political question of whether the financial accounting standard for these costs should be designed to promote the policy of encouraging the discovery of new knowledge to keep U.S. industry progressive and to strengthen the national economy. The FASB's consistent response to this question asserts that its role is to ensure that the capital markets are provided with information that is not designed to lead or mislead users into making or not making desired decisions. This response is clearly stated in SFAC 2's definition of *neutrality*, which is a contributor to information's reliability.

In the 1950s, most organizations were conservative and expensed research and development costs in the period in which they were incurred. However, a few companies capitalized some or all of these costs. One such company was Convair, a division of General Dynamics Corporation that produced aircraft for commercial transportation and that capitalized large sums of research and development costs by the early 1960s. When General Dynamics decided to get out of the commercial aircraft industry, the previously capitalized costs were recognized as an expense in a single year. This expense was the largest write-off of previously capitalized costs in the history of accounting up to that time and was a major impetus to the Accounting Principles Board's decision to begin studying accounting for research and development costs in the early 1960s.

Although the APB did not resolve the issue, it sponsored and published Accounting Research Study No. 14, "Accounting for Research and Development Expenditures," just before it went out of existence in 1973. This study defined research and development costs and suggested which costs might be capitalized.

The FASB put accounting for research and development costs on its initial agenda as a follow-up to the work performed by the APB. The first discussion memorandum (DM) published by the FASB was on research and development costs. SFAS 2, "Accounting for Research and Development Costs," was issued in October 1974 and made mandatory the common practice of expensing research and development costs.[1] The Board members apparently arrived at this conclusion for a variety of reasons, not the least of which must have been the desire to avoid the virtually impossible task of developing criteria that would specify when and how much to capitalize and expense without opening loopholes to preparers who would want to manipulate their financial statements. Although SFAS 2 was issued before any concepts statements, its approach is consistent with the Conceptual Framework, first in terms of its recognition of an expense instead of capitalizing a questionable asset, and second in terms

---

[1] More detailed information about this and other authoritative documents referenced in this chapter is presented in a separate section beginning on page 143.

of the Board's stance that it could not create a standard based on the political goal of encouraging companies to perform research and development.

Interest Costs

Traditionally, interest incurred on debt was reported as an expense. However, as early as 1917, some accountants advocated capitalization of interest because it is as necessary for the acquisition of an asset as any other capitalized costs, including purchase and installation costs. In general, this argument did not affect practice.

In contrast to most companies in other industries, many utility companies capitalized interest costs. Because their rates are supposed to recover their costs, they argued that expensing the interest incurred while constructing assets would be unfairly charged against the customers who use the utility's services during the construction period. Thus, they would choose to defer the interest expense by capitalizing it as part of the cost of the assets. This technique's popularity was boosted by the fact that it also increases the balance of the total assets that serves as a utility's rate base. In simple terms, the company's total asset measure is multiplied by an acceptable rate of return in order to define the amount of allowable income under state regulations. By adding interest cost to the rate base, the company increases the amount of allowable income that can be earned in excess of expenses, including the amortized interest cost. The inclination to postpone expense is constrained, of course, by the fact that the decision to capitalize interest increases reported income in the short run and thereby makes any rate increases appear less necessary.

In the 1960s and 1970s, many companies that were not utilities began to capitalize interest costs with a corresponding increase in their net income, assets, and equity. In 1974, the Securities and Exchange Commission (SEC) placed a moratorium on the capitalization of any additional interest cost until the FASB could study and resolve the issue. Five years later, in 1979, SFAS 34 was issued after a 4–3 vote. It requires capitalization of certain interest costs incurred in acquiring assets that are constructed for a company's own use, or constructed as a discrete project for sale or lease to another company. A company must expense any interest incurred after the asset is placed into service.

The Board's reasoning on this issue was not guided by the Conceptual Framework because only SFAC 1 had been published when SFAS 34 was released. The discussion in the standard makes it clear that the majority had reached their conclusions for different reasons. Some reasoned by analogy to the acceptable treatment of other costs and simply asserted that interest is a necessary cost that should, therefore, be capitalized. Others in the majority asserted that interest should be capitalized to cause the recognized cost to come closer to management's estimate of the net present value of the future cash flows from the assets. The three dissenting Board members agreed among themselves that interest is the cost of getting cash and is appropriately reported as expense without regard to what the cash is used for.

The Board might have been assisted by a clear concept of which attribute of the asset should be recognized and measured. If a present value of management's predicted future cash flows is considered to be relevant, then accountants should attempt to measure it directly instead of merely adding interest and other amounts to the purchase price. On the other hand, if the asset's current value is considered to be relevant, then accountants should attempt to determine that amount without regard to the costs incurred to acquire or produce it. And, if the asset's historical cost is considered to be relevant, then the standards setters would need to identify which kinds of costs should be added and why. Even if SFAC 5 on recognition and measurement had been issued when SFAS 34 was being deliberated, its compromise concepts would not have provided any guidance for resolving the interest capitalization issue. This situation clearly illustrates the inadequacy of descriptive concepts for guiding standards setters to new solutions.

Software Development Costs

The growth of the computer industry has greatly increased the number of companies developing and marketing software. Many of these companies are small and struggling for survival, with the result that the capital market tends to impose a risk penalty on them by demanding a higher rate of return from their securities.

Because these companies incur large costs for personal services and have very few tangible assets, their balance sheets usually present a weak financial position. To strengthen this appearance, many companies want to capitalize their product development costs instead of expensing them. One drawback of this practice is that there is little dependable evidence of the software's value until it has been successfully marketed and implemented. Accounting for software by deferring and amortizing its cost is complicated further because its useful life is often so short that it is no longer an asset by the time that its existence and value can be proven.

As a result of the large increase in software development in the 1970s and the ambiguity of SFAS 2 on the question of whether software costs meet the definition of research and development costs, the FASB issued Interpretation No. 6 in 1975. It allowed capitalization of costs incurred to develop software for use in administration or sales activities and costs incurred to buy or lease software from other companies. However, the costs of developing software to be used in research and development activities could not be capitalized. The Board was not able to definitively resolve the issues concerning the treatment of the costs of other types of software, and provided only general guidance that some could be capitalized and some could not.

The situation remained unsettled until 1983, when another round of growth created many new software companies that attempted to register new securities with the SEC. The Commission's staff grew uneasy about the widespread use of capitalization and imposed a moratorium on any new adoptions of that approach pending the establishment of more definitive guidance from the FASB. In 1984, the Board issued an exposure draft that proposed more rigorous tests for determining whether a particular type of expenditure should be capitalized or expensed. Substantial opposition was expressed in comment letters and in testimony at hearings conducted in 1985. SFAS 86 was issued in August of that year; it allows capitalization of only certain costs incurred after the marketability of software has been established. Although this practice is used, it should be clear that the controversy will continue.

Oil and Gas Accounting

Oil and gas companies also face a capitalization versus expense issue with respect to the cost of the many dry holes drilled for every producing well.

One view is that the costs of dry holes should be expensed because these wells did not generate any assets. Thus, only the costs of successful wells would be capitalized and then amortized over their useful life. This accounting approach is known as *successful efforts*. In contrast, another view holds that *all* drilling is necessary to find productive wells. The argument is made, therefore, that the costs of all wells should be capitalized, even those incurred in drilling dry holes. This accounting approach is known as *full costing*. A compromise position between the two methods would apply full costing to individual oil fields. By considering the local field to be the reporting unit, it would be possible to capitalize the costs of drilling dry holes within the field and then amortize their costs against the revenues from the productive wells in the same field. If every well in a field turned out to be dry, then the capitalized costs would be written off when the company abandoned the project. In effect, only the costs of successful fields would be capitalized.

The issue of how to account for oil and gas costs had been of low priority until the mid-1960s. However, an APB committee raised the issue because many smaller oil companies had adopted the full-cost method, whereas many large oil companies used successful efforts.

Because the oil and gas industry and the Big Eight auditing firms were divided on the question, the APB could not issue an opinion. The project was not included on the FASB's initial agenda; instead, the issue came to the top of Congress's list of priorities in the mid-1970s, when efforts were being made to develop a national policy to ensure adequate supplies of energy. One facet of that policy was the monitoring of the profits of energy producers, which in turn demanded satisfactory measures of profits. At that point, the diversity of practice for accounting for oil and gas costs became a stumbling block, and the Securities and Exchange Commission was instructed to develop an appropriate solution. The SEC turned to the FASB, which undertook an effort to settle the controversy.

The outcome was SFAS 19, "Financial Accounting and Reporting by Oil and Gas Producing Companies," which was issued in 1977. The successful efforts approach was selected over much opposition from smaller oil and gas companies, but with support from larger ones and most of the Big Eight. The SEC, conscious of its own constituencies, rejected SFAS 19 in 1978 with ASR 253, 257, and 259, and allowed both the successful efforts and full-cost methods to be used. The SEC then proposed "reserve recognition accounting" (RRA), which would recognize income when oil is discovered and when oil prices are increased rather than waiting until the oil is actually produced.

Thus, the SEC was able to avoid the troublesome capitalization versus expensing controversy only by discarding traditional accounting concepts. Under RRA, all drilling costs would be deducted from income in the year they were incurred. Accordingly, a company that did not discover any oil or gas would not recognize an asset on the statement of financial position and would report a loss on the income statement. On the other hand, if the company were successful, it would show an asset equal to the value of the oil that was discovered and the income statement would reflect income equal to the difference between the value of the discovered resources and the costs incurred in finding them. The SEC's original proposal in 1978 was that RRA would be used only in supplemental disclosures for several years but would then become the primary basis of reporting. The proposal met opposition from the industry and auditors. Their arguments generally stated that there were no feasible methods of reliably determining the value of reserves. The SEC dropped its plan in 1981 not only because of these arguments but also because the newly elected Reagan administration was committed to deregulation and because public interest in the development of an energy policy was waning.

Because SFAS 19 was rejected by the SEC, it was substantially rescinded by SFAS 25, with the result that both full costing and successful efforts are still acceptable. When the SEC dropped its plans to make RRA mandatory, it encouraged the FASB to develop a standard to provide supplemental information similar to what would be produced by RRA. The Board completed this project in 1982 with the issuance of SFAS 69.

Another round in this controversy occurred in October 1986, when the SEC rejected a proposal from its chief accountant that successful efforts be established as the only acceptable method. Even if the Conceptual Framework had been completed when SFAS 19 was being developed, and even if it had established a definitive measurement concept, it seems extremely likely that an oil and gas standard based on that concept would have been rejected because of the complex political and economic factors that affect these companies and their regulators. Thus, it appears that the capitalization versus expensing issue will remain unresolved in this industry.

OFF-BALANCE-SHEET FINANCING

Various issues have also been raised over the acceptability of accounting practices that effectively allow a corporation to borrow without reporting a liability on the statement of financial position. The apparent advantage to a corporation of these *off-balance-sheet-financing* practices is that the presentation makes the company appear more solvent than it really is. From one perspective, the omitted liability may prevent unsophisticated investors and creditors from becoming alarmed by a diminished solvency. From another, an off-balance-sheet-financing arrangement might allow the company to borrow additional funds without triggering special clauses in other debt contracts that restrict the ratio between recognized debts and equity. In most cases, however, sophisticated investors and creditors are aware of the possibility of unrecognized debts and design their analyses and contracts to allow for their effects on their financial decisions. Thus, it is extremely likely that the company's cost of capital (and the prices of its securities) will reflect the higher risk, whether the financing is reported on the balance sheet or not.

Despite the doubtfulness of the benefits, many corporations and financial institutions have made numerous efforts to set up debt arrangements that allow a company to avoid reporting a liability. The following discussion considers two primary situations: leases and unconsolidated finance subsidiaries.

Leases

A lease is an agreement whereby the owner of an asset allows another party to use it in exchange for a rental fee. For a simple lease, the arrangement is entered into for the convenience of the user, who in this way can avoid buying an asset that is used only infrequently or temporarily. Accounting for such simple leases is straightforward—the user (called the *lessee*) does not recognize an asset or liability on the balance sheet and reports only rent expense on the income statement.

The acceptability of these accounting practices created an opportunity for off-balance-sheet financing to take place. By leasing an asset that would ordinarily be purchased, the lessee would not recognize either the asset or the debt for any unpaid rents. However, by making the lease cover a longer term, the lessee becomes the de facto owner of the asset, while the legal owner of the asset (called the *lessor*) merely acts as a secured lender.

In October 1949, the Committee on Accounting Procedure released ARB 38, which later became Chapter 14 of ARB 43. It required the footnotes of the lessee's financial statements to describe the amounts and timing of the annual payments to be paid and any other important terms of leases. These requirements responded to a growing number of "sale-and-leaseback" transactions in which a company built an asset, sold it to another company, and then immediately leased it back. In economic substance, the seller-lessee has borrowed the so-called selling price from the buyer-lessor, and the nominal rentals are nothing more than payments on the loan. Furthermore, the property has not been surrendered to the buyer, but has only been pledged as collateral against the loan. However, by applying acceptable practices, the asset was omitted from the balance sheet, no liability was recognized, and rent expense was reported instead of depreciation and interest expense.

The Committee on Accounting Procedure had been studying accounting for leases when it was disbanded in 1959, and the APB decided to continue working on the project. The APB recognized the topic's importance and made it one of the first five to be studied by the AICPA's newly created Accounting Research Division. The outcome was Accounting Research Study No. 4, "Reporting of Leases in Financial Statements," which was issued in 1962. Between 1962 and 1973, the APB issued four opinions (Nos. 5, 7, 27, and 31) dealing with leases. These four opinions essentially continued the same footnote requirements that had been established in ARB 38. Although Opinion 7 called for the capitalization of some leases, the APB was not able to generate a sufficient consensus to develop a rigorous set of criteria that would significantly increase the number of lease agreements being reported on lessees' statements of financial position.

In the 1970s, the SEC got involved in accounting for leases because it appeared that the APB had not done enough to curb the excesses. Opinion 31, "Disclosure of Lease Commitments by Lessees," was a stopgap, last-gasp effort by the APB in response to concerns of the SEC.[2] In October 1973, just after APB Opinion 31 was released, the SEC issued Accounting Series Releases Nos. 132, 141, and 147. These rules required disclosures similar to those in APB Opinion 31 as well as additional mandatory footnote disclosures of the present value of certain lease commitments and the impact on net income that would have been reported if the company had capitalized leases that were in substance purchases of assets.

Despite the existence of one Accounting Research Bulletin, one Accounting Research Study, four APB Opinions, and three SEC Accounting Series Releases, many inconsistencies remained in lease accounting prac-

---

[2] Opinion 31 was the last one issued by the APB. In fact, it was actually issued in September 1973, several months after the APB was officially disbanded and while the FASB was already in operation. To avoid confusion, the opinion is dated June 1973.

tices. Consequently, the FASB placed accounting for leases on its agenda in 1973. The FASB issued a discussion memorandum in July 1974 and held public hearings in November 1974. The Board received 306 responses to the discussion memorandum, and 32 presentations were made at the public hearings. The Board issued an exposure draft in August 1975, and received 250 additional comment letters. Modifications to the original exposure draft were made, and a second exposure draft was issued in July 1976. This time, the Board received 282 comment letters.

SFAS 13, "Accounting for Leases," was issued in November 1976. The FASB adopted a very detailed approach in response to demands from the profession for specific guidance. As indicated in Chapter 3, accounting for leases continued to be an issue for the FASB. Altogether, the Board has issued 8 standards, 6 interpretations, and 10 technical bulletins on lease accounting. The issues were resurrected in 1984 as part of concerns over "standards overload," but the Board decided against adding the project to its agenda. This decision was popular with preparers because the leaning of the Board was to capitalize all leases and thereby close off the loopholes that many corporations were using to omit liabilities from the balance sheet.

Through the following definition of *assets*, the conceptual framework does provide some guidance for lease accounting:

> Assets are probable future economic benefits obtained or controlled by a particular entity as a result of past transactions or events. (SFAC 6, par. 25)

Specifically, the definition's reliance on "control" instead of ownership means that a lessee can obtain an asset through a lease without holding legal title to physical property. In addition, the discussion in SFAC 6 explains that liabilities may exist without a legally enforceable contract. This point supports the conclusion that a lessee can have a liability under a cancelable lease agreement. Therefore, the general requirement under SFAS 13 for the lessee's recognition of an asset and a liability is consistent with the conceptual framework. In addition, the framework also supports the Board's tentative conclusion in 1984 that every lease creates an asset and liability that could be recognized.

Unconsolidated Finance Subsidiaries

From the 1950s into the late 1980s, a popular device for achieving off-balance-sheet financing was the wholly owned unconsolidated subsidiary company, which was often referred to as a *finance subsidiary*. Specifically, a parent company would own an investment (usually 100 percent) in the stock of the subsidiary. In accordance with the superficial legal form of the arrangement, the parent would report its investment in the shares in the investment section of the balance sheet. In economic substance, however, the parent actually controlled all of the subsidiary's assets and was obligated to pay its liabilities. But, by reporting nothing more than the net investment in the subsidiary's stock, the parent's balance sheet did not reflect the full amount of these liabilities or the additional assets.

For example, suppose that a company presents the following statement of financial position (assume that all amounts are in millions):

Cash	$ 50	Debt	$300
Accounts receivable	200		
Other assets	350	Equity	300
Total	$600	Total	$600

Notice that the ratio of the debt to the equity is 1.00.

Now, suppose the management wants to borrow $200 million. If it does, the company's cash will be $250 million, total assets will be $800 million, and the debt will be $500 million. As a consequence, its debt-equity ratio will go to the less desirable level of 1.67 ($500 ÷ $300).

As an alternative, the management could set up a new subsidiary corporation, and have the parent corporation buy all of its stock for $1 million cash. The parent's balance sheet will appear as follows:

Cash	$ 49	Debt	$300
Accounts receivable	200		
Investment	1		
Other assets	350	Equity	300
Total	$600	Total	$600

Thus, there is no significant change in the parent company's apparent financial position.

At this point, the parent can have the subsidiary borrow the needed $200 million cash, which is transferred to the parent by selling the accounts receivable to the subsidiary for that amount. After this second event, the parent's balance sheet will look like this:

Cash	$249	Debt	$300
Accounts receivable	0		
Investment	1		
Other assets	350	Equity	300
Total	$600	Total	$600

Thus, the debt-equity ratio remains at 1.00, even though $200 million has been borrowed.

In contrast, suppose that the accounting rules require the economic substance of the relationship between the parent and subsidiary to be the basis for the financial statements instead of the legal form. By this view, there would be no investment in stock on the parent's balance sheet, the sale of the receivables would not be treated as a real transaction, and the subsidiary's $200 million of debt would be considered to be the parent's liability. The *consolidated* balance sheet would look like this:

Cash	$250	Debt	$500
Accounts receivable	200		
Other assets	350	Equity	300
Total	$800	Total	$800

This picture is the same that would be presented if the subsidiary had never been created in the first place. Notice that the debt-equity ratio has climbed to 1.67 ($500 ÷ $300).

In most parent-subsidiary situations, this latter treatment is required because accountants have accepted the concept that the financial statements of the two companies should be consolidated. The reasonableness of this approach was so widely accepted that it was rarely debated. However, in the course of conducting a 1956 survey of accounting practices related to consolidations, the research department of the AICPA found that some companies were not consolidating the assets and debts of special finance subsidiaries such as the one described above. Because the primary mandate of the Committee on Accounting Procedure was to describe acceptable practices rather than to resolve controversies, it issued ARB 51 as a description of what many companies seemed to be doing. With respect to the question of whether all subsidiaries should be consolidated, the Bulletin says without much explanation that it "may be preferable" to present separate statements for finance companies that have a parent company engaged in manufacturing.

In the eyes of many managers, this exception created a loophole with the result that a large number of finance subsidiaries were created in subsequent years. Furthermore, the finance subsidiaries grew to the point that they dwarfed their parents. It was not unusual, for example, to find that the off-balance-sheet debts of an unconsolidated subsidiary would equal 300–500 percent of the reported debts of the parent with the consequence that the reported debt-equity ratio might be less than one while the consolidated ratio would have exceeded three or four.

In 1982, the FASB created an agenda project to consider a number of conceptual and practice issues related to the *accounting entity*. Included among those issues was the question of whether a finance subsidiary's assets and liabilities should be consolidated with the parent's assets and liabilities. After publishing an exposure draft in 1986, the Board issued SFAS 94 in 1989. This standard requires the consolidation of the assets and liabilities of all controlled subsidiaries without regard to the nature of their business. After it became effective, SFAS 94 greatly altered the financial statements of the many large corporations with managers who had relied on unconsolidated finance subsidiaries to achieve off-balance-sheet financing. For example, General Motors Corporation owns its finance subsidiary, General Motors Acceptance Corporation, which holds essentially all of GM's receivables from its dealers for inventory purchases and all of the receivables from individual customers who finance through GMAC's plans. At the same time, GM uses GMAC to issue virtually all of its debt securities, especially short-term debentures. Prior to the issuance of SFAS 94, GM's balance sheet did not consolidate GMAC's assets and liabilities. GM's balance sheet for 1985 showed total liabilities for the parent company of only $25 billion and $30 billion of equity, or a debt-to-equity ratio of 0.83. However, by 1990, GM was required to consolidate GMAC's assets and liabilities, and its balance sheet for that year reported total liabilities of $148 billion even though the company's equity had remained essentially constant at only $30.6 billion. This higher level of debt raised GM's debt-to-equity ratio to 4.83, which is nearly six times higher than it was before SFAS 94 took effect.

EMPLOYEE COMPENSATION

Other recurring issues have involved the accounting by an employer for compensation paid to its employees. This area has been sensitive for two main reasons. First, some forms of compensation have been preferred because they were not completely charged against the employer's income. Thus, the employer could compensate its employees without fully reporting the expense on the income statement. This omission not only produced higher reported earnings but allowed employees (especially management) to receive more compensation than might be apparent. Second, many companies offered various forms of deferred compensation that require large future cash outflows. For example, pension agreements are designed to compensate employees for their current services with future cash payments after they retire from active service. By deferring both the payment and the reporting of the expense, companies were able to build up huge unreported liabilities for these *post-retirement benefits*. This section briefly describes four controversial issues involving employee compensation: compensated absences, pensions, other post-employment benefits, and compensation paid with stock.

Compensated Absences

After World War II, many U.S. companies began to offer or expand paid
vacations and sick leave for their employees. Under these arrangements,
employees can simply not report for work and still receive the same pay
that is received when they do work. As a matter of convenience, companies continued to charge payroll expense with the amount paid to the
employees without reflecting the fact that no work was received from
them during the vacation or sick leave.

In response to a request from the AICPA in the late 1970s to undertake a project on compensated absences, the FASB studied the issues and
determined that an employer should accrue additional expense each pay
period above the amount paid currently to its employees for future vacation and sick leave compensation. The project led to SFAS 43, which was
issued in 1980. It requires an employer to report expense and recognize a
liability for these compensated absences. In effect, the standard increases
compensation expense in the time periods in which the employees earn
the right to the payments and decreases it in the later periods in which the
absences occur.

Two significant points can be observed from this project. First, the
requirements are very consistent with long-established practices for ac-
cruing other incurred but unpaid expenses. Nonetheless, it was necessary
for the FASB to produce a specific standard to force preparers to report
their expenses more completely. The second significant point relates to
the Conceptual Framework and its equalization of the importance of the
balance sheet with the income statement. In fact, once the new accruals
are accomplished, there should be no significant impact on total compensation expense or net income because the vacation expense recognized in
one year should be approximately equal to the amount of vacation pay
earned in prior years but paid out in the current year. However, the
employer's balance sheet is more complete because it reports a new liability for the accrued and unpaid compensation that was simply not recognized before SFAS 43.

Pensions

Under a pension contract, an employer agrees to compensate its employees for work done in the present or past by making payments to them after
they retire. In effect, services are obtained from employees but paid for
later. On the surface, it appears that the employer has a liability to its
employees. However, an opportunity to defer the expense and use off-
balance-sheet financing could arise if the liability could be left out of the
financial statements.

Indeed, that omission was the established practice for many years. APB Opinion 8, issued in 1966, made an unsuccessful attempt to have corporations place a pension liability on their balance sheets. The amounts omitted from the balance sheet grew very large, and many statement preparers became even more strongly opposed to the idea of recognizing a liability. Others opposed recognizing the liability because they thought that the measurement of the amount payable to employees in the future was too uncertain and, as a result, too unreliable to merit recognition. This view was shared by many preparers, auditors, and users.

The FASB put employer accounting for pensions on its agenda in 1974 for two primary reasons. First, the Employees' Retirement Income Security Act of 1974 (ERISA) raised the general public's interest in pensions. Second, news articles identified the problem and criticized pension accounting and corporations with large amounts of omitted liabilities. Stopgap measures were issued in SFAS 35 covering the financial statements for the actual pension plan (an entity legally separate from the employer) and in SFAS 36 requiring the employer to provide additional footnote disclosures of certain pension items. Both standards were issued in 1980.

In February 1981, the Board published a discussion memorandum on pensions and received 193 responses. In July 1981, the Board heard 37 presentations at public hearings. The FASB proposed recognition of a liability (net of investments committed to a pension investment fund) in a 1982 Preliminary Views document. This publication generated huge opposition from all quarters.

After more hearings and an intensive effort to find compromises among themselves that would satisfy the vocal constituencies, four Board members agreed to issue SFAS 87 in December 1985.

SFAS 87 is unusually complicated because of the unfamiliar concepts that were used to develop it and the compromises that were reached. In brief, it requires pension expense to be calculated *as if* the employer has recognized not only a full pension liability, but also assets for the pension fund investments and a type of employee goodwill purchased by promising to pay them more in the future. However, the employer does not have to recognize more than a so-called *minimum liability*, which is far below the full amount. In addition, the Board invented techniques to arbitrarily smooth out income and defer the effects of changing to the new methods. The compromises were so pervasive that the Board's explanation of the basis for its conclusions includes the highly unusual warning that ". . . the most current and most relevant information [is excluded] from the employer's statement of financial position. That information is, however, included in the disclosures required [by the Statement] . . ." (par. 104).

Other Post-Employment Benefits

In the process of identifying and resolving pension accounting issues, the FASB determined that similar unrecognized expenses and liabilities existed for employers who had committed to pay other post-retirement benefits to their former employees, primarily promises to keep paying their medical expenses. These benefits had become especially common in the 1970s and 1980s. As the project developed, it became painfully apparent that these liabilities were often so large that they exceeded a company's pension obligation.

To avoid a delay in issuing the pension accounting standard, the Board created a separate agenda project to deal with *other post-employment benefits* (often referred to as OPEB). This project eventually led to the issuance of SFAS 106 in 1990. The requirements of the Statement are similar to the ones established in SFAS 87, with some new differences to accommodate the demands of some constituents. For example, SFAS 106 allows an employer to recognize the entire transition adjustment in one year's income instead of spreading it over the future as required by SFAS 87 for pensions. However, SFAS 106 embraced the same off-balance-sheet treatment of the liability that was used in SFAS 87. The effect of the transition charges was so large that the national media directed their attention to the FASB in a way that had never happened before. For example, the press gave significant attention to the $20 billion dollar charge against income that General Motors reported for 1992.

As an indication of the importance of financial reporting, the time since the issuance and implementation of SFAS 106 has seen virtually every company reconsider the medical benefits plan offered to its retirees in order to find ways to reduce the cost and the liability. By forcing employers to acknowledge the full effect of their benefit plans, it is clear that SFAS 106 helped businesses avoid a major future crisis. Another effect that is likely to occur is a modification of income tax laws to allow employers to deduct current contributions to medical benefit funds, just as they are allowed to do for their contributions to their pension funds.

The Board's basic solutions for pensions and medical benefits were consistent with the financial statement elements described in the Conceptual Framework. Under the initial approach considered by the FASB, an employer would have recognized a liability for the amount owed to employees for their pension and medical benefits. In addition, the company's assets in the pension or other funds would have been recognized on the balance sheet and the employer's annual expense would have equaled the increase in the liability less the increase in the market value of the fund, after adjusting for paid benefits. However, the lengthy and heated political process produced so much opposition to this conceptual approach that the Board had to find a more popular solution. As a result, there is relatively little in the employer's financial statements prepared under SFAS 87 and 106 that is consistent with the fundamental accounting theory described in the Conceptual Framework.

Compensation Paid with Stock

With the great growth and development of public capital markets, and as a result of favorable income tax treatment for both employees and employers, another phenomenon of the post–World War II economy was the rapid expansion of plans that compensated employees with outright shares of the employer's stock, with rights to acquire shares at future dates (called *stock options*), and other variations, including *stock appreciation rights* that entitle a manager to be paid a bonus equal to the increase in the value of the company's stock over a specified time period. These compensation plans are often justified on the basis that they achieve congruence between the goals of managers and stockholders by encouraging actions that increase the stock's market value.

Issues arose in the late 1940s as accountants began to cope with the problem of accounting for noncash compensation. In effect, the result of using stock to compensate employees is a decrease in earned capital and an increase in contributed capital. As a consequence, many argued that all that happens is a transfer within equity and that no expense should be reported. Others argue that reliable measurement of some forms of stock options is so difficult as to be virtually impossible. Despite these objections, however, it remains true that issuing stock to employees dilutes the ownership share of existing stockholders and many others thought that this effect should be reflected in the income statement.

These issues were first attacked by the Committee on Accounting Procedure and its efforts led to the issuance of ARB 37 in 1948. Its principles were included in Chapter 13B of ARB 43 in 1953. A central idea in the bulletin is that stock plans fall into *compensatory* and *noncompensatory* categories. The first group consists of plans that are intended to reward managers for their performance. The second group consists of plans that are intended to allow the corporation to raise new capital without offering shares for sale to the public. For compensatory plans, compensation was to be recognized as of the date the options are granted, but only if the option price was *below* the stock's current market value. For example, suppose that a company's stock was worth $25 per share on the grant date. If the option price was $25 or above, no compensation expense would be recorded. While there is an appealing simplicity in the logic behind this approach, it ignores the financial truth that longer term options with exercise prices above the current market price can have value. That value lies in the ability to participate in future price increases without making a cash investment. For example, options with an exercise price of $25 have the potential of returning a huge reward to their holder when the price goes above that level. But, if the price stays at $25 or even drops to $10 per share, the option holders have not lost anything because they did not have to invest any cash. If the employees actually bought the stock at $25, they would enjoy the reward of any value increases but they would run the risk of losing all or part of their investment if the price declined.

The Accounting Principles Board attempted to resolve the stock compensation issue by publishing Opinion No. 25 in 1972. Although the APB's authority gave its pronouncements more weight and influence than ARB 43, the members could not agree on a measurement method that would provide a value for options with exercise prices in excess of the stock's current market price. This shortcoming weakened the opinion, despite the APB's careful attention to more complicated compensation plans involving variable numbers of shares that could be issued according to the company's performance.

The FASB began a project in the mid-1980s that was designed to bring more complete accounting for the costs and other effects of compensation paid with the company's stock, or with stock-related financial instruments. It did not take long before the Board ran up against the same measurement obstacles that had defeated its predecessors. In addition, the preparer community was virtually unanimously opposed to recognizing any costs. Despite the Board's clear declaration of its obligation to report neutral information, preparers continued to predict undesirable consequences for business in general and small emerging businesses in particular if stock option grants would be reported as compensation expense. In response to the pressure and in acknowledging that the Board members were not coming to a consensus, the project was shelved by merging it with a slow-moving and low-priority project on identifying and accounting for the differences between debt and equity and between various categories of equity.

However, the issues could not stay buried because of growing public concern in the late 1980s and early 1990s that the large amounts of compensation paid to top managers were not justified. As each year showed that more executives were receiving tens and even hundreds of millions of dollars through stock options, other pressures mounted on the FASB to produce a standard that would show how these plans affect a corporation and its stockholders. In 1992 and early 1993, the Board experienced an unprecedented avalanche of opposition to its apparent intent to press ahead with a project that would lead to recognizing compensation expense equal to the value of options granted to managers, even if the option price exceeded the stock's price on the grant date. Over a six-month period, the FASB received more than 500 comment letters, even though the project was still in the preliminary deliberations stage and no comments had been requested through a discussion memorandum or an exposure draft. The dissatisfaction was not confined to the preparer community but also included unanimous opposition from each of the Big Six public accounting firms and even from a variety of financial statement users. Nonetheless, the Board expressed its resolve in April 1993 to move ahead with a plan to initially require disclosure of the compensation cost for a three-year period following the issuance of a standard. At the end of the three years, companies would be required to recognize the expense in their income statements. The decision to move ahead was bold in light of the comments, but it was also encouraged by support from some members of Congress who had seen the executive compensation controversy as an issue that they could use for their own political purposes.

In 1993, as this book's manuscript is being prepared for publication, the eventual outcome of the FASB's efforts is still unknown. However, the issuance of an exposure draft in June suggests that change is likely to come to practice after nearly 50 years of dissatisfaction with the partial solution described by the Committee on Accounting Procedure.

INCOME TAXES

On the surface, accounting for income taxes seems to be a fairly straightforward problem. Once the tax for a given year is calculated on the tax return, it might appear that the amount should be recognized as an expense on the income statement. To the extent that the tax has not been paid or has been overpaid, a liability or a receivable would be recognized.

Deferred Taxes

Accounting for income taxes is not that simple, however, because of differences between the definitions of income under GAAP and under the tax code that put revenues (or expenses) in different time periods. That is, a transaction may produce a revenue (or expense) on the current year's income statement under GAAP while no revenue (or expense) is recognized on the same year's tax return because the tax code would recognize it in some future period or periods. The result is that there is often no obvious relationship between the amount of GAAP income for a year and the amount of tax actually paid.

This lack of correlation is of special concern to management because reporting the actual tax payable as expense would tend to produce volatility in reported after-tax income from year to year. It is also of concern to users because a company can make an election for the tax return (such as accelerated depreciation) that merely *postpones* the payment of taxes rather than permanently reducing them. Thus, users are concerned that profits might be overstated and liabilities understated.

The earliest authoritative discussion of accounting for income taxes is found in ARB 2 (issued in 1939), which dealt with accounting for refunded debt. The bulletin suggested that the cost of refunding debt should be amortized over the life of the new debt. Because all refunding costs were deductible for tax purposes in the year of the refunding, it also indicated that there might be an effect for income taxes on the financial statements. It offered no suggestion, however, on how to account for this effect.

ARB 18, issued in 1942, also dealt with refunding debt. This bulletin recognized the fact that the accounting for the refunding transaction might be different under GAAP than under the tax code and described a method of accounting for the effect on income taxes that would recognize the tax expense in proportion to the reported income.

Another situation that involved accounting for income taxes was the country's transition to a peacetime economy after World War II. Specifically, the wartime tax code allowed the cost of so-called emergency facilities to be written off over only five years on the tax return. ARB 27, issued in 1946, discussed how companies should account for the amortization and depreciation of these facilities. Additional material was included in ARB 42, issued in 1952, and then restated in ARB 43, which combined many previous bulletins, including ARB 23 dealing with various tax accounting issues. ARB 43 described how to account for the tax effects of using a longer period of write-off for financial reporting than the five years allowed for tax purposes. The bulletin suggested a combination of the techniques now known as the *net of tax* and *liability* methods.

Accounting for income taxes was also discussed in ARB 44, "Declining-Balance Depreciation," which was issued in October 1954. Although the declining-balance method had been used in England for many years, its use in the United States had been limited. When the Internal Revenue Code of 1954 liberalized its acceptability for tax purposes, interest in its use grew significantly. ARB 44 identified the circumstances in which declining-balance depreciation might be appropriate for financial reporting and suggested that accounting recognition might be given to the effects on income taxes when the declining-balance method was used for tax purposes and some other method of depreciation was used for the financial statements. It indicated, however, that such recognition was not necessary in ordinary situations.

In July 1958, a revised version of ARB 44 was issued. It addressed the tax issues related to accelerated depreciation more directly, and suggested that recognition be given to *deferred taxes* on the current year's reported income that would be paid in the future. The members of the Committee on Accounting Procedure indicated that they had observed and studied cases involving the application of the original version of ARB 44 and had concluded that recognition of deferred taxes was needed to obtain an appropriate matching of costs and revenues and thereby avoid income distortion. Dissenters to the revised ARB 44 expressed their concern over the use of a bulletin on depreciation to create an accounting standard on deferred taxes.

After the release of the new ARB 44, questions were raised about the CAP's intent in using the phrase *deferred tax* for the account credited with the postponed income tax effects. In April 1959, the CAP issued an interpretation letter indicating that the account was meant to be either a deferred credit or a liability account but stating that it could not be reported as a credit to earned surplus (the previously acceptable term for *retained earnings*) or any other stockholders' equity account. As a result, the AICPA was sued by Appalachian Power Company, which had been reporting the credit balances as adjustments to earned surplus. The case eventually went to the U.S. Supreme Court, with the AICPA prevailing.

In 1966, the APB released Accounting Research Study No. 9, "Interperiod Allocation of Corporate Income Taxes." This study led to the issuance of APB 11, "Accounting for Income Taxes," which required the use of the deferral method and prohibited increasing stockholders' equity for deferred taxes. Furthermore, it addressed other tax issues, including the treatment of the tax benefits arising from the deductibility of a current year's loss from prior and future years' taxable income. APB 11 also established the practice of *intraperiod* tax allocation, which disaggregates the total tax expense into portions associated with different categories of income identified on the income statement.

All in all, Opinion 11 proved highly acceptable for a number of years. However, the FASB began its own project on tax accounting in the early 1980s. One reason was the incompatibility of the deferred tax account with the Conceptual Framework's definitions of elements of financial statements in SFAC 3. Specifically, the deferred taxes account was not consistent with the definition of a liability. A more compelling reason was growing criticism that Opinion 11's approach had become too complicated as a result of the increasing complexity of the tax law. Some felt that the ever-increasing size of the balance of deferred taxes on the statement of financial position invalidated the basic assumption that the account balance would decline as time passed.

The FASB's first step was a research report that identified many of the problems in reporting income taxes.[3] This publication was followed in 1983 by a discussion memorandum and public hearings. Somewhat unexpectedly, the comment letters expressed satisfaction with the status quo. Generally, they reflected concern that the Board might actually make practice more complex or might bring back more volatility in reported income by simplifying the procedures.

From this controversial beginning, the Board's income tax project went on to be long and difficult to bring to a conclusion. After five years of

---

[3] Dennis Beresford, et al., *Accounting for Income Taxes: A Review of Alternatives* (Norwalk, Conn.: FASB, 1983).

intensive effort and due process, SFAS 96 was issued late in 1987. This standard applied the *liability* method, under which the taxpayer looks to future tax cash flows related to presently owned assets and presently owed liabilities. If the company is expected to experience future cash outflows for taxes, it has a deferred tax liability. Consistent with the Conceptual Framework's definition of expense, SFAS 96 specified that the annual tax expense equals the sum of the change in the deferred tax liability plus the actual taxes paid or payable for the year. Thus, the total expense exceeds the tax paid or payable if the ending deferred tax liability is larger than the beginning balance.

Significantly, SFAS 96 did not allow a company to recognize an asset for an expected net reduction in future taxes because of deferred deductions. This requirement was rooted in the Conceptual Framework's definition of an asset that requires a company to control future benefits through a past transaction. For income taxes, the Board concluded that the company could not control the future cash benefits because control over them depends on future income events rather than past transactions.

Following the issuance of SFAS 96, there was a substantial amount of dissatisfaction and turmoil as the preparer constituency resisted its requirements, with the main issue being the nonrecognition of the deferred tax asset. Efforts to overturn the Statement even included an attempt by several U.S. senators to pressure the SEC to reject it. The debate extended well beyond anyone's expectations, with the result that the FASB began to lose confidence in its consensus, and issued three Statements (SFAS 100, SFAS 103, and SFAS 108) that postponed the effective date of SFAS 96 in order to allow the Board to regroup and deal with the issues again.

Finally, the FASB simply reopened its deliberations on the tax asset issue and began to develop a more popular resolution. This effort led to the issuance of SFAS 109 in 1992 that reversed SFAS 96 by allowing deferred tax assets to be recognized in many situations, even though the taxpayer must assume sufficient future income to allow the deferred deductions to be realized. The decision was rationalized by falling back on the traditional *going-concern assumption* that is not included in the Conceptual Framework. If the company is sufficiently uncertain about the validity of the assumption, it must provide an allowance that reduces the book value of the deferred tax asset and increases income tax expense for the year. The change can be viewed as a triumph of politics over theory, although FASB and the preparer community both characterize it as a pragmatic compromise that reflects the shift in the tax law toward postponing deductions instead of accelerating them.

Perhaps the biggest theoretical shortfall in accounting for deferred taxes is the failure to use discounting to reflect the relative economic advantages of deferring payments farther out into the future. As a simple example, a company is substantially better off it if postpones $100,000 of taxes for 10 years instead of paying them at once or postponing them only 2 or 3 years. However, SFAS 109 forces the company to report $100,000 of tax expense in all three situations. The Board justified not using discounted amounts on the basis of simplicity, but the result is likely to be that the information produced under SFAS 109 is not as useful for investment and credit decisions as it could be.

However, it is not likely that the FASB will reconsider accounting for income taxes because the prolonged due process was so contentious and because the carefully crafted solution is so dependent on compromises that would be hard to modify and hold together.

The Investment Tax Credit

Another income tax-related accounting problem was the *investment tax credit*, which was a special reduction in taxes that the taxpayer qualified for simply by buying particular types of assets (generally not real estate). The accounting issue was how to report the savings from the tax credit. Three different positions were popular: (1) reduce the cost of the asset by the savings; (2) reduce tax expense in the year of the purchase; and (3) reduce tax expense over the life of the asset.

The APB attempted to deal with the investment tax credit in 1962 as an accounting issue instead of a political issue. Initially, the APB concluded in Opinion 2 that the first position (called *cost reduction*) was most consistent with the traditional accounting model that attempted to spread benefits over the useful lives of assets. However, the APB had not reckoned with the political strength of corporate managers who wanted quick improvements in their reported profits. The investment tax credit was created to help stimulate business activity in the middle of a recession when corporate profits were depressed. A number of corporate managers appealed to the SEC, which disagreed with the APB position. Only a few weeks after Opinion 2 was issued, the SEC stated in Accounting Series Release No. 96 that the second method (called *flow through*) was also acceptable for financial statements filed with the Commission. Fifteen months later, the APB issued Opinion 4, which acknowledged that the flow-through method was acceptable, as well as the cost reduction method and the third method listed above (called *deferral*).

The initial investment tax credit lapsed, but it was restored by Congress in the early 1970s. At that time, the APB started another project to resolve the issue. However, Congress included a provision in the Revenue Act of 1971 that a taxpayer could not be bound by anyone's decision as to how to present the savings from investment tax credits in the financial statements. This provision is generally considered to be the result of lobbying by strong corporate interests that were trying to protect their profit pictures. Consequently, the FASB could not meaningfully address the issue in its income tax project. The Tax Reform Act of 1986 eliminated the investment tax credit and the issues were made moot. However, they will surface again if and when Congress decides that the credit should be restored.

CHANGING PRICES

Perhaps no other accounting issue has generated as much controversy and emotion as the one that asks whether financial statements should be based on the amounts originally spent and received or on measures that reflect the *current values* of the statement items. In fact, some evidence of disagreement appears in the literature as early as 1918.[4] If prices were stable, there would be no issue. However, prices are anything but stable and the controversy has always attracted much attention.

Price-Level Adjustments

A middle-ground position keeps the original cost amounts but expresses them in terms of *constant dollars*. This process reflects only the effects of inflation, which is the change in the purchasing power of the dollar. The historical cost of an item is adjusted by a general price index that measures the change in purchasing power.

This price-level-adjusted approach tended to be popular with auditors because it would allow them to continue using the same basic verification procedures that they use for additional historical cost accounting systems. Price-level adjustments were not favored by preparers because the process usually increases the reported cost of goods sold and depreciation while leaving revenues unchanged. Thus, reported income is virtually always reduced. It also diminishes the results of their performance in operating the corporation by increasing assets and equity. This effect combines with the lower income level to produce a substantial reduction in the return on assets.

A complete description of price-level adjustments was articulated by Henry Sweeney in the 1930s.[5] The widespread interest in the problem is reflected in the fact that the Rockefeller Foundation funded a study during the 1940s by a group of accountants, economists, labor leaders, and bankers on business income, including alternative methods for reflecting the effects of inflation. The APB considered the possibility of requiring price-level-adjusted financial statements but could not get the two-thirds majority needed to make them mandatory. The nonauthoritative APB Statement 3 was issued in 1969 and recommended that historical cost financial

---

[4] Livingston Middleditch, "Should Accounts Reflect the Changing Value of the Dollar?" *Journal of Accountancy,* February 1918, pp. 114–20.

[5] Henry W. Sweeney, *Stabilized Accounting* (New York: Harper & Row, 1936).

statements be supplemented by general price-level-adjusted information. Its recommendations were almost totally ignored.

The FASB added accounting for changing prices to its agenda and issued an Exposure Draft in 1974 that would have required price-level-adjusted information in the footnotes to the financial statements. Before the standard could be issued, the SEC intervened in 1976 by issuing Accounting Series Release No. 190, which required the largest registrants to provide a different type of disclosure based on current values.

The Board deferred issuing a statement on price-level-adjusted (or "constant dollar") accounting until it had progressed further on its Conceptual Framework project and until additional studies and hearings could be held on the issues. In 1979, the Board issued SFAS 33, "Financial Reporting and Changing Prices," which put the technique of price-level adjustments into use as supplemental information (the standard also included current value requirements). However, the constant dollar requirements were dropped from the standard when it became apparent that the approach lacked support from any constituent group. This was accomplished late in 1984 through SFAS 82.

Because the Conceptual Framework project deteriorated into a description of existing practices, SFAC 5 on recognition and measurement does not either encourage or discourage price-level adjustments.

Current Value

In contrast to price-level adjustments, the *current value* approach would report the changed price of an item whether the change was related to inflation or to shifts in specific prices. The intent of this approach is to describe the amount of wealth controlled by the reporting entity by reflecting the full results of changes in supply and demand for all of its assets and liabilities. This approach is supported because it provides more complete and more relevant information than historical cost-based approaches. For example, if an item cost $1,000 when it was purchased and 10 percent inflation has occurred since then, price-level adjusted accounting would report its cost as $1,100. However, because of a low supply of the item (or a high demand for it), the current value of the item might be $1,300. Thus, neither the original cost nor the price-level adjusted amount would provide complete information about the item or the income effects experienced by the company while holding the asset when its value increased.

Using current value leads to recognizing these holding gains and losses that arise from owning assets (or owing liabilities) when prices increase or decrease. This approach tends to be unattractive to auditors because of the unfamiliar risks that it creates for them by requiring them to verify amounts that are not documented through transactions involving their clients.

Preparers tend to argue against the use of current values because it causes them to incur the costs of implementing a new accounting system. More to the point is the fact that it also causes them to lose control over some of the information that flows to users. Furthermore, it tends to create fluctuations in reported income as values change. Perhaps most significantly, it causes them to report lower income from operations because the cost of goods sold and depreciation expense tend to be higher.

Despite the many arguments raised in favor of the current value approach, it was not accepted as part of common practice until SFAS 33 was issued in 1979. This standard created a partial application of the approach by requiring the reporting of supplemental current value information by approximately 1,500 large public corporations that met specified size criteria. As described in Chapter 4, the issue of whether current values should be used more extensively eventually became the focus for the recognition and measurement phase of the Conceptual Framework project.

Because of the cautious posture adopted by the Board in Statement of Financial Accounting Concepts No. 5, it appeared unlikely that much would be done to increase the use of current values. However, perhaps because of some membership changes, the Board made the following announcement in the October 8, 1985, issue of *Status Report*:

> The Board has concluded that the information about the effects of inflation and changes in specific prices is important in assessing the amounts, timing, and uncertainty of prospective cash flows. The Board also agrees that the present requirements for the disclosure of the effects of changing prices has not met that need. As a result, the Board has determined it should continue to strive to improve the disclosures and has tentatively approved a continuing agenda project having the objective of developing more effective and useful disclosures of the impact of changing prices on enterprise performance, resources, obligations, and financial capital. The FASB staff is working to develop the scope and content of that project.
>
> The Board has concluded that the present disclosure requirement contained in Statement 33, "Financial Reporting and Changing Prices," as amended, should be retained during the continuing agenda project period.

Despite this resolve in 1985, the coalition of Board members supporting current value experimentation fell apart late in 1986 in frustration over finding a direction for future development. Shortly thereafter, SFAS 89 was issued, and changed the remaining requirements of SFAS 33 to voluntary guidelines to be used by those preparers who wanted to provide the information. Given the approach's lack of popularity with preparers, virtually no companies have continued to provide this information.

However, this decision by the FASB did not make the current value issue disappear. Instead, the late 1980s saw the United States begin to realize that it would incur the huge cost of making good on the losses experienced by the savings and loan industry. Although many factors contributed to the losses (including deregulation, inflation, recession, fluctuating interest rates, managerial ignorance, and corruption), it was abundantly clear that corrective steps were initially delayed because the savings institutions published financial statements that concealed their weaknesses instead of revealing them. In an effort to prevent similar problems in the future, many began to call for the use of current values in financial statements. The advantages of what came to be known as *mark-to-market* accounting were especially promoted by the chairman of the SEC, Richard Breeden, and the SEC's chief accountant, Walter Schuetze.[6] The SEC and the AICPA strongly encouraged the Board to undertake a project to create standards that would cause financial statements to provide more complete information about companies' assets and liabilities.

This request fell on receptive ears because the FASB had an ongoing major project on accounting for *financial instruments*, and one of the directions being pursued in this project was the disclosure of the market value of such things as a company's receivables, payables, and investments in securities. The Board pressed ahead, and issued SFAS 107 in 1991, which requires large companies to disclose this market-based information supplementally, unless the company's management has no idea what the market values are. If they do not have this information, they must disclose why they do not. Of course, in making that disclosure, they must admit that they do not know some very basic and relevant information about their companies.

The FASB next created a more specific project to require balance sheet recognition of the fair value of investments in marketable equity and debt securities and changes in that value as gains and losses on the income statement. (This project was the subject of the news articles presented in the Prologue and several of the discussions in Chapter 3.) In response to pressure that was coming virtually exclusively from the banking industry (including the chairman of the Federal Reserve Board, Alan Greenspan), the FASB fashioned a major compromise in SFAS 115 that allows a company to divide its investment portfolio into three parts. Two of the subportfolios are accounted for using fair values while the investments held in the third (consisting of debt securities expected to be held to maturity) are accounted for at amortized historical cost, just as they always have been. The holding gains and losses from one subportfolio are reported on the income statement while those experienced on the other are reported as unrealized in the equity section of the balance sheet.

This highly compromised piecemeal solution does not accomplish much of the progress that could have been made, and should serve as a continuing reminder that the preparer community and its representatives

---

[6] Schuetze was a charter member of the FASB and served from 1973 through 1975.

continue to hold a strong position in the FASB's political system. More progress will undoubtedly come, but only in the face of forceful and continuing resistance from corporate managers.

This controversial issue about the use of current values was, of course, the one that derailed the FASB's efforts to deal with recognition and measurement in its Conceptual Framework project. Because SFAC 5 expresses a relatively weak and compromised position that describes practice, it does not provide a conceptual position that could be used to support the expansion of current values beyond the basic objective in SFAC 1 that asserts that financial statements should provide information useful for decision making.

SUMMARY

The FASB has faced numerous controversies during its lifetime. Some have been new, but most of them have been merely new forms and variations of issues that existed earlier. By being familiar with the history of these issues, the readers will find it easier to cope with new issues that emerge in order that they will be more capable of evaluating the adequacy of newly proposed solutions.

SELECTED READINGS

BARTLEY, JON W., AND LEWIS S. DAVIDSON. "The Entity Concept and Accounting for Interest Costs." *Accounting and Business Research,* Summer 1982, pp. 175–87.

BIELSTEIN, MARK M., AND EDWARD W. TROTT. "The New Approach to Accounting for Income Taxes." *Management Accounting,* August 1992, pp. 43–47.

BURNS, GARY W., AND D. SCOTT PETERSON. "Accounting for Computer Software." *Journal of Accountancy,* April 1982, pp. 50–58.

BYINGTON, RALPH J., AND PAUL MUNTER. "Disclosures about Financial Instruments." *CPA Journal,* September 1990, pp. 42–48.

COLLEY, J. RON, AND ARA G. VOLCAN. "Business Combinations: Goodwill and Push-Down Accounting." *CPA Journal,* August 1998, pp. 74–76.

DIETER, RICHARD. "Is Now the Time to Revisit Accounting for Business Combinations?" *CPA Journal,* July 1989, pp. 44–48.

DUNNE, KATHLEEN M. "An Empirical Analysis of Management's Choice of Accounting Treatment for Business Combinations." *Journal of Accounting & Public Policy,* Summer 1990, pp. 111–13.

GRAY, DAVID. "Do We Need a New Way to Measure Pension Fund Performance?" *Financial Executive,* November/December 1988, pp. 50–53.

JOHNSON, L. TODD. "Research on Disclosure." *Accounting Horizons,* March 1992, pp. 101–3.

JONES, JEFFERY C. "Financial Instruments: Historical Cost vs. Fair Value." *CPA Journal,* August 1988, pp. 57–63.

KIRSCH, ROBERT J., AND SACHI SAKTHIVEL. "Capitalize or Expense." *Management Accounting,* January 1993, pp. 38–43.

LANDER, GERALD H.; ALAN REINSTEIN; AND AUGUSTIN K. FOSU. "An Evaluation of Agency Theory Influence in Pension Accounting." Winter 1991–1992, *Journal of Applied Business Research,* pp. 13–16.

LUSK, LAURIE A. "Creativity in Pension Accounting." *Management Accounting,* March 1992, pp. 31–35.

MILLER, PAUL B. W. "The New Pension Accounting (Part 1)." *Journal of Accountancy,* January 1987, pp. 98–108.

MUNTER, PAUL. "The Financial Instruments Project Marches On." *CPA Journal,* July 1992, pp. 30–36.

NAIR, R. D., AND J. J. WEYGANDT. "Let's Fix Deferred Taxes." *Journal of Accountancy,* November 1981, pp. 87–102.

RAYBURN, FRANK R. "Discounting of Deferred Income Taxes: An Argument for Reconsideration." *Accounting Horizons,* March 1987, pp. 43–50.

READ, WILLIAM J., AND ROBERT A. J. BARTSCH. "The FASB's Proposed Rules for Deferred Taxes." *Journal of Accountancy,* August 1991, pp. 44–53.

————. "Accounting for Deferred Taxes under FASB 109." *Journal of Accountancy,* December 1992, pp. 36–41.

SUNDER, SHYAM. "Properties of Accounting Numbers under Full Costing and Successful Efforts Costing in the Petroleum Industry." *The Accounting Review,* January 1976, pp. 1–18.

SWENSON, DAN W., AND THOMAS E. BUTTROSS. "A Return to the Past: Disclosing Market Values of Financial Instruments." *Journal of Accountancy,* January 1993, pp. 71–77.

SWINDLE, BRUCE, AND DARYL BURCKEL. "Accounting for Software Development Costs: Has SFAS 86 Lived Up to Its Promise?" *Practical Accountant,* October 1992, pp. 40–49.

SYMONDS, EDWARD. "Oil and Gas Accounting—What Has the FASB Achieved?" *Accountancy,* November 1982, pp. 53–55.

VANCIL, RICHARD F. "Inflation Accounting—The Great Controversy." *Harvard Business Review,* March–April 1976, pp. 58–67.

WALKER, DAVID M. "Statements 87 and 88: The ERISA Implications." *Financial Executive,* September/October 1988, pp. 10–14.

PUBLICATION REFERENCES

AMERICAN INSTITUTE OF CPAs

Committee on Accounting Procedure—Accounting Research Bulletins

No. 2   Unamortized Discount and Redemption Premium on Bonds Refunded, September 1939

No. 18   Unamortized Discount and Redemption Premium on Bonds Refunded (Supplement), December 1942

No. 23 Accounting for Income Taxes, December 1944

No. 27 Emergency Facilities, November 1946

No. 37 Accounting for Compensation in the Form of Stock Options, November 1948

No. 38 Disclosure of Long-Term Leases in Financial Statements of Lessees, October 1949

No. 42 Emergency Facilities: Depreciation, Amortization, and Income Taxes, November 1952

No. 43 Restatement and Revision of Accounting Research Bulletins, June 1953

No. 44 Declining-Balance Depreciation, October 1954

No. 44 (Revised) Declining-Balance Depreciation, July 1958

No. 51 Consolidated Financial Statements, August 1959

Accounting Principles Board—Opinions

No. 2 Accounting for the "Investment Credit," December 1962

No. 4 (Amending No. 2) Accounting for the "Investment Credit," March 1964

No. 5 Reporting of Leases in Financial Statements of Lessee, September 1964

No. 7 Accounting for Leases in Financial Statements of Lessors, May 1966

No. 8 Accounting for the Cost of Pension Plans, November 1966

No. 11 Accounting for Income Taxes, December 1967

No. 25 Accounting for Stock Issued to Employees, October 1972

No. 27 Accounting for Lease Transactions by Manufacturer or Dealer Lessors, November 1972

No. 31 Disclosure of Lease Commitments by Lessees, June 1973

Accounting Principles Board—Statement

No. 3 Financial Statements Restated for General Price-Level Changes, June 1969

Accounting Research Studies

No. 4 John H. Myers, "Reporting of Leases in Financial Statements," 1962

No. 9 Homer A. Black, "Interperiod Allocation of Corporate Income Taxes," 1966

No. 14   Oscar S. Gellein and Maurice S. Newman, "Accounting for Research and Development Expenditures," 1973

FINANCIAL ACCOUNTING STANDARDS BOARD

Statements of Financial Accounting Standards

No. 2   Accounting for Research and Development Costs, October 1974

No. 13   Accounting for Leases, November 1976

No. 19   Financial Accounting and Reporting by Oil and Gas Producing Companies, December 1977

No. 25   Suspension of Certain Accounting Requirements for Oil and Gas Producing Companies (an amendment of FASB Statement No. 19), February 1979

No. 33   Financial Reporting and Changing Prices, September 1979

No. 34   Capitalization of Interest Cost, October 1979

No. 35   Accounting and Reporting by Defined Benefit Pension Plans

No. 36   Disclosure of Pension Information (an amendment of APB Opinion No. 8), May 1980

No. 43   Accounting for Compensated Absences, November 1980

No. 69   Disclosures about Oil and Gas Producing Activities (an amendment of FASB Statements 19, 25, 33, and 39), November 1982

No. 82   Financial Reporting and Changing Prices: Elimination of Certain Disclosures (an amendment of FASB Statement No. 33), November 1984

No. 86   Accounting for the Costs of Computer Software to Be Sold, Leased, or Otherwise Marketed, August 1985

No. 87   Employers' Accounting for Pensions, December 1985

No. 89   Financial Reporting and Changing Prices, December 1986

No. 94   Consolidation of All Majority-Owned Subsidiaries, October 1987

No. 96   Accounting for Income Taxes, December 1987

No. 100   Accounting for Income Taxes—Deferral of the Effective Date of FASB Statement No. 96, December 1988

No. 103   Accounting for Income Taxes—Deferral of the Effective Date of FASB Statement No. 96, December 1989

No. 106   Employer's Accounting for Post-Retirement Benefits Other Than Pensions, December 1990

No. 107   Disclosures about Fair Value of Financial Instruments, December 1991

No. 108   Accounting for Income Taxes—Deferral of the Effective Date of FASB Statement No. 96, December 1991

No. 109   Accounting for Income Taxes, February 1992

No. 115   Accounting for Certain Investments in Debt and Equity Securities, June 1993

Exposure Drafts of Statements of Financial Accounting Standards

Financial Reporting in Units of General Purchasing Power, December 1974

Accounting for Stock-Based Compensation, June 1993

Statement of Financial Accounting Concepts

No. 1   Objectives of Financial Reporting by Business Enterprises, November 1978

No. 2   Qualitative Characteristics of Accounting Information, May 1980

No. 5   Recognition and Measurement in Financial Statements of Business Enterprises, December 1984

No. 6   Elements of Financial Statements of Business Enterprises, December 1985

Interpretation

No. 6   Applicability of FASB Statement No. 2 to Computer Software (an interpretation of FASB Statement No. 2), February 1975

Discussion Documents

Discussion Memorandum—An Analysis of Issues Related to Accounting for Research and Development Costs, 1973

Discussion Memorandum—An Analysis of Issues Related to Accounting for Leases, 1974

Discussion Memorandum—An Analysis of Issues Related to Accounting for Pensions and Other Post-Employment Benefits, 1981

Preliminary Views on Major Issues Related to Employers' Accounting for Pensions and Other Post-Employment Benefits, 1982

Discussion Memorandum—An Analysis of Issues Related to Accounting for Income Taxes, 1983

SECURITIES AND EXCHANGE COMMISSION

Accounting Series Releases

No. 96   Accounting for the "Investment Tax Credit," 1963

No. 132   Reporting Leases in Financial Statements of Lessees, 1973

No. 141   Interpretations and Minor Amendments Applicable to Certain Revisions of Regulation S-X, 1973

6

A Look into the FASB's Future

The preceding chapters have shown how the Financial Accounting Standards Board works toward its overall goal of improving the practice of financial accounting. In doing so, the book has described the people, the process, and the politics of the FASB and has provided some insights into the history of standards setting. At this point, it is appropriate to look ahead to the future of the Board and to examine the factors that are likely to affect its ability to keep operating successfully. The following issues are discussed:

- Public versus private standards setting
- Standards overload versus timely guidance
- International accounting standards and issues
- Statement preparer participation versus dominance

In addition, this chapter provides an overall evaluation of the outlook for the FASB's future.

PUBLIC VERSUS PRIVATE STANDARDS SETTING

Throughout the 55-year history of financial accounting standards setting, many people have debated whether the process should be carried out in the public sector of the economy or within the private sector. In most cases, the consensus has been that it is far more preferable to have it within the private sector.

In one sense, this issue may not be worth debating because the process is already very much in the public sector. The preceding chapters have shown that the FASB's due process allows all participants to express their beliefs on the questions before it. The Board is designed to be independent of each of them while being dependent on all of them. Furthermore (and very importantly), the primary sources of the FASB's authority are the endorsements of its standards by the Securities and Exchange Commission and by state boards of public accountancy.

Thus, the issue might be better stated as whether the SEC should have direct responsibility for this public standards-setting process instead of merely having a position of *oversight*. In evaluating the issue, it is helpful to determine what the SEC gains by having the FASB in operation.

First, *accounting standards are being established.* Controversial issues are debated at the FASB and many of them are eventually resolved, with the result that the SEC has the guidance it needs for its registrants.

Second, *the SEC is able to influence the FASB's agenda.* Thus, the Commission is able to have its most urgent issues resolved.

Third, *the SEC is potentially able to influence the outcome* of the process through its authority to establish its own rules for its registrants if it disagrees with the FASB. This ability is exercised through the SEC's formal and informal communication of its desires to the FASB described in Chapter 5. The ultimate threat of a veto (like the one exercised on SFAS 19, "Financial Accounting and Reporting by Oil and Gas Producing Companies") is always there to help ensure that the Board remains conscious of its need to satisfy the SEC.

Fourth, the arrangement *allows the SEC to shift critics' attention from itself to the FASB.* By passing issues along to the Board for resolution, the heat of public scrutiny is focused on the Board and taken off the Commission, which has other controversial tasks to accomplish. This ability to direct attention to the FASB was described in the June 27, 1991, article on page 4 in the Prologue for the mark-to-market project. When the SEC identified the problem, it expressed its concerns to the FASB, and then waited for the Board to carry out its due process and resolve the issues.

Fifth, *the SEC does not have to bear many costs of the process.* None of the Financial Accounting Foundation's funds for the FASB's budget come from the SEC or any other government agency. In effect, the only costs the SEC incurs are related to communications with the Board and occasional transportation costs to enable its personnel to observe and participate in various meetings.

Sixth, *the SEC obtains the services of many people who might not be willing to work under government salary scales.* For example, SEC Commissioners are paid between $108,000 and $148,000 per year, in contrast to the $305,000 paid to FASB members. The SEC's chief accountant earns $115,000, while the FASB's director of research and technical activities makes $305,000. The salaries of the chief acountant's professional staff range from $62,000 to $93,000, whereas FASB's project managers earn between $85,000 and $125,000. Although working at the SEC may provide an intangible benefit from performing a public service, it seems unlikely that the Commission would be able to consistently locate, hire, train, and retain people whose talents and backgrounds are equal to those of the people at the FASB and who are also willing to make a long-term commitment.

Given these six advantages of the present system, the SEC is unlikely to voluntarily assume full responsibility for the tasks that the FASB accomplishes. Thus, any motivation to take over the job will probably have to come from outside the Commission. In turn, that development can happen only through a strong consensus in Congress that something is wrong with standards setting and that it can be remedied only by direct government control. Furthermore, that consensus can be developed only if events occur that raise sufficiently high concerns in Congress to cause the issue to rank above other problems that currently have a higher priority, such as the reduction of the deficit, tax reform, defense spending, foreign relations, and critical local issues.

A potential source of heightened congressional interest in standards setting might be a repeat of the savings and loan collapse for large banks that would significantly injure or inconvenience a large number of voters. Even then, it would be necessary to draw a strong connection between these ill effects and financial accounting standards, and to demonstrate that having standards setting take place outside the direct responsibility of the SEC significantly contributes to the problem. Finally, it would have to be shown that putting the process directly under the SEC would create lower costs and better results than modifying the existing process to eliminate its shortcomings.

In conclusion, it seems extremely unlikely that the FASB will be disbanded in favor of a system subject to direct governmental control. Of course, there are degrees of control over the FASB that the SEC might exert, such as a more visible involvement in the due process, representation on the Board of Trustees, and partial funding of the Board's budget. At present, however, there does not appear to be much interest in even these simple steps.

Congressional Attention

As described briefly on page 121 in Chapter 4, congressional investigations in the mid-1970s called attention to the accounting profession and the FASB. The primary leaders were Senator Lee Metcalf of Montana and Congressman John Moss of California. Their subcommittees examined a number of issues, and some changes were made in 1977 as a result of the investigation. For example, the FASB's due process was opened to more observation and public participation. The AICPA's influence on the Financial Accounting Foundation and the FASB was significantly reduced. The AICPA also went through a restructuring that distinguished between those members whose clients include SEC registrants and those whose clients are not registrants. However, hindsight has shown that there was no real possibility that any legislation could have been passed, possibly because of the reforms that were instituted, but more likely because Metcalf and Moss were not able to generate enough enthusiasm among their colleagues to raise the priority of the issues sufficiently high to cause them to pass new laws.

Beginning in 1985, congressional attention was again focused on the public accounting profession as a result of an investigation conducted by Congressman John Dingell (of Michigan) through his Oversight and Investigations Subcommittee of the House Committee on Energy and Commerce. One issue initially pursued by the subcommittee was the question of whether the existing standards-setting process shares any of the blame for a number of business failures that had inconvenienced many depositors of banks and savings and loan associations. Among those testifying at the first session of the hearings was FASB Chairman Don Kirk. Although that session of the hearings directed some attention to the standards-setting process, the FASB quickly passed from the center of attention as it became apparent that there was no clear link between its activities and the problems that had been encountered.

In 1993, it did not appear that there would be any legislative or other significant pressure to move the FASB's activities directly under government responsibility. However, it is always possible that attention directed at the SEC will increase the intensity of its participation in the Board's due process. It is also possible that the Clinton administration could alter this situation through its appointments of the new SEC chairman and commissioners.

STANDARDS OVERLOAD VERSUS TIMELY GUIDANCE

Like other regulatory institutions, the FASB has to tread a fine line between doing too much and doing too little in its standards setting. If it does too much, it takes away the flexibility and judgment that allow accountants to cope with the specific situations they encounter in describing different companies in different industries. The presence of too many standards also makes practicing accountants learn new material, with the result that their costs increase, both in terms of educating themselves and in the risks that they face for practicing without being up to date.

On the other hand, doing too little creates the problem of excessive flexibility, such that the desired uniformity and comparability can be lost. This flexibility also increases the likelihood that some managers and audi-

EXHIBIT 6–1 The FASB's Dilemma of Multiple Sources of Authority

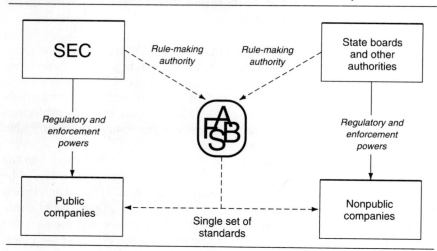

tors could more easily abuse the system. Additionally, having too little guidance might make it more difficult for other auditors to stand up to strong clients who are trying to push the standards to their limits or take advantage of loopholes in the standards.

Another factor the Board must consider is the interaction among its sources of authority. Exhibit 6–1 illustrates a significant conflict that arises because the different organizations that have endorsed the FASB have authority over different parties. Specifically, the Board gets authority from the SEC to establish many of the standards used by registrants in their filings with the Commission. These companies are larger, their securities are widely held and actively traded, and their financial reports are distributed among many investors and creditors. They are more likely to engage in complex transactions and have large and sophisticated accounting staffs that can implement new standards fairly easily. Furthermore, many of them are audited by major auditing firms that also have more sophisticated personnel.

The FASB also gets authority from state boards of public accountancy and the AICPA. These organizations have authority over both SEC registrants and nonregistrants through the control that they can exert over independent auditors. The auditors of nonregistrant companies often have smaller practices and tend to be less sophisticated. Nonregistrants engage in fewer complex transactions, distribute their reports far less widely, and have smaller accounting staffs who are less capable of implementing new standards.

These differences between registrants and nonregistrants create a dilemma for the FASB when it sets standards that apply to both public and

EXHIBIT 6–2 Pronouncements Published by the FASB

Year	Standards	Interpretations	Concept Statements	Technical Bulletins	Total
1973	1	0	0	0	1
1974	2	3	0	0	5
1975	9	4	0	0	13
1976	2	8	0	0	10
1977	6	5	0	0	11
1978	4	8	1	0	13
1979	10	2	0	19	31
1980	10	3	3	2	18
1981	9	3	0	6	18
1982	18	0	0	2	20
1983	7	1	0	0	8
1984	4	1	1	4	10
1985	6	0	1	6	13
1986	3	0	0	2	5
1987	6	0	0	3	9
1988	4	0	0	2	6
1989	3	0	0	0	3
1990	2	0	0	1	3
1991	2	0	0	0	2
1992	5	1	0	0	6
Total	113	39	6	47	205

nonpublic companies. If the Board deals only with the SEC's needs in regulating registrants, it will tend to produce complex standards that are too sophisticated for the needs of nonregistrants and strain the abilities of the nonregistrants' accountants. But, if the FASB pays too much attention to the limitations of nonregistrants, its standards will not meet the SEC's needs and its authority will be jeopardized.

Standards Overload

Many observers seem to believe that the FASB has indeed issued too many standards or has focused too narrowly on the SEC's needs to the detriment of the needs of nonregistrants. To these people, there is a problem of *standards overload*.

As a crude sort of evidence, many critics have pointed to the high level of the Board's output in the late 1970s and early 1980s. To illustrate the grounds for this complaint, Exhibit 6–2 shows the number of each of the four types of pronouncements that the FASB produced in each complete year since 1973. Exhibit 6–3 on page 154 presents the same data in graphical form. The Board started slowly as it was getting established but then moved into a faster pace for 1979 through 1982. The total figure for 1979 is distorted by the large quantity of Technical Bulletins issued during that year. Chapter 3 explains that this burst of output includes

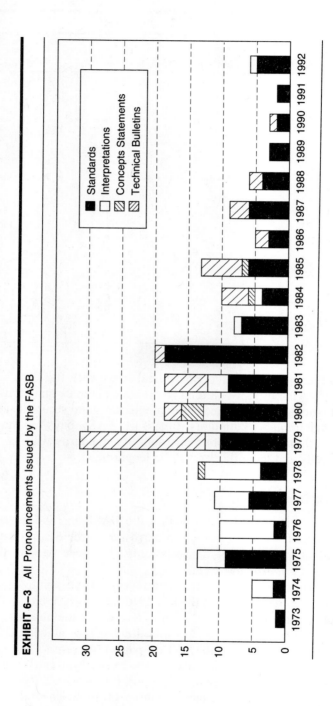

EXHIBIT 6–3 All Pronouncements Issued by the FASB

Standards
Interpretations
Concepts Statements
Technical Bulletins

the answers to constituents' questions from earlier years that could not be published before Technical Bulletins were created in 1979. Subsequently, the level of output subsided.

But it is not enough to look merely at the quantity of output. Other critics have criticized the *specialized* nature of the standards as weakening the apparent significance of all standards. Examples of standards that might be overly specialized include SFAS 31, "Accounting for Tax Benefits Related to U.K. Tax Legislation concerning Stock Relief"; SFAS 44, "Accounting for Intangible Assets of Motor Carriers"; and SFAS 73, "Reporting a Change in Accounting for Railroad Track Structures." Because many of the standards produced in 1979–82 were either highly specialized like these, or extracted from AICPA publications to make the practices officially generally accepted, the numbers can be misleading. By the authors' reckoning, the level of output of significant and broadly applicable standards is substantially lower. The graph in Exhibit 6–4 on page 156 shows that, on the average, fewer than three significant standards have been issued each year, with as many as seven in only two years. In fact, the analysis shows that the FASB did not issue any broadly significant standards in 1988 or 1989. This pattern is far different from the one depicted in Exhibit 6–3, and should defuse the criticism that was aimed at the Board for its high volume. The Board has definitely slowed its pace since 1986. On the other hand, this reduced level of output raises the opposite issue of whether the FASB is creating as many significant standards as it ought to in light of the many shortcomings in financial reporting practice.

Still others have disparaged the Board for specifying detailed procedures instead of providing broader guidance that can be interpreted and applied by accountants and auditors who are closer to specific problems. As examples, they point to SFAS 13, "Accounting for Leases," and the many later pronouncements that were issued to modify and interpret its rules; SFAS 35, "Accounting and Reporting by Defined Benefit Pension Plans"; SFAS 66, "Accounting for Sales of Real Estate"; and SFAS 87, "Employers' Accounting for Pensions." This criticism was also heard in the Board's deliberations and was documented in one Board member's dissent to SFAS 66, which begins with these words: "Mr. [Ralph] Walters dissents to the issuance of this Statement because he objects to incorporating these complex, rigid, and detailed rules into accounting standards."

At a relatively high philosophical level, there is no problem accepting the idea that an overload condition can be created. However, it is just as certain that people will disagree as to whether enough accountants have been sufficiently overloaded to justify a slowing or other change in the Board's level of activity. In evaluating this question, some insight may be gained in looking at other fields. For example, doctors do not complain that drug companies are producing too many new kinds of drugs. Rather,

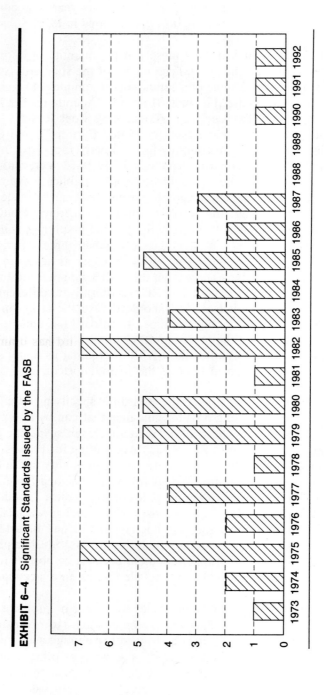

EXHIBIT 6–4 Significant Standards Issued by the FASB

they tend to want all the different drugs that they can use to relieve their patients' discomfort. Similarly, ambitious mechanics generally do not demand that manufacturers quit applying new technologies in designing cars. Instead, they simply learn how to service the new products to gain a competitive advantage over others who are less adaptable. We would also be unlikely to find top tax accountants complaining to Congress about the complexity of the tax laws. Even if they do complain, they still keep learning the new laws to serve their clients and earn more fees.

On the other hand, complaints of a condition similar to standards overload have been heard from the managers of companies that have had to comply with the Occupational and Safety Health Act (OSHA) or the reporting requirements of the Employees' Retirement Income Security Act (ERISA).

Consequently, there is no simple answer to the question of whether overload has been reached for financial accounting. Because of their limited resources, companies that are not SEC registrants (and their auditors) are more likely to argue that they are overloaded. Of course, some managements of SEC registrants are likely to complain of overload because they generally prefer less regulation to more, and because they prefer the flexibility provided by the status quo to the restrictions created by a new standard. Regardless of the various ways that the facts can be interpreted, the evidence is quite clear that the Board has dramatically slowed its pace of output.

Timely Guidance

For those accountants and other observers who believe that the FASB has not issued enough standards or has not acted with sufficient speed to resolve new issues, there exists the problem that has been called *timely guidance*.

In effect, these critics complain that the due process takes so long that the reporting and accounting problems are no longer important by the time standards are finally issued. For example, the Board took two years and two Exposure Drafts to issue SFAS 77, "Transfers of Receivables with Recourse." Without faster resolutions, the Board's critics argue, preparers and auditors are left without guidance for too long, and those who are so inclined are given an undesirable opportunity to abuse the existing standards and mislead statement users.

On the other side of this issue, it has been argued that speeding up the due process would undermine the credibility of the consensus that the Board members finally reach. It is also argued that auditors should be sufficiently independent and intelligent to interpret the existing literature to resolve most reporting problems without relying on special pronouncements. One response to the potential problem of abuse by some managers or auditors could be based on the premise that the abuse is an *ethical* issue that is not related to accounting standards. If so, the issue is beyond the scope of the FASB's responsibilities and clearly within the responsibilities of the preparer and auditor constituencies.

The FASB's Response

Regardless of their positions on these questions about standards overload and timely guidance, the members of the FASB cannot afford to ignore these criticisms; indeed, the politics of the situation make it essential for the Board to acknowledge in some way its concern about the complaints.

One response would be an attempt to develop two distinct sets of accounting principles; a more complex set would apply to SEC registrants, while a simpler and less costly one would be used by nonregistrants. This approach has often been labeled *Other Comprehensive Basis of Accounting,* or *OCBOA* for short.[1] It has also been described as *differential measurement.*"[2] It is known less formally as *Big GAAP versus Little GAAP.*

The Board has applied a variation of this strategy in some of its standards by limiting their applicability. For example, SFAS 21 exempts "nonpublic companies" from the requirements of APB Opinion 15 (for earnings per share disclosures) and SFAS 14 (for reporting information about segments of a company). The Statement defines a nonpublic company as "an enterprise other than one (*a*) whose debt or equity securities trade in a public market on a foreign or domestic stock exchange or in the over-the-counter market (including securities quoted only locally or regionally) or (*b*) that is required to file financial statements with the Securities and Exchange Commission" (par. 13). Similarly, the FASB eliminated a cost for most companies by requiring that SFAS 33, "Accounting for Changing Prices," be applied only to the largest public companies (about 1,500) that met specified size criteria.

A widespread application of this Big GAAP/Little GAAP approach would produce its own set of problems. For example, it would be necessary to deal with the transition that would have to occur when a company grew in size or otherwise had to adopt Big GAAP and abandon Little GAAP. It is also possible that statement users would have a lower level of confidence in Little GAAP statements because they would represent a low-cost compromise. As a result, any savings in accounting costs might be overshadowed by a higher cost of capital that would reflect the higher risk created by less useful financial information.

---

[1] An evaluation of one such alternative basis is described in Barry P. Robbins, "Perspectives on Tax Basis Financial Statements," *Journal of Accountancy,* August 1985, pp. 89–100.

[2] See Rholan E. Larson and Thomas P. Kelley, "Differential Measurement in Accounting Standards: The Concept Makes Sense," *Journal of Accountancy,* November 1984, pp. 78–90.

Because of these difficulties (and the results of a survey[3]), the FASB has decided against pursuing a full differential measurement system as a solution to the standards overload problem. However, its members have taken other steps to bring some relief. For example, the current Board seems less willing to place items on the agenda; there are not nearly as many projects on the 1993 agenda as there were in 1979 through 1982. Also, as described in Chapter 3, the Board has stated its intent to use Technical Bulletins more frequently to shorten the due process for projects that are not likely to affect many companies. To help solve the timely guidance problem, the Board created the Emerging Issues Task Force (EITF) in 1984; its purposes and operations are discussed below.

The Emerging Issues Task Force

The specific impetus for the creation of the EITF was a recommendation from the Structure Committee of the Financial Accounting Foundation trustees. Because of its permanence, the EITF differs from other task forces created for the limited purpose of advising the FASB staff on a single project or related projects. It consists of 14 members, including technical experts from each of the Big Six public accounting firms, three from other public accounting firms, and four preparers, including one selected by the Business Roundtable. The remaining member (and chairman) is the FASB's director of Research and Technical Activities. The meetings are also attended by the assistant director of RTA and one or more Board members. Very significantly, the SEC's chief accountant attends each meeting and participates actively in the deliberations. Apart from the chief accountant, there is no representation from the statement user constituency.

The basic purpose of the EITF is to identify new accounting and reporting issues related to new and different types of transactions. In debating these issues, the members try to reach a consensus; there are three possible outcomes of these debates:

- *A consensus[4] that a single treatment is preferred.*   In these cases, no further action is necessary. When the EITF was formed, the SEC's chief accountant at the time, Clarence Sampson, stated that he would accept this consensus as authoritative support for practices used in financial reports filed with the SEC. This position has not been altered by either of his successors, Edmund Coulson or Walter Schuetze.

---

[3] The results are included in the FASB's 1983 Research Report entitled *Financial Reporting by Private Companies: Analysis and Diagnosis.*

[4] In general, a consensus is considered to exist when no more than two members of the EITF disagree with the proposed accounting.

- *No consensus on the best treatment but agreement that the problem is narrow.* In these cases, no additional deliberations or resolutions are needed because the problem does not affect enough companies to justify the additional effort.
- *No consensus on the best treatment but agreement that the problem is important.* In these cases, the EITF determines that the problem merits attention from the FASB because of its potentially widespread occurrence and its significance. In dealing with the problem, the Board may choose to let the staff issue a Technical Bulletin to resolve the issues or it may decide to add a project to its agenda.

Despite the EITF's high potential for allowing the Board to provide guidance more quickly, its history shows that some difficulties were encountered in the process of reaching its current level of authority.

Perhaps the most important obstacle to overcome was the question of whether the task force could legitimately act as an authoritative standards-setting body. Prior to the creation of the GAAP hierarchy described in Chapter 3, the only sanction of its authority came from the SEC's chief accountant, with the consequence that there was substantial doubt about the EITF's ability to set GAAP for nonpublic companies. With the action by the Auditing Standards Board, this uncertainty was eliminated because a consensus is identified as a third-level pronouncement (10c).

Another problem concerned the medium for publishing the results of EITF deliberations and resolutions. For a number of years, the minutes of the meetings were not published, although they were available upon request. As a result, it was considerably difficult for practicing accountants to even know that a consensus had been reached and even more difficult to learn the contents of a consensus. This problem has been overcome by the Board's decision to publish highly condensed summaries of consensus positions in an annual volume. With this distribution system in place, the results are more readily available to all practitioners.

Although some question existed in the past about the long-term survivability of the EITF, it appears that it has become a permanent fixture in standards setting. Its work has proven to be useful to both the Board and the constituent groups and two serious threats to its legitimacy and effectiveness have been successfully addressed. Thus, the EITF is not likely to be challenged in the future in the same way that it was in the past.

Summary

There will always be a fine balance between issuing too many and too few standards, and the members of the Financial Accounting Standards Board will always have to tread carefully. It is quite possible that the Board did issue too many pronouncements in the late 1970s and the early 1980s. Since then, it has clearly moved in the other direction, perhaps even to

the extent that it may have overcompensated by providing too l
thoritative guidance.

As is true for so many complex problems, there is no easy solution to
the standards overload and timely guidance problems; success in coping
with them will be achieved only through a careful and ongoing monitoring
of the situation.

INTERNATIONAL ACCOUNTING STANDARDS AND ISSUES

The decade of the 1980s produced a major challenge for the FASB that is
certain to last well beyond the end of the 20th century. Because of a
number of factors, including improved computer and communications
technology, more efficient transportation, huge economic growth, and a
less confrontational diplomatic environment, the world has developed a
global economy that includes transnational capital markets. Because of
the improved ability to move capital across borders quickly and safely
and the desires of investors to invest in other economies, there has arisen
the issue of whether regulated financial reporting is as necessary in this
arena as it has been within individual domestic capital markets.

From one perspective, regulation may not be necessary if participants
in the international markets are already sufficiently sophisticated to understand their risks and to use existing private and public information
sources. On the other hand, the need for all investors to diversify their
portfolios and the increasing attractiveness of many international investment opportunities have combined with effective computer and communication technologies to make it feasible and desirable for even less sophisticated investors to gain access to these markets. If these trends continue,
it is certain that pressure will grow to provide at least some protection
similar to that provided by domestic financial reporting systems.

However, effective international regulation of any activity has always
been difficult, and financial reporting promises to be similar. For example,
securities regulators in many countries, including the United States, have
already developed intricate domestic regulatory systems and have accu-
mulated enforcement and other political power to keep those systems
effective and in place. The stability of these individual systems is threatened if companies from other countries are able to obtain capital from
local investors without complying with the regulations that domestic companies must follow. For example, a French company might want to obtain
funds from U.S. investors. Would it be consistent with the best interests
of U.S. investors for the SEC to prohibit their purchase of the French
securities unless the company provides financial reports equivalent to
those required of U.S. companies? But would this level of regulation
discourage the French company from coming to the U.S. market and,
thereby, cause the investors to lose a good investment opportunity? As a
compromise, should the SEC be willing to accept financial statements

from the French company prepared in accordance with French accounting practices? If the foreign statements are accepted, would U.S. investors be vulnerable to being misled and would the French company be operating at an advantage over U.S. companies that must comply with the stringent U.S. requirements?

Another set of issues arises for the French company if it wants to offer its securities in 10 different countries. Should it be forced to prepare separate financial statements and securities filings in accordance with 10 different GAAP and regulatory systems? Or, would it be possible to prepare one set of statements to be used in all 10 countries?

The dilemma in both situations is that too little regulation exposes investors to high risks while too much regulation may produce diminished competition in capital markets with a resulting loss of efficiency.

In fact, these issues have actually been under consideration for many years. In 1973, the same year that the FASB was established, the leading professional accounting organizations of the major trading nations joined together to form the *International Accounting Standards Committee* (IASC) to begin to identify and deal with some of these problems. The IASC is headquartered in London, but its 14 part-time members come from literally all over the world. Since its creation, the primary thrust of the IASC's efforts has been to identify preferable accounting principles for specific practice areas in order to eliminate those that do not provide useful information. The political environment is substantially more complex than the relatively well-defined one faced by the FASB, and the IASC has seldom been able to reduce any set of existing alternatives down to only a single acceptable practice. For example, consider the difficulty that would be faced if the IASC attempted to eliminate last-in, first-out (LIFO) as an acceptable inventory accounting practice. Because of its advantages for income tax reporting, LIFO is considered to be acceptable in virtually only the United States. However, even in this case, it would be very difficult for the IASC to overcome the political power that would be brought to bear in favor of maintaining LIFO's acceptability even though it is widely acknowledged that it produces incomplete financial information and measures of income and assets that are not comparable with amounts reported under other inventory systems. In spite of problems such as these, the IASC has been able to reduce many sets of acceptable practices to the point that they contain relatively few alternatives.

Since it was founded, the IASC has grown in importance because capital market participants and regulators have expressed much interest in using International Accounting Standards in financial statements used in multinational securities offerings. The ultimate goal is to reduce a company's costs and delays in getting access to capital by allowing it to accomplish multinational security offerings with only one set of financial statements prepared in accordance with international standards. This approach would reduce the company's costs but would still allow sophisticated investors in each country to modify and analyze the reported data with some protection from misleading and incomplete information.

One major barrier to elevating IASC standards to this degree of acceptability is the possibility that managers of domestic companies will claim that they are disadvantaged by having to comply with domestic GAAP that cause their financial statements to present a less favorable picture of their profits and financial position than they would if they used international standards. Thus, it would not be surprising to find these managers seeking relief from more stringent and less favorable principles created by a domestic standards-setting body (such as the FASB) so that they can compete on a level playing field with companies from other countries. For example, only U.S. companies are presently required to report an expense for accrued post-retirement health care benefits. Also, U.S. companies are required to amortize purchased goodwill against reported earnings over a period of no longer than 40 years while companies in other countries do not amortize the goodwill or simply record the debit to retained earnings instead of a goodwill account. Managers in the United States might want relief from these kinds of requirements in order to improve their ability to compete for capital. However, seeking or granting this "relief" would be acting on unjustified premises that (*a*) these reported expenses are not real, and (*b*) that investors are so naive that they would not modify and supplement the information in the reports from all companies (domestic *and* foreign) to make it useful for their decisions. Neither premise seems appropriate in light of the facts. Indeed, U.S. managers could find that more stringent reporting requirements put their companies at a competitive advantage because the greater amount of information in their reports reduces investors' needs to rely on less reliable and more costly private information sources. Based on this analysis, U.S. companies could actually face a lower cost of capital because of more stringent reporting requirements instead of a higher cost of capital that preparers worry about.

The effort to produce international accounting standards has been characterized by some observers as a threat to the FASB's power and influence. Their concern is that the Board's work and authority would be undermined and diminished if IASC standards were to be endorsed by the SEC and other countries' regulators as constituting GAAP suitable for multinational financial reporting. However, these negative expectations are counteracted by the fact that the IASC and other regulators are actually looking to the FASB and the SEC for leadership. Indeed, IASC standards tend to reflect U.S. GAAP, with a few exceptions (such as the LIFO example described earlier). As a consequence, it is more appropriate to view the situation as an opportunity to allow the FASB to expand its influence well beyond U.S. borders. Because the Board and other U.S. leaders have seen both the opportunity and the risk, the FASB and the

SEC have worked with the IASC and other countries' securities regulators to begin to identify the many political and technical issues so that they can eventually resolve them. In any case, it is certain that efforts will continue long into the future as the FASB develops and expands its leadership role in dealing with international accounting standards and issues.

STATEMENT PREPARER PARTICIPATION VERSUS DOMINANCE

One cornerstone of the FASB standards-setting system is that improvement of financial accounting practice through changes in generally accepted accounting principles will eventually lead to a *more efficient allocation* of resources in the capital markets.

Another fundamental and important purpose for GAAP is to *constrain managers* against biased reporting that makes their performance or condition appear better than it actually was. This tendency is not necessarily an outgrowth of an unethical frame of mind but may be the result of a perfectly normal desire to present a good image.

Another cornerstone for the FASB's operations is its policy of having an open discussion and debate of the issues at hand. Thus, the due process allows everyone to participate and make their views known to the Board, even if these views are coming from the management that is to be constrained against bias.

But this freedom to participate also creates the significant risk that any particular interest group might obtain the upper hand in the Board's deliberations and infringe on the legitimate interests of the other groups. If this situation were to arise, the purposes for having GAAP might be compromised or even completely defeated. This problem would be especially troublesome if financial statement preparers were to become the dominant group because they are the ones who are being regulated. The possibility that this *preparer dominance* problem could arise is suggested by what some observers believe has happened in other situations in which the regulated industries have taken over control of the regulatory mechanism. For example, this condition has been alleged to exist for some state public service commissions that are charged with regulating various utilities.

Therefore, it is appropriate to consider whether the FASB could fall, or has already fallen, under the dominance of preparers. In the view of many, there is ample evidence that this condition already exists.

From one perspective, preparers have established a very high profile in Board activities. With respect to comment letters received in response to discussion documents and exposure drafts, more always come from preparers than from any other group. Although Board members deny that they are persuaded by a count of the responses for or against a position, it certainly would be understandable if they were to feel overwhelmed by a large number of letters opposing a preliminary position.

Another indication of a high profile for preparers is the fact that approximately 60 percent of the Financial Accounting Foundation's donated funds come from industry.[5] Again, Board members are supposed to be immune from being swayed by this fact because they do not have any responsibilities for raising funds; however, they might be influenced by threats that a particular position on an issue would result in the elimination of donations. The potential for this susceptibility to financial pressure was described by Stephen Zeff shortly after the FASB's Rules of Procedures were amended in 1978 to give preparers more influence while the AICPA's influence was diminished.[6] An example of this problem occurred early in the Board's deliberations of the project to revise SFAS 33. Specifically, Board member Frank Block said (first in a closed meeting with staff members, and later in a public meeting) that many corporate donors did not like the disclosures required by the standard and that he was inclined to think that they should be accommodated.

Another indication of dominance is the fact that 8 out of 16 (50 percent) of the Foundation's trustees come from preparer backgrounds. Sixteen members (53 percent) of the Financial Accounting Standards Advisory Council are preparers. Preparers also hold 31 percent of the seats on the Emerging Issues Task Force.

Other Evidence of Preparer Dominance

The preceding paragraphs describe various statistics that show how preparers' interests affect the FASB. In addition to those statistics, there is other evidence that strongly suggests that some of the leaders in the preparer community have pursued a strategy of gaining a strong hand in the Board's governance with the goal of limiting the Board's ability to require corporations to report additional information. By limiting this ability, the efforts also weaken the Board's capacity for protecting and promoting the public's interest in more effective and more complete financial reporting. If this conclusion is true, a significant threat has been created and proponents for private sector standards setting should take action to deal with it.

The evidence exists primarily in an eight-year long series of events that are listed in Exhibit 6–5 together with their dates. While some sort of plausible explanation might exist for each of them taken individually, examining the whole series suggests that the leadership of the preparer

---

[5] This category also includes an unidentified (but reportedly small) portion from banks and similar financial institutions. Because banks are both preparers and users of financial statements, a more exact determination of the percentage from preparers is difficult to make.

[6] See Stephen Zeff, "The Rise of Economic Consequences," *Journal of Accountancy*, December 1978, p. 60.

EXHIBIT 6–5 Series of Events Indicating the Pattern of Preparer Dominance

Date	Event
Summer 1985	FEI White Paper demands more representation on Board; justified by assertion that preparers are really users; trustees appoint a second preparer to the Board.
Fall 1986	Trustees reject Leisenring as FASB chairman and select Beresford.
Summer 1987	Art Wyatt resigns as Board member.
Fall 1987	Business Roundtable establishes a task force to deal with FASB's structure and process.
Early 1988	Business Roundtable task force contacts Foundation trustees; Business Roundtable members advised to silence praise for FASB coming from their chief financial officers.
Summer 1988	Business Roundtable proposes a superoversight committee that would have the power to remove items from the FASB agenda and reject standards.
May 1990	FAF trustees reinstate two-thirds majority voting rule for FASB.
Late 1990	Ray Lauver resigns as Board member.
Late 1990	Tom Jones, assistant to John Reed, chairman of Citicorp and head of Business Roundtable task force, appointed as a trustee.
Early 1991	Trustees close the Washington office of FASB.
Spring 1991	Without explanation, the trustees announce that one-term board member, Art Northrop, formerly of IBM, will not be reappointed; sources suggest that he was not supported by the Financial Executives Institute.
Late 1992 Early 1993	Trustees Dennis Dammerman (senior vice president for finance of General Electric and president of FAF trustees) and Michael Cook (chief executive officer of Deloitte & Touche) exert direct lobbying efforts on the Board and SEC on specific issues.

constituency have a clear agenda in mind. This section of the chapter describes and analyzes these events.

The first event described in Exhibit 6–5 seems relatively innocuous, but it is significant because it represents the first effort by the preparer community to make a demand for a change in the FASB's structure. Preparers had long used the open communication process with the Board to comment on specific technical issues under deliberation. In contrast, this particular communication from the Financial Executives Institute in 1985 was an unsigned committee report that essentially demanded that the trustees increase the number of preparers in Board positions from one to three. The questionable rationale put forth by the committee was that preparers are really the most important group of financial statement users. While managers might indeed be users, the report overlooked the fact that managers have an interest in their own financial statements that is contrary to the interests of investors, creditors, and the general public. Despite this weak basis, the trustees accepted the demand in the report and appointed a second preparer, Art Northrop, to the Board position vacated by Frank Block, who had spent a career in banking and financial analysis.

The second event in the series occurred in 1986 as the trustees began to consider who would replace Don Kirk as the Board's chairman. The leading candidate throughout the first part of the year was Jim Leisenring, who was then serving as the Board's Director of Research and Technical Activities, and who had proven to be an effective representative and leader for the Board. However, his independence and apparent willingness to support major reform in financial reporting made him unattractive to the leaders in the preparer community. In considering their choice, the trustees of the Financial Accounting Foundation (FAF) discounted strong support for Leisenring (and Board member Art Wyatt) and eventually selected Denny Beresford, who had been nominated by the Institute of Management Accountants. The significance of this event lies in the fact that the trustees were willing to use their appointment powers to try shaping the direction of the Board's activities in accordance with the preparers' needs.

In the following year, 1987, another event signaled the severity of the preparers' encroachment on the Board's independence. Specifically, Board member Art Wyatt resigned from his position in response to what he characterized as the growing improper influence of preparers on the Board. Although some attributed his resignation to his personal disappointment over not being appointed chairman, Wyatt was not as interested in having that position as they suggested. The significance of this event is that it was a clear signal that the Board was feeling substantial pressure from preparers. Ironically, Wyatt was replaced by Leisenring, who was named the vice chairman of the Board. This appointment, plus the appointment of Clarence Sampson, still gave the Board a fairly solid four-vote majority of individuals who were considered to be inclined to bring reform to accounting practice. Their strength was bolstered by the selection of Tim Lucas as the director of Research and Technical Activities to replace Leisenring. Lucas was closely identified with the Board through his years of service as a project manager, and had demonstrated strong leadership in bringing to fruition the difficult pensions and Conceptual Framework projects.

In response to this residual independence in the Board and the effects of a series of major standards that the Board had issued, the next step in the series was taken by the Business Roundtable, which is an organization composed of the chief executive officers of approximately the 200 largest public corporations in the United States. Although the Roundtable calls itself a "forum for the exchange of ideas" among top managers, it has a tremendous amount of influence over national policies through the economic and political power of its members. This group was critical of the changes brought upon it by the FASB, and appointed a small task force of

CEOs in 1987 to study the FASB and to develop a strategy for slowing and otherwise weakening its efforts. The chair of the task force was John Reed, the CEO of Citicorp, the largest bank in the United States. He was assisted by Tom Jones, one of the top accounting executives of Citicorp, and a member of the Emerging Issues Task Force. The significance of the creation of the task force is that it represents a colossal strengthening of the power being brought to bear against the FASB by preparers.

One of the first steps that Reed took was to contact the leaders of the FAF trustees first to express the displeasure of the Roundtable and then to gain influence with the group. Accordingly, he met with the trustees' former president, Rholan Larson, and their current president, Jack Ruffle, early in 1988 to present the Roundtable's concerns. According to this excerpt from a memorandum signed by Reed and distributed to members of the Roundtable, Reed received a sympathetic response at the meeting:

> Larson and Ruffle were genuinely concerned about the business community's growing lack of confidence in the FASB and seemed interested in exploring possible steps that might be taken to address the concerns. They mentioned that the FAF is currently reviewing the standard-setting process and the responsibilities of the Board of Trustees. *They also expressed an interest in having a representative of the Business Roundtable fill a trustee-at-large position that is currently open.* [Emphasis added.]

The memo is also notable for the following paragraph in which Reed instructs other CEOs to restrain their chief financial officers from speaking favorably about the FASB:

> The FAF representatives [Larson and Ruffle] commented that the FASB and FAF have received mixed signals regarding the FASB's recent performance. While CEOs have been very negative, CFOs and controllers who work more closely with the FASB have been more supportive of the FASB's actions. *This lack of a consistent posture within the business community, while somewhat understandable, is undermining the Task Force's efforts and the Roundtable members should get their CFOs and controllers on board with our views on the FASB.* [Emphasis added.]

The last sentence clearly suggests that the task force's goal would be more easily met if the entire preparer community could be perceived as having a unified view that the Board's efforts were inappropriate. It would be illuminating to learn just what unfolded as Roundtable members began to instruct their accountants to ignore their ethical responsibilities to promote the public's interest. Were the CFOs persuaded to get "on board" by reason or by intimidation? In any case, this instruction shows that the Roundtable was playing a high stakes game with no holds barred.

During the summer of 1988, Reed made a bold proposal to the chairman of the SEC for a super-oversight committee that would be composed of an SEC commissioner, the chief accountant, the chairman of the FASB, and representatives of the preparer and auditing constituencies.

This committee would be given the power to add or delete projects from the FASB's agenda or to reject any of the Board's standards after they had been passed. Commission Chairman David Ruder quickly and firmly rejected the proposal as usurping the SEC's oversight. But Reed was not willing to give up the quest to slow down and divert the FASB.

In May 1990, the FAF trustees made a major move in the direction of the Roundtable's goal by changing the FASB's voting rule to a two-thirds majority from the simple majority that had existed since 1978. This change was implemented over the objections of the chief accountant, all active Board members, and virtually every former Board member, on the basis that it would protract the process and produce more compromised standards. Perhaps those were the results that the trustees wanted.

In 1990, the Board was presented with another Board member change when Ray Lauver resigned, effective as of December 31. It was clear to all observers that his departure, like Art Wyatt's three years before, was hastened by his frustration with the relentless growth of the influence of financial statement preparers over the process.

Later in the year, continuing sympathy for the Roundtable's attack on the FASB was demonstrated when Tom Jones, Reed's assistant in the task force's efforts to dismantle the Board's abilities to reform accounting practice, was appointed as one of the trustees. Regardless of his professional credentials, Jones's close identification and involvement with the task force's objectives and methods cause his selection as a fiduciary of the standards-setting system to be inappropriate.

Early in 1991, the trustees made the unexpected move of closing down the FASB's office in Washington, D.C., which had worked for many years to build effective relationships with federal regulators and legislators that would ensure that the Board's mission and efforts were understood and supported. Despite the success of these efforts, the office was closed, ostensibly to reduce operating costs. However, the authors believe that this decision was another in the series that was intended to weaken the Board's power that it had gained from sources other than the preparer constituency. At the very least, this step promoted the negative image that the Foundation believed that it did not need to maintain a presence in the capital because it did not have any accountability to the public. At the worst, it made it nearly impossible to gain the support of government leaders for the Board's initiatives. No financial savings, especially not the relatively small amount used to operate what was essentially a one-person office, could justify the damage that was inflicted by this decision.

In 1991, Board member Art Northrop's first term was scheduled to come to an end as of June 30. During the spring, the trustees began to consider whether he should be reappointed for a second five-year term. Despite his willingness to continue serving, unanimous support from the other Board members, and substantial praise for his work, the trustees simply announced without further explanation that he would not be reappointed. According to sources close to the situation, Northrop's reappointment was not supported by the Financial Executives Institute because he had disappointed leaders of the preparer constituency by not always taking positions on the issues that they expected, despite the fact that he had spent more than 40 years with IBM. This decision is significant because it shows that the trustees were again willing to use their appointment powers to try to shape the outcome of the Board's process to meet their own needs.

Page 32 in Chapter 2 describes this provision of the bylaws of the Financial Accounting Foundation:

> . . . the Trustees shall *not*, by or in connection with the exercise of their power of approval over annual budgets or their periodic review of such operating and project plans, direct the FASB or GASB to undertake or omit to undertake any particular project or activity or *otherwise affect the exercise by the FASB or GASB of their authority, functions, and powers in respect of standards of financial accounting and reporting.* (Chapter A, Article I-A, Section 1) [Emphasis added.]

The willingness of the trustees to overstep this limit was made abundantly clear in 1992 and 1993 when Foundation President Dennis Dammerman (senior vice president for finance of General Electric) and Vice President Michael Cook (chairman and chief executive officer of Deloitte & Touche) both decided to make direct attacks against the Board's tentative conclusions in the stock compensation project that was described in Chapter 5. Their actions have been defended by the assertion that they are entitled to express their opinion like anyone else. However, it is quite clear to the authors and others that their position as trustees means that they do not have that privilege. The restriction in the bylaws is unambiguous on this point. Furthermore, the common-law concept of trusteeship holds that a trustee is to be a trustworthy advocate for the interests of the organization in clear precedence over his or her own interests. Just as a trustee of a trust must give up the right to purchase its assets to avoid any conflict of interest, the trustees of the Foundation must give up their right to participate in the due process to avoid any conflict of interest. In effect, the trustees must choose between serving as trustees or expressing their points of view through the process. It is incompatible for them to attempt to wear both hats at the same time.

Summary

This series of events does not promote an optimistic view that the Board will be able to quickly bring about improvements in financial reporting that would cause statement preparers to begin reporting substantial amounts of new useful information. This obstacle exists despite the clear public interest in having additional and more useful information made available to the capital markets. Based on the authors' observations and interviews with Board and staff members, they have concluded that the organization is feeling substantial pressure from preparers, but especially from the trustees. Thus, the situation is the exact opposite from the one that was contemplated when the FASB was created and when the SEC delegated its rule-making authority to the Board. While the authors do not have any doubt about the determination of most or all of the Board members to resist these immense pressures, the situation does not promote their ability to independently analyze and resolve the issues, and does promote a strong negative impression that preparers dominate the process. The integrity of the Board members was demonstrated in June 1993 when they voted to issue an exposure draft in the stock compensation issue (see Chapter 5) in the face of unanimous opposition from major corporations and the Big Six public accounting firms.

Despite this serious threat to the Board's independence, two important groups have been noticeably silent and otherwise reluctant to confront it. The auditing constituency, despite its clear mandate to protect and promote the public interest in useful financial statements, has not acted to blunt the preparers' efforts and, especially in the stock compensation project, chose to apply pressure to the Board in concert with their clients. Perhaps they are reluctant to risk alienating their clients by speaking out, but it was a similar perception of auditors' close alignment with their clients' interests that discredited the Accounting Principles Board and caused its dissolution. Even the American Institute of Certified Public Accountants, the main representative group of the auditing profession, has been completely silent on these matters even though it would not be concerned with any client relationships.

The government regulator constituency, including the SEC and members of Congress, also has not demonstrated much concern over the mounting influence of preparers. Despite a strong letter that Congressman John Dingell sent to SEC Chairman Breeden in 1990 expressing his support for the FASB's independence from preparer pressures, he seems to have completely withdrawn his objections, as indicated by his virtual silence since then.

The ultimate irony of the preparers' campaign to control the FASB and its standards is that any victory will be hollow. While preparers might think that controlling their own reporting practices will allow them to reap huge benefits from presenting favorable financial statements, the fact remains that the capital market is capable of perceiving that those statements would lack dependability and other useful qualities. Thus, instead of enjoying a lower cost of capital by presenting favorable reports, corporate managers will surely incur a higher cost of capital because the market will not accept those reports at face value. In short, their control of the process will not provide them with the benefits they seek and will actually increase their costs instead of decreasing them.

Reversing the Trend

There should be no doubt that the Board's existence is reasonably secure, despite the many threats to the contrary that are frequently heard, particularly with regard to the stock compensation issue. Certainly, the Board will be able to continue to operate and carry out its due process. However, if the pressures from preparers continue to be unchecked, that process will not be able to continue the progress that has been made toward serving the public interest through improved financial reporting.

What, then, can be done to break the momentum toward preparer domination? It should be clear that no "quick fix" will be able to undo all the damage that has been done. However, one relatively simple change could do much to blunt and even reverse the trend. One very important characteristic of the FASB's due process is the fact that its meetings and deliberations are conducted in public. It is frequently said that "sunshine" is an effective political disinfectant because it makes those in power reveal their true motives and methods. Even though all FASB meetings must be open to the public, the trustees of the Foundation still conduct private meetings when they consider appointments and reappointments of trustees and members of the FASB. Perhaps holding these meetings in public would mitigate the Board's clear vulnerability to dominance by preparers (or any other group, for that matter). This change is likely to be resisted on the grounds that appointments are sensitive decisions that are better made in private. However, it can be more persuasively argued that this sensitivity means that public meetings are imperative so that all constituents can be certain that their interests and the public's interest are not being damaged.

In order for any solution to be implemented, there must be a widespread acknowledgment that the problem exists. This step can occur through exposure in the press and other news media. Then, if conscientious leaders from the government, user, auditor, and preparer constituencies will act with integrity, the pressures can be overcome and the public interest served. Otherwise, the problem is sure to get worse before it gets better.

WILL THE FASB SURVIVE?

Perhaps the ultimate question to be asked about the FASB's future is whether it *ought* to have one. Some academic accountants have argued that the capital markets are their own best regulators because providers of capital will require higher rates of return from companies that do not provide useful information to compensate for the higher risk inherent in such situations. Thus, these people would prefer a situation in which there would be no requirements for external reporting or any standards that would specify the contents of any external reports. Others have argued that the ready availability of massive data processing capabilities has made regular public reporting obsolete. They suggest that corporations should make all of their accounting data available in electronic form to allow users to access the parts they think are relevant and reliable instead of depending on decisions made by standards setters, auditors, and statement preparers.

While these ideas are intellectually interesting and certainly worthy of debate, the authors have concluded that they are unrealistic because they do not take into consideration the political factors that have brought the SEC and the FASB into existence and kept them operating. Thus, we believe that the responsibility placed on the FASB is legitimate and important.

The authors also conclude that the FASB has made a positive contribution to financial accounting; thus, by the linkage described in Chapter 1, there is adequate evidence to support the conclusion that the FASB contributes to the well-being of the U.S. economy and should be allowed to exist into the future.

Once it is determined that the FASB *ought* to have a future, the next question is whether it *will* have one. This question cannot be answered without first noting that the Board has the very difficult job of resolving complex and controversial issues in the midst of groups of powerful participants who often have conflicting interests. Given this task and this setting, it is always possible that a few changes could bring the system down, even if the good intentions of the participants are that it continue.

Although these difficulties have existed throughout its history, the Board has been able to survive longer than the APB with a far greater influence on the practice of accounting. The FASB has achieved this record like any other survivor in *politics* because its *people* have been sensitive to the needs of their constituents and the environment, and the *process* has been sufficiently flexible to adapt to changes in those needs. If the sensitivity and the flexibility continue into the future, there is every reason to expect the FASB to continue to exist and to have a major effect on financial accounting.

SELECTED READINGS

BERESFORD, DENNIS R. "Internationalization of Accounting Standards: The Role of the Financial Accounting Standards Board." *CPA Journal*, October 1988, pp. 78–83.

FLEGM, EUGENE H., AND DONALD J. KIRK. "The Limitations of Accounting: A Response." *Accounting Horizons*, September 1989, pp. 90–104.

FOUST, DEAN. "It's Time to Free the FASB Seven." *BusinessWeek*, May 3, 1993, p. 144.

GIESEN, DAVID W. "FASB Chairman: Our Aim Is to Aid Not Attack." *Savings Institutions*, November 1988, pp. 72–78.

HEATH, LOYD C. "How about Some Constructive Input to the FASB?" *Financial Executive*, September–October 1990, pp. 54–56.

KING, ALFRED M. "Let's Make America Competitive." *Management Accounting*, May 1992, pp. 24–27.

KIRK, DONALD J. "FASB Standards: Too Many or Too Few?" *Journal of Accountancy*, February 1983, pp. 75–80.

LARSON, RHOLAN E., AND THOMAS P. KELLEY. "Differential Measurement in Accounting Standards: The Concept Makes Sense." *Journal of Accountancy*, November 1984, pp. 78–90.

MCGOUGH, ROBERT. "Blood Will Run in the Streets." *Financial World*, May 12, 1992, pp. 16–19.

MOSSO, DAVID. "Standards Overload—No Simple Solution." *Journal of Accountancy*, November 1983, pp. 120–38.

ROBBINS, BARRY P. "Perspectives on Tax Basis Financial Statements." *Journal of Accountancy*, August 1985, pp. 89–100.

SEIDLER, LEE J. "What Ails the FASB." *CPA Journal*, July 1990, pp. 46–49.

SYMONDS, EDWARD. "FASB—Still Young, but under Pressure to Slow Down." *Accountancy*, September 1984, pp. 159–61.

THOMAS, BARBARA S. "Timely Guidance: What Role for the SEC and FASB?" *Financial Executive*, October 1983, pp. 34–39.

Review Questions and Exercises

PROLOGUE AND CHAPTER 1

Review Questions

1. List 10 key points illustrated by the news stories in the Prologue.
2. In general, why is financial accounting considered important?
3. How does financial accounting contribute to a smooth-running, efficient U.S. economy?
4. Many resources of an entity are generated internally through its own profitable activities. How does an entity acquire resources externally?
5. What mechanism is used in capital markets to allocate available resources among those competing for them?
6. Through what medium are providers of external resources matched with consumers of resources?
7. Why is much of the information for making capital markets decisions financial in nature?
8. Consumers and providers consider alternative sources and investments in capital markets. Decisions are reached and contracts entered into. Why is information the lifeblood of all rational decision making?
9. In order to make rational decisions, what do providers and consumers of capital need to know?
10. Identify several types and sources of financial information.
11. What is one major type of financial information that is prepared and distributed by corporations?

12. What is likely to happen to the economy if decisions in capital markets are made in light of useful financial information?

13. Identify five groups that have an interest in financial accounting and indicate the reason for each group's interest. Are these groups' reasons for interest in financial accounting different?

14. Discuss the concepts of uniformity and comparability as they relate to financial accounting. Why are these concepts considered important in financial accounting?

15. How do financial accounting rules seeking uniformity affect users of financial accounting information? Corporate management? Auditors?

16. What term is used to describe the set of chosen rules and guidelines for preparing financial statements?

17. What mechanism has been established to resolve differences on which rule or guideline should be established for a particular problem in financial accounting?

18. The Financial Accounting Standards Board is the operating part of a three-part structure. What are the other parts?

19. What is the main role of the Financial Accounting Foundation (FAF)?

20. How many trustees administer the FAF?

21. How are FAF trustees appointed?

22. What impact does the FAF have on the standards-setting work of the FASB?

23. What is the primary role of the Financial Accounting Standards Advisory Council (FASAC)?

24. In what year was the FASB founded?

25. Prior to the founding of the FASB, what groups were responsible for financial accounting rule-making?

26. What authority does the FASB have in establishing generally accepted accounting principles? Can the FASB enforce GAAP? If not, who can?

27. Has the SEC ever indicated a preference for the FASB to establish GAAP? If so, how?

28. What other organizations have added to the authority of the FASB and how?

29. What organizations have added to the influence of the FASB even though they have not added to its authority?

30. The FASB follows a set of procedures collectively called the *due process*. Describe the process of the FASB *in general*.

31. According to Don Kirk, former FASB chairman, what kinds of issues are generally debated by the FASB?

32. Distinguish between the two common definitions of politics.

33. Discuss an alternative to standards setting by means of a political process.

34. How does the FASB's structure capture the advantages of both the participative and the autocrat approach to standards setting?

35. List the three levels on which the FASB encounters the need for political action.

36. Describe four implications of the fact that GAAP are developed through a political process.

Exercises

1. The term *information* was used in this chapter and tends to be used extensively in accounting. What is information? What characteristics make information useful? Is there a difference between information and data? Do the financial statements and footnotes include information that might not be useful? What factors might cause this result to occur?

2. Identify three decisions that might be based on financial accounting information. Also, identify the financial accounting information relevant to those decisions. How can the Financial Accounting Standards Board identify the information needed in financial statements for decision making?

3. The controversy over accounting for securities investments was presented in the Prologue. Review the articles and identify the organizations and people participating in the discussions and decisions. Also identify why each organization or person was participating.

4. A manager in your firm has been asked to present a short speech on an accounting controversy at a local business luncheon. The manager has asked you to assist in preparing the talk. You are to review relevant business publications such as *The Wall Street Journal* and *BusinessWeek* to identify the following:

a. A financial accounting topic that is "in the news."

b. The importance of the topic to the financial statements (e.g., mark-to-market accounting affected the amount of assets reported on the balance sheet and resulted in gains and losses on the income statement).

c. The parties participating in discussions about the topic.

d. The status of the accounting for the event.

The manager has asked you to prepare a memo on your findings.

5. Identify three groups that you belong to and describe the political processes that are used to govern each group. An example of a group might be your accounting class.

CHAPTER 2

Review Questions

1. What is the intent of the structure of the FASB?

2. List the three components of the entire FASB organization.

3. Discuss the three primary activities of the Financial Accounting Foundation.

4. What limitations are placed on the activities of the FAF and what is the purpose of those limitations?

5. Provide some examples of changes that have occurred in the practices of the FASB as a result of the FAF's review procedures.

6. Identify the organizations that provide FAF trustees.

7. What percentages of the donations to the FASB come from preparers of financial statements, auditors, and users of financial statements?

8. To what three tasks is the structure of the FASB directed?

9. What steps have been taken to help Board members preserve their independence?

10. How long may a Board member serve?

11. What characteristics might qualify a candidate to be a Board member?

12. Identify some of the duties that the chairman of the Board performs in addition to the duties performed by other Board members.

13. What is the sole purpose of the Financial Accounting Standards Advisory Council? Identify the two areas that the Council generally addresses in meeting this purpose.

14. How many members serve on FASAC? How long do they serve? What salary are they paid? What are their backgrounds?

15. In addition to FASAC regular members and Board members, who attends all FASAC meetings and what is this person's role?

16. Identify some of the tasks carried out by the Research and Technical Activities staff of the FASB.

17. Discuss the role and status of the director of the Research and Technical Activities staff.

18. Identify the positions at the second level of the Research and Technical Activities staff and discuss the primary responsibilities of the positions.

19. Discuss the qualifications and responsibilities of a project manager.

20. What is the purpose of the "fellow" programs of the FASB? Identify the various types of fellows who participate in the program.

21. What action caused the formation of the Committee on Accounting Procedures?

22. Indicate the type of pronouncement that the CAP issued and discuss the authority of the CAP.

23. What is the content of ARB 43 and what is its present status?

24. Why was the Accounting Principles Board established?

25. What were the official pronouncements of the APB? What is their status today?

26. What factors led to the dissolution of the APB?

Exercises

1. Assume that you are a trustee on the Financial Accounting Foundation. Today, you received a phone call from the chairman of the board of a major corporation who is concerned about the possible reappointment of an FASB member who has consistently taken stands on standards that have resulted in

lower earnings for the corporation. What factors would you consider in responding to the chairman? Prepare a brief reply.

2. On two occasions, the Financial Accounting Foundation thought it important to change the number of assenting members of the FASB needed to approve a standard.

   a. Discuss arguments for and against the *five*-member and *four*-member requirements.

   b. The Board now has seven members. Discuss the size of the Board and the advantages and disadvantages of increasing or decreasing it. Recall that both of the FASB's predecessors, the CAP and APB, were larger groups.

3. Assume that you are a member of the FASB. A good friend and former classmate of yours is now the chief financial officer for a major corporation and has asked you to attend an annual retreat that the corporation holds in Bermuda to update corporate executives and to plan corporate strategies. You would speak to the group for about 30 minutes following dinner, on whatever contemporary accounting topic you considered useful to the audience. All of your expenses would, of course, be paid by the corporation. It is known to you that the outcome of an accounting issue presently under study by the Board could have an adverse effect on the company's financial statements. Will you accept or not accept, and why?

4. As a senior accounting major, you have expressed an interest in being an FASB graduate intern. Prepare an essay describing what you would gain from this experience. Assume that the essay is one of the criteria that the FASB will use in selecting interns.

5. This exercise requires class participation and simulates the process by which an FASB project manager builds a Board consensus. Assume that an issue being addressed by the Board appears to have four potential solutions—A, B, C, and D. You are to specify which of these four alternatives you consider: (1) strongly preferred, (2) acceptable but not preferred, (3) barely acceptable, and (4) not acceptable. You must assign each alternative a different ranking. One member of your class, serving as project manager, will ask two randomly selected members of the class for their rankings. See if you can identify a consensus based on these rankings. Then, add a third member's ranking and again try to reach an agreement on the alternative you would select. You may repeat this process under several different project managers.

CHAPTER 3

Review Questions

1. What is the meaning of the term *due process*?
2. What are the five broad goals of the FASB's due process?
3. Why is due process considered essential by the FASB?
4. Identify the five categories of GAAP described in SAS 69.
5. What actions unambiguously designate Statements of Financial Accounting Standards as generally accepted accounting principles?

6. What document must precede all final SFASs?

7. How many Board members must vote in favor of a standard before it can be issued?

8. Are FASB Interpretations part of GAAP, and if so, what is the source of their authority?

9. Discuss the purpose of an FASB Interpretation.

10. Compare the due process steps for an SFAS with the due process steps for an Interpretation.

11. How many Board members must vote in favor of an Interpretation before it can be issued?

12. Do Statements of Financial Accounting Concepts (SFAC) create GAAP? Why or why not?

13. What are the purposes of a Statement of Financial Accounting Concepts?

14. What due process procedures were followed in the development of SFACs?

15. Identify the topics of the six SFACs.

16. Do Technical Bulletins create GAAP?

17. What is the purpose of a Technical Bulletin?

18. Identify the circumstances that lead to the issuance of a Technical Bulletin.

19. Discuss the due process followed for the development of a Technical Bulletin.

20. Identify the six basic steps in the due process for an FASB project.

21. Discuss some of the ways used to uncover the problems that the Board attempts to solve.

22. Discuss the three factors that the Board always considers when deciding whether to add a project to its agenda.

23. What are some activities that might take place during the early deliberations stage of the Board's due process?

24. What documents might be published in the tentative resolution stage of the due process?

25. After the analysis of responses to an Exposure Draft and further discussions by the Board, what are the three possible outcomes of the further deliberations stage of the due process?

26. What circumstances would cause a project to be terminated after an exposure draft has been issued?

27. What activities occur in the final resolution stage of the due process?

28. Briefly identify the activities that might take place in the subsequent review stage of the due process.

29. Why is the public relations function a useful part of the FASB's operations?

30. Identify the newsletters published by the FASB.

31. Identify FASB public relations publications or activities other than newsletters.

32. Identify some of the characteristics of effective communication with the FASB.

Exercises

1. Assume that you are the chief financial officer of a major corporation. The FASB has recently released an exposure draft that would cause the reported earnings of your corporation to plummet if it becomes a standard. What avenues would you use to respond to the FASB? Would your answer change if your corporation's reported earnings were expected to rise sharply as a result of the standard?

2. Obtain a copy of a discussion memorandum or an exposure draft, and prepare a comment letter. It is important that you attempt to incorporate the characteristics of an effective comment letter that were described by Board and staff members. Your instructor will indicate whether you should use a specific document or one that you select.

3. Several general steps are included in the due process followed by the FASB for establishing accounting standards. This process is followed to ensure that the interests of the FASB's constituents have been considered.

   a. What were the major due process steps associated with the establishment of SFAS 76, "Extinguishment of Debt," issued in November 1983?

   b. What were the major due process steps associated with the establishment of SFAS 87, "Employers' Accounting for Pensions," issued in December 1985?

   c. Compare the due process steps used in SFAS 76 and SFAS 87.

4. Exhibit 3–3 presents five actual letters that the FASB received in response to the exposure draft for SFAS 115.

   a. Identify the basic position taken by each respondent. Do you agree or disagree with the position? Is sufficient support presented for the argument? Did the writer use the Conceptual Framework? If so, was it used well? What is the overall effectiveness of each comment letter?

   b. Select one comment letter and suggest how any deficiencies in its arguments or presentation could be corrected. You should not suggest a change in the basic position for or against the Board's proposal.

CHAPTER 4

Review Questions

1. Why is the FASB's Conceptual Framework considered to be important?
2. List three general reasons for developing a conceptual framework.
3. What is one main goal of a descriptive conceptual framework?
4. Why is a descriptive framework also called *bottom-up*?
5. Describe the advantages and disadvantages of a descriptive framework.
6. Explain why a descriptive framework often does not provide guidance to a standards-setting body such as the FASB.
7. What is one main goal of a prescriptive conceptual framework?
8. Why is a prescriptive framework also called *top-down*?

9. Describe the advantages and disadvantages of a prescriptive framework.

10. Explain why it is difficult for an authoritative body to establish a prescriptive framework.

11. What are two advantages of having a conceptual framework that defines commonly used terms?

12. What difficulty is encountered in applying definitions that are part of a conceptual framework?

13. What are three objectives of the FASB's Conceptual Framework? Was the framework intended to be prescriptive or descriptive?

14. Many accountants would prefer to leave the status quo intact. Is this preference unique to accountants? What difficulty does it tend to cause in efforts to produce a conceptual framework?

15. What did the FASB state in Statement of Financial Accounting Concepts No. 5 that shows that the Conceptual Framework is at least partially descriptive?

16. Identify the broad accounting issues that were originally established for the *recognition and measurement* phase of the Conceptual Framework project. What other controversial issue seemed to draw the most attention?

17. What action is described as "peeking," and why did it interfere with the development of the Conceptual Framework?

18. Why would it be important to issue a Statement of Financial Accounting Concepts (or any other pronouncement based on a consensus) *before* a Board member was replaced after the end of his or her term?

19. Why did an open due process make it difficult to develop the Conceptual Framework? Despite this problem, why was it considered essential to have one?

20. Describe the shifts in the "balance of powers" that occurred during the life of the Conceptual Framework project.

21. Pages 101 and 102 present a quote from SFAS 87 on pensions in which the Board members describe their real preference and the reasons why they were not proposing a standard consistent with that preference. Discuss the implications of this paragraph for the Board's ability to resolve controversial issues.

22. What are the two major contributions of the FASB's Conceptual Framework?

23. How many Statements of Financial Accounting Concepts were issued by the FASB? What are their titles?

24. According to SFAC 1, what is the primary objective of financial reporting? What is the political significance of this objective?

25. What type of financial statement user did the FASB identify as being most important? Why is this choice significant?

26. According to SFAC 2, what are the two primary qualities of useful information?

27. Why is there little guidance in a policy that states that the benefits of providing information should exceed its costs?

28. Identify the 10 elements of financial statements defined in SFAC 3. Which

two are the most primary? Why might this status of these elements be considered revolutionary?

29. List some examples of not-for-profit organizations. Why have not-for-profit accounting issues been difficult for the FASB to resolve?

30. Identify the five financial statements described in SFAC 5. Explain the difference between the two types of income statements.

31. List the four recognition criteria defined in SFAC 5. How do they repeat SFAC 2? Why are two of these criteria redundant?

32. What is the primary modification that SFAC 6 makes to SFAC 3?

33. What term does SFAC 6 use to describe the element equivalent to owners' equity for not-for-profit organizations?

34. List the classes of net assets of not-for-profit organizations identified in SFAC 6.

Exercises

1. There is a difference between descriptive and prescriptive approaches to developing a theory. Use these approaches to describe the way an activity is carried out at your school and to prescribe the way you think it should be carried out. For example, you might select the registration process, the allocation of parking, the allocation of sports tickets, the granting of tenure, or the scheduling of placement interviews.

2. Suggest at least two broad objectives for financial accounting other than the one selected by the FASB. Discuss the implications of these alternative objectives for resolving accounting issues.

3. One alternative to accounting for assets at cost on the balance sheet would be to report them at some measurement of their current value. Identify the parties you think would participate in the FASB's due process and why they would participate if the following assets were to be reported at current values:

   a. For agricultural products only.

   b. For assets of manufacturing companies only.

   c. For all assets.

4. The text identified *A Statement of Basic Accounting Theory* as a top-down (prescriptive) framework for financial accounting published by the American Accounting Association. Obtain a copy of this publication, perhaps from your library, and describe its resolution of the issue on whether financial statements should be based on historical costs or current values.

CHAPTER 5

Review Questions

1. What is the fundamental issue regarding capitalization versus expensing?

2. Preferences for capitalization or expensing differ among those interested in financial statements. Describe the general preferences of preparers, users, and auditors.

3. What two factors contribute to the capitalization versus expensing controversy in accounting for the costs of research and development?

4. Identify the event that led the APB to begin studying accounting for research and development costs.

5. Describe the treatment of research and development costs specified in SFAS 2.

6. State the primary reason for capitalizing interest costs.

7. Why did utility companies begin capitalizing interest cost before other corporations?

8. SFAS 34 requires the capitalization of interest costs associated with what kinds of activities?

9. What caused software companies to prefer capitalization of development costs?

10. Discuss the similarities and differences between software development costs and research and development costs and between the accounting treatments prescribed for them.

11. Summarize the major differences between the successful efforts and full-cost accounting methods used by oil and gas companies.

12. In the 1970s, the SEC took a more active role in establishing accounting policy for oil and gas companies. What events brought on the SEC's involvement, and what was the nature of its action?

13. The SEC's proposal for accounting for the exploration activities of oil and gas companies was reserve recognition accounting (RRA). In some respects, it is a rather novel approach to the capitalization versus expensing problem. Describe RRA accounting, and characterize the accounting profession's general reaction to it.

14. What is the possible benefit for a company in arranging off-balance-sheet financing?

15. Explain how leasing can be used by a lessee to obtain the benefits of an off-balance-sheet financing arrangement.

16. Under ARB 38, what disclosures concerning leased assets were to be made?

17. What is one major advantage of not consolidating a subsidiary?

18. What type of subsidiary of a manufacturing company was often not consolidated?

19. Why is accounting for employee compensation a sensitive issue?

20. Describe how vacations and other compensated absences were accounted for prior to SFAS 43 and how they are to be accounted for now.

21. What were the two primary reasons why the FASB placed pensions on its agenda in 1974?

22. What, in general terms, does SFAS 106 require and what has been the consequence of its release?

23. What is unusual about the large number of comment letters received on the stock compensation project and what does it suggest about the nature of the project?

24. Provide arguments for and against recognizing a pension liability on the balance sheet.

25. What causes the income taxes of a company for a given year to be different on the financial statements and on the tax return?

26. Define deferred taxes.

27. Give three reasons why the FASB undertook an income taxes project.

28. What was the investment tax credit, and what accounting issues did it create?

29. What precluded the FASB from limiting acceptable methods of accounting for investment tax credits?

30. Name and describe the two alternatives to historical cost accounting that account for changing prices.

31. In using the current value approach, holding gains arise. What are holding gains, and why do auditors face difficulty in auditing them?

32. What was the purpose of SFAS 89?

Exercises

1. The following chart presents the agenda of the FASB as of June 30, 1993. The chart indicates each project and its status. Determine the current status of the projects and update the chart. Also include new projects added to the agenda.

2. This chapter included a discussion of five areas of accounting controversies: capitalization versus expensing, off-balance-sheet financing, employee compensation, income taxes, and changing prices. Review your additions to the agenda in Exercise 1, and identify whether any of the new projects are related to these controversies.

3. A history of five accounting controversies was included in this chapter to demonstrate the role of people and politics in the process for setting standards. Select (or your instructor might assign) one of the following accounting issues, and prepare a brief history of the controversy. The issues are: foreign currency accounting, components of income (current operating versus all inclusive approaches), and extinguishments of debt.

4. Obtain one or more *Intermediate Accounting* or *Accounting Theory* textbooks and find their discussions of several of the issues described in this chapter. Analyze the presentations to determine whether the issues and their resolutions are described in terms of political or theoretical factors, or both. Do the descriptions correspond to those presented in this book? Try to explain any differences that you uncover. What reasons might cause textbook authors to leave out politics in their discussions of these and other issues?

Project	Status as of June 30, 1993	Status as of _____
1. Consolidations: Policies and procedures New basis Unconsolidated entities	Early deliberations Early deliberations Early deliberations	
2. Financial instruments: Liabilities and equities Hedging	 Project on hold Early deliberations	
3. Impairment of assets	Tentative resolution	
4. Present value-based measurement	Early deliberations	
5. Stock compensation	Tentative resolution	
6.		
7.		
8.		
9.		

CHAPTER 6

Review Questions

1. Even though the FASB is not a governmental agency, how can it be argued that setting financial accounting standards is a public sector process?

2. Describe six benefits that accrue to the SEC by having the FASB set accounting standards.

3. What difficulties would have to be overcome to create a governmental agency for setting accounting standards?

4. What is standards overload? What is timely guidance? Can they both occur at the same time? Explain.

5. What problem is created for the FASB by the fact that it gets authority from the SEC, the AICPA, state boards of public accountancy, and state societies of CPAs?

6. What events contributed to the perception that standards overload existed and was the FASB's fault?

7. Are other activities subject to the possibility of standards overload? What do participants in those activities do about it?

8. What are the advantages and disadvantages of having two sets of GAAP?

9. What is the composition of the Emerging Issues Task Force? What constituent group is not directly represented?

10. Why would it be controversial to have the EITF creating GAAP?

11. What risk is created by having a due process that allows a regulated group to participate in the development of regulations? What are the advantages of this relationship?

12. What factors have led to the issue of whether there is a need for regulated international financial reporting?

13. Provide examples of how international regulation of financial reporting may prove to be difficult.

14. What is the IASC and what has been its primary thrust since it was formed?

15. Does the IASC operate in a political environment similar to the FASB?

16. What financial activity has led to the growing importance of the IASC?

17. Why might managers of domestic companies be a barrier to the elevation of the acceptability of IASC accounting standards?

18. Does the development of the IASC provide a threat to the power and influence of the FASB?

19. What signs indicate that preparers dominate the FASB and its processes?

20. What could the SEC do to counteract dominance by preparers?

21. How are preparers benefited and threatened by their dominance of the standards-setting process?

Exercises

1. Assume that you are a CPA practicing as a sole practitioner with clients who are not under the regulations of the SEC. Prepare a letter to the FASB either (1) requesting it to consider separate accounting standards for your type of clients or (2) indicating why separate standards are not necessary.

2. Review *The Wall Street Journal,* the *Journal of Accountancy*, and other accounting-related sources to identify corporate failures and frauds during the last several years. Determine whether the problem appeared to be a result of poor management, inadequate accounting standards, inadequate auditing standards, or some other factors. Do your results suggest to you that the setting of accounting standards in the private sector is not succeeding?

NAME INDEX

SUBJECT INDEX